Cotillo

ARCHITECTURAL STONE

ARCHITECTURAL STONE

Fabrication, Installation, and Selection

Mark A. Chacon

JOHN WILEY & SONS, INC.

New York • Chichester • Weinheim • Brisbane • Singapore • Toronto

For my girls,
Gina, Gabriela, and Rachel.

Without their love, support, and patience,
this book would not have been possible.

This book is printed on acid-free paper. ♾

Copyright © 1999 by John Wiley & Sons, Inc. All rights reserved.

Published simultaneously in Canada.

No part of this publication may be reproduced, stored in a retrieval system or transmitted in any form or by any means, electronic, mechanical, photocopying, recording, scanning or otherwise, except as permitted under Sections 107 or 108 of the 1976 United States Copyright Act, without either the prior written permission of the Publisher, or authorization through payment of the appropriate per-copy fee to the Copyright Clearance Center, 222 Rosewood Drive, Danvers, MA 01923, (978) 750-8400, fax (978) 750-4744. Requests to the Publisher for permission should be addressed to the Permissions Department, John Wiley & Sons, Inc., 605 Third Avenue, New York, NY 10158-0012, (212) 850-6011, fax (212) 850-6008, E-Mail: PERMREQ@WILEY.COM.

This publication is designed to provide accurate and authoritative information in regard to the subject matter covered. It is sold with the understanding that the publisher is not engaged in rendering professional services. If professional advice or other expert assistance is required, the services of a competent professional person should be sought.

Library of Congress Cataloging-in-Publication Data:

Chacon, Mark.
    Architectural stone : fabrication, installation, and selection / Mark Chacon.
        p.   cm.
    Includes bibliographical references and index.
    ISBN 0-471-24659-X (alk. paper)
    1. Building stones.   2. Building, Stone.   I. Title.
TA426.C45 1999
691'.2 — dc21   99-25460

Printed in the United States of America.

10 9 8 7 6 5 4 3 2 1

Contents

Preface

As a young designer in a large architectural office, I was called upon to participate in the design of complex, high-profile retail projects. Of the many tasks that I was assigned, the selection of the marble used as flooring and selection of granite used for exterior cladding were among my favorites. I did not have any previous experience with natural stone beyond the slide shows presented in Architectural History in college, yet I appreciated the feel and perceived strength of the material. In the early 1980s the use of thin stone tile was gaining momentum, but this material was still available only from limited sources and the same stones seemed to be used on most projects. Therefore, my projects and those produced by my office used the same stones that I am certain were used by everyone else in the United States, primarily marbles and granites from Italy and Spain. We were fortunate that our retail and shopping center clients continued to build stores and centers through the 1980s, and the use of stone has increased dramatically each year.

As I began writing *Architectural Stone,* it occurred to me that through all of the projects I designed incorporating the use of stone, we never had a failure. In my early design years there were few stone material options, yet those that were available had been used with repeated success. Our studio had adopted a design philosophy (somewhat imposed by our client) that we did not want to be first to try a new idea — yet we did not want to be last — which also applied to the selection of stone. We required that installations of a proposed stone be observed first-hand and researched thoroughly to determine the stone's suitability for our application. We reviewed the maintenance procedures that were used for our examples and evaluated the available test data to support our decisions, but in the end we relied more on the experiences of comparable installations of our proposed stones.

As we began to seek new stone options, following the same unwritten procedures for selection, the industry continued to grow, bringing new options to our attention, many without ever being proven in "same kind" installations. In my effort to qualify new materials, I found it difficult to locate reliable sources of information or industry guidelines to assist in my evaluation. I began to realize that the selection of stone was more art than science.

Technology has dramatically changed the stone industry in the past 25 years, after its remaining relatively unchanged for several hundred years. This technology has enabled producers to process stone into thin modules, reducing waste, and through improved delivery systems, decreased the cost of a material once considered very expensive to a level that the general public can now afford. Because of the combined advances in fabrication technology and transportation systems, new stone types are introduced to the market each year. The exportation of new stones from emerging markets such as China, India, Southeast Asia, and, soon, the former Soviet Union is giving a greater choice to architects and designers. Unfortunately, the decision to use a specific stone is usually based on the visual aesthetics of the sample presented to the architect, rather than on a review of the past use of the material and its history of success.

The use of stone in architecture is on the increase, yet it is hard to believe that there are few guidelines or references for those who select natural stone. There is no single test or combination of tests that, when performed, yield data that can be used as a guide to determine the suitability of a stone. There is no single point of reference to assist in the evaluation of stone, nor is there a reference that describes the process or issues to be considered in selecting stone. The results of bad decisions can cost an owner, and consequently the architect, installer, and supplier, thousands and in some cases millions of dollars to correct.

Because the subject of natural stone is enormous, this book is intentionally organized in a general format to cover as much subject matter as possible. I believe that this approach will expose the architect and designer to as many issues as possible. Currently, *Architectural Stone* is the only single-source "go to" reference that discusses all the issues that need to be considered in the selection of stone.

The book focuses on three main points:

1. *What are the characteristics of stone?* How is stone formed geologically; what are the differences between a marble and a granite? How does the formation of each type of stone have an impact on the way the stone will appear and perform?
2. *What limitations are to be anticipated in the use of stone as a result of the fabrication process?* For example, if the material is a slate that is removed from its quarry by hand, it then becomes clear that the overall size of the slate will be severely limited.
3. *How are the different types of stone installed?* For instance, if a stone cannot be calibrated because of its dimensional structure, then the stone cannot be thin set, which is the lowest-cost method for installing stone tile. Variation in a stone's thickness will require a mortar bed of a depth that can accommodate the variation.

The understanding of these three areas is critical to the most important issue relating to the use of stone: *selection.* Chapters 2 through 4, which discuss the characteristics of building stone, stone fabrication, and methods of installation, are the foundation to the main point of the book, which is to offer guidelines for the selection of stone, as presented in Chapter 6.

In 1996 I left the design profession to pursue my passion for stone and my desire to go into business. I have found that my experience with stone from the design perspective has been a valuable asset as a supplier of architectural stone, and in the evaluation of materials for my clients. In the process of building my business, I have accumulated a large collection of references on stone and related technical data from around the world. Interestingly, when asked to make recommendations for a specific project, I am not able to go to one book or source in my library; I must resort to examples from several sources to base my proposals. Drawing on what I have learned on both sides of the fence, I have assembled *Architectural Stone* as a gift to my friends in the design profession, which I hope will become their single resource and guideline when evaluating stone for their projects.

Acknowledgments

Consultants, Coaches, and Mentors

Tim Syverson
Geologist, Environmental Consultant
Characteristics of Building Stone
Consulting

Phil Loubere
Graphic Designer / Illustrator
Illustrations

Gerhard Ruf
Stone Supplier / Consultant
Characteristics of Building Stone and Stone Fabrication
Consulting & Photography

Ryan Bruce
Architect
Installation Methods
Installation Details

Skip Kuhn
TrizecHahn
Installation Methods, Thin-set Installations
Consulting

Don Quackenbush
Architect
Installation Methods
Anchored Veneer and Curtain Wall Installations
Consulting

John Swolgaard
Architect
Installation Methods
Curtain Wall Installations
Consulting

Lou Couillard
Mapei
Installation Methods, Mortars, Setting Materials, and Grout Systems
Consulting

Craig Corbin
Mapei
Installation Methods, Mortars, Setting Materials, and Grout Systems
Consulting

Brad Williamson
Architect
Installation Methods, Specifications
Consulting and Contributor

Joseph Salvo
Miracle Sealants and Abrasives
Protection and Maintenance of Stone Installations
Consulting

Michael Reis
Stone World Magazine
Glossary
Contributor

Scott Huntley
Architect
Coach and Mentor

Luigi Biagini
Stone Consultant and Photographer
The artistic side of the stone business

Luigi Di Cola
Stone Consultant
My early training

Geoffrey Milspaw
Associated Imports
For sharing the passion

Special thanks to all of my friends at Callison Architecture

ARCHITECTURAL STONE

1

Introduction

THE STONE TRADITION

Stone has always been valued as a material of great durability and permanence. The use of stone has been traced to humankind's beginnings in pursuit of shelter. Fieldstones were collected by hand and set side by side, then stacked one upon another to create walls. Wood timbers were used to support roofs composed of split stone, such as slate if available, or flat stones. As societies developed, the use of stone increased to solve basic problems, such as in defining property with stacked stone walls, paving roads with cobblestone to bring goods to market, and building monuments to honor the gods. Much of our recorded history has been learned through our study of the art and architecture produced by ancient civilizations; these examples exist today because the edifices of those early cultures were constructed of stone. The history of civilization has been captured in stone, a material used originally as simple protection and later evolving to a symbol of wealth, strength, and status.

The methodology used for the extraction and processing of stone is basically the same today as it was in ancient times. When the early builders discovered outcrops of slate and cliff faces of sandstone exposed through natural weathering, they learned that larger units of stone could be removed from these deposits than they had been able to gather from the fields by hand. Techniques were developed whereby the natural faults could be exploited to aid in the extraction of stone from their deposits. Slate faces could be split into thin sheets and used as roofing material. Sandstone boulders could be pried from their benches with levers, and

Figure 1-1. View of the Apuan Alps.
The Apuan Alps on the west coast of Italy, parallel to the Mediterranean Sea, where the quarries producing Bianco Carrara, Bianco Statuario, and many other famous white Carrara marbles extend from the area north of Pisa to the area north of Carrara. White tailings of marble debris, resulting from 2,000 years of continuous quarrying, are apparent at the base of the mountains.

smaller stone blocks could then be shaped with metal pick axes. These small blocks could be used to build load-bearing walls for homes and places of gathering. These are the same basic techniques that are used today for quarrying natural stone; the difference, however, is that we have 4,000 years of experience to drive the high technology available to us today.

Figure 1-2. The roads to the quarries of Bianco Carrara.
The roads to the quarries located near the summit of several peaks within the Apuan Alps of Italy. The roads switch back their way over the tailings to the quarries under production today. These are the same quarries that produced the marble for Michelangelo's David, more than 500 years ago.

The marble quarries of Carrara have been in continuous operation for more than 2,000 years, the quarriers passing on the tools and traditions generation after generation. As the Romans built their empire conquering new lands, prisoners of the various campaigns were often brought to work the quarries of Carrara for the rest of their lives as slaves. Today it is not uncommon to see quarry workers who have strong Nordic features, whose ancestors have lived in the Apuan Alps Alps for centuries working the quarries, originally for the emperor of Rome. In the early days, wood wedges were driven into the natural cracks of a marble deposit and wet with water. As a wedge expanded, it was replaced with a larger wedge, and so on, continuing for days, until the block separated from the quarry ledge. The irregularly shaped blocks were squared with hammer and chisel, then rolled over logs to the base of the mountain (see Figures 1-1 and 1-2).

Yesterday's quarryman has been replaced by modern-day geologists who survey stone deposits with lasers and sonic devices and plan the sawing of a deposit based on the naturally occurring faults within the quarry bench. Continuous wire loops are embedded with diamonds and driven by pulleys almost effortlessly, sawing a smooth-faced rectangular block from the deposit in a matter of hours. The blocks are transported by truck to nearby processing plants, which fabricate the stone to specific dimensions as directed by an architect, possibly from another continent.

The nature of stone being of large mass and weight has historically dictated its use as large scale masonry units and facings within the composition of a grand-scaled building. For this reason, the stone trades have evolved very slowly for several thousand years until the end of the nineteenth and toward the beginning of the twentieth century, when the ingenuity that blossomed during the industrial revolution began to modernize the equipment of the stone industry. It was not until the introduction of the skyscraper that dramatic change was realized in the industry, with its requirement of thinner and lighter-weight materials. The development of highrise architecture introduced the concept of attaching a non-load bearing skin to a steel building frame, which turned the stone industry on its head. To meet the demands of high-rise buildings, stone had to be sawn to uniformly thin dimensions; slabs were needed that could be produced in thicknesses of ¾ in. and 1 ⅛ in. These challenges have been met by technology, which has changed the processes of quarrying, processing, and fabricating natural stone faster in the past 60 years than has been witnessed in the previous 2,000 years.

HISTORICAL USE OF STONE AS A BUILDING MATERIAL

The early shelters built by ancient peoples were round huts, which were easy to construct using flat stones stacked to form walls without the use of mortar; this technique is referred to as *rubblestone* construction. A round hut design was easier to build than squared buildings with complicated corners, and where slate deposits were found, thatched roofs were replaced with pieces of slate (see Figure 1-3). Interestingly, this type of construction has regained popularity in modern design, using split-face stone as a decorative masonry facing, and is referred to as *dry stack*. In those early times when transportation as we know it did not exist, builders were limited to using indigenous materials. Every region had its own

Figure 1-3 The Trulli stone houses southern Italy.
The Trulli, round huts of ancient design, are still in use today. The Trulli are built of indigenous limestones stacked one upon another to form a single space below each of the conical stone roof structures. They were built as homes thousands of years ago, in round form so as to avoid the use of corners for simplicity.

stone types, which were quarried or collected by hand. The buildings produced with local materials blended with the landscape and expressed the color and character of the geologic region. As these techniques developed and more buildings were erected of the same indigenous stones, whole villages took on the characteristic appearance provided by the use of stones from the surrounding landscape. With more experience, builders were able to incorporate larger stones into their structures, using them as oversized jambs and headers to create focal points at the entries of their homes. Early forms of cement were developed, and plaster was mixed to cover the rubblestone walls; however, the feature stones continued to be expressed, which is the origin of quoining at building corners.

As trade flourished between villages, roads were built to connect them. Originally, the walking surfaces between villages were of beaten earth; later the surfaces were covered with crushed rock. The earthen streets of the villages were surfaced by burying cobblestones — stones found in nature, usually found in stream beds or gravel deposits. As stones were discovered that were capable of being split, such as porphyries, roads were built of hand-split cubes set in a bed of sand or fine aggregate.

The use of stone in construction was increasingly appreciated, and rulers of ancient civilizations understood the permanence of stone edifices. The great pyramids of Giza and the nearby Sphinx, constructed more than 4,000 years ago, are among the grandest monuments of humankind, and a testament to the durability of stone. The pyramids of Giza were constructed of limestone, and the Great Sphinx was carved from sandstone. The limestone used for the Great Pyramids was quarried across the Nile and transported by boat to the desert valley. Most likely, timbers were used as rollers to drag the blocks to the site of the pyramid. The same technique for rolling blocks was used in the quarries of Carrara for centuries to follow.

Temple building continued through the rise of Greek and Roman civilizations. Many temples were built at the threshold of the classical period of Greek civilization. Temples whose primary purpose was to house images of the gods and to preserve the offerings of the faithful were built of stone using post and lintel construction techniques. Temples such as the Temple of Aphaia, built of limestone circa 500 B.C., and the Temple of Hera II, also constructed of limestone, circa 460 B.C., are examples of the development of Greek architecture incorporating the massive use of stone. The most famous of all stone edifices, the Parthenon, was built on an enormous limestone rock overlooking Athens. The entire structure was built of Pentelic marble, including the roof tiles, and is considered to be one of the greatest buildings of the world. The post and lintel structural system was pushed to its limits; refining the Doric order by using slender columns of additional height added grace to the colonnade, and reducing the mass of the entablature increased the temple's proportion of height.

The Roman Empire was expanding, and great civic centers were planned throughout its reaches. Its planners solved problems of water supply for many of the new towns by diverting nearby springs and building grand aqueduct systems to transport the water. The largest of these is the Segovia aqueduct in Spain, which is built of granite blocks without the use of mortar and is 2,400 ft long and 95 ft tall. The Romans discovered a method for the production of concrete that used a drier mixture of cement, with rubblestone added as aggregate. This enabled their builders to move beyond the limitations of post and lintel construction, producing structures with tremendous spans. During this period one of the more adventurous uses of stone was as facings or claddings of concrete and stone structures, such as in the Coliseum at Rome. Although today the exterior of the Coliseum has the appearance of being bullet ridden, in actuality the holes in the surface are the locations of the original anchors that attached marble veneer panels to the structure.

The products of quarries were often so easily available and quarried that the stones were used for the ballasts of ships. The trading ships of Britain, during the seventeenth and eighteenth centuries, carried sandstones as ballast that were offloaded when they reached the southern states of America, where the ships were then loaded with cotton. Many of the buildings found in the old commercial centers of the United States were built of sandstones from Britain. The town centers of early America were paved with solid blocks of limestone and granite, and many country roads were surfaced with crushed stone.

An early use of limestone was for agricultural purposes. Small limestone blocks were collected and burned in makeshift kilns. Upon firing, the resulting material, calcium oxide, was raked out and mixed with water to produce calcium hydroxide, or lime. This material, when spread over farmland, acted as a fertilizer by counteracting the natural buildup of acidity from humus deposits, thus promoting healthy plant growth.

MODERN USE OF STONE AS A BUILDING MATERIAL

During the past two centuries the use of stone in construction was limited to government buildings, large-scale public gathering places, and homes of the wealthy. The reason was that the same labor-intensive stone-processing techniques used for centuries previous were still practiced, making the use of stone exclusive because of its high cost. Nearly every train station of the urban centers of the world, every state capital in the United States, and monuments of major significance, such as the Lincoln Memorial and the Washington Monument, were built of stone. All of these stone structures were built of massive load-bearing masonry units. The heights of buildings were limited, because the mass required at the base increased as a building grew taller, reducing the useable areas at the lower levels. The walls grew thicker, and openings for windows and doors were reduced in size and quantity. Yet the real estate markets were demanding the opposite: larger windows with views and open floor areas for retail use at the pedestrian levels. The solution was introduced during the latter half of the nineteenth century: iron and steel structural frames that supported a lighter-weight exterior skin or facade. Now buildings could go taller without consuming so large a proportion of the floor area. The masonry industry jumped on the concept and developed the early panelized wall systems built of brickwork attached to a frame that could be installed at the perimeter of the building structure. The stone industry, however, was slow to follow the requirements of the emerging American skyscraper.

As architects of the day explored newer materials to achieve the design generated by the international movement, multimaterial curtain wall systems were developed using various metals, terra-cotta, glass, and masonry. Many of the systems were successful, but some were not. The appetite for the beauty of natural stone was growing stronger, and the stone industry was finally caught up in the momentum. Stone producers developed new methods of block extraction, and fabricators invented more efficient equipment to process stone with precision, and most important, thinner dimensions. Stone producers realized the increased market potential of thin dimensional stone resulting from lower material and shipping costs. By the middle of the nineteenth century the integration of stone veneers within true curtain wall systems had begun.

Technology has dramatically changed the stone industry in the past 25 years and has enabled producers to process stone into thin modules, thereby reducing waste. And because of improved delivery systems, a material that was once considered a luxury, is now available to the general public. To produce a stone floor as recently as 1950 required a stone module of a minimum ¾ in. thickness and utilizing a full mortar bed, for a total of 2 to 3 in. overall thickness. The finishing of this floor required grinding and polishing the stone in place, which was time-consuming and costly. A stone floor could be installed only in government buildings or for the very wealthy. Through technology, machinery has been developed capable of producing uniformly thin stone modules to a now standard dimension of ⅜ in., which can be thin-set in a mortar bed of ⅛ in., at a price that the average construction budget can accommodate.

2

Characteristics of Building Stone

GEOLOGIC FORMATION OF BUILDING STONE

When buildings composed of marble, granite, or limestone are completed and occupied, they are appreciated for their beauty and their appearance of luxury and enduring value. To the average person the building material is usually referred to as, and thought to be, "marble," which is a common misconception. Historically, stones that were capable of producing a shine or polished surface were called "marbles." This concept is reinforced by the origin of the word *marble,* derived from the Greek verb *marmaro,* which is translated as "to shine" This definition is far too general when applied to building stone, inasmuch as there are many types of stone that can achieve a polish or shine, such as granites, limestones, some quartzite, and even a few types of slate. From the perspective of an architect who is integrating stone with a design concept or a builder who is executing the stonework, the most important issue is how the stone will react in the intended application. This is why an understanding of how rocks are formed from the earth and the process they undergo to become marble, granite, or limestone, is useful in trying to anticipate the behavior of a particular stone when it is introduced into the built environment.

All stones are classified in three categories, based on the manner in which they were formed: igneous, metamorphic, and sedimentary. There are variations

Figure 2-1 Fossil Fish.
Fossil fish found within a piece of Solnhofen limestone dating from the Jurassic Period. The fossil was found by a quarrier while excavating the limestone for paving stone, October 1998, near the village of Solnhofen Germany.

within each of the groups, which sometimes approach the characteristics of another group; however, these are the generally accepted categories. All stone, regardless of its category, is a product of naturally occurring events relating to the evolution of the earth. Common theories, or models, used to describe how various geologic features and stones are created include plate tectonics, sea floor spreading, and mountain building. Each of these models describes dynamic events that can be used to explain the origin of one or more of the three stone types (igneous, sedimentary, and metamorphic).

Continental Drift, Plate Tectonics, and Sea Floor Spreading

The related theories of continental drift, plate tectonics, and sea floor spreading describe the creation of new stone and the reclaiming of existing stone on a global scale. The theory of continental drift was introduced in the early 1900s by Alfred Waegner, who proposed the idea that the continents are built on plates that are not fixed, but "float" on the surface of the earth. He proposed that at one time all of the continental plates were joined to form one large land mass, called Pangea. More than 300 million years ago Pangea began to break up into smaller continents, which drifted apart. Through this process several land masses became islands and eventually collided with other land masses. This collision of the land masses and the plates below caused uplifts that created mountain ranges, such as the Himalayas, when the India of today collided with the Asian continent. Similarly, the island that is now Italy collided with the mainland of Europe to form the Alpinni range as a continuation of the larger Alps. Today this concept is identified as plate tectonics, which accounts for the dynamic plate activity along the margin of the continental plates (see Figure 2-2).

For evidence to support his theory, Waegner pointed to the jigsaw fit of the continents of South America and Africa, which has recently been confirmed through the use of computer-generated mapping systems. In addition, Waegner presented evidence of similar fossils and minerals found on both sides of the Atlantic Ocean; he believed that it would have been impossible for them to have existed if the two separate continents were not at some time joined together.

The theory of continental drift was challenged at the time and was not recognized until World War II, when more sophisticated equipment was developed to map the ocean floor using sonic depth recording. Ridges were discovered in the middle of the ocean that rose to a height of 3,000 meters and were 2,000 kilometers wide, larger than the Himalayas. The mapping of the sea floor showed that there is a deep trench that bisects the length of the underwater mountain range, whose depth is more than 2,000 meters. Further research showed that the temperature of the material at the crest of the ridge was greater than the temperature farther away from the ridge. The difference in temperature of the material within the trench, as compared with the temperature of the material outside, is significant in reinforcing the concept of the conduction of hotter magma from the earth's core to the cooler surface through the trench within the midoceanic ridge.

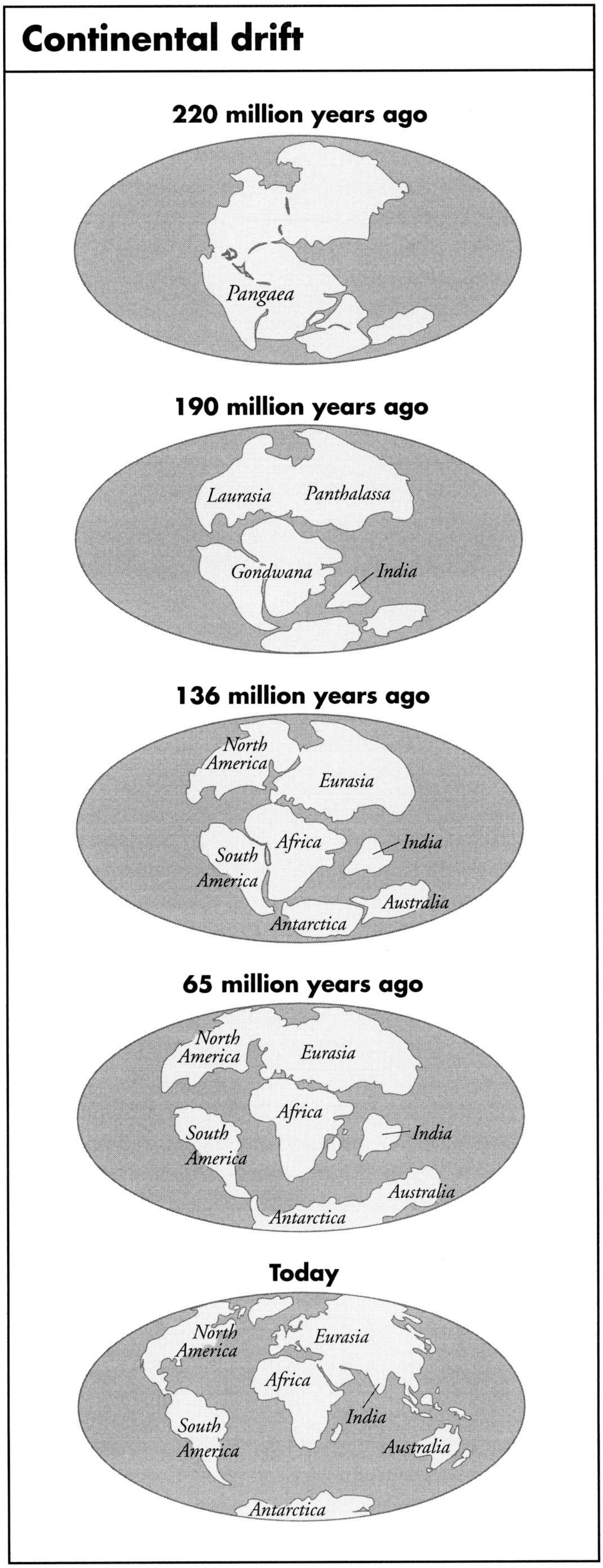

Continental drift

220 million years ago

Pangaea

190 million years ago

Laurasia   Panthalassa

Gondwana   India

136 million years ago

North America   Eurasia

South America   Africa   India

Antarctica   Australia

65 million years ago

North America   Eurasia

South America   Africa   India

Antarctica   Australia

Today

North America   Eurasia

Africa

South America   India   Australia

Antarctica

Figure 2-2 The theory of continental drift. The theory of continental drift proposed the idea that the continents are built on plates that are not fixed but float the surface of the earth. It was proposed that at one time all of the continental plates were joined to form one large land mass called Pangea. More than 300 million years ago, Pangea began to break up into smaller continents, which drifted apart. Through this process several land masses became islands and eventually collided with other land masses. This collision of the land masses and the plates below caused uplifts that created mountain ranges, such as the Himalayas, when the India of today collided with the Asian continent. To support the theory, the jigsaw fit of the continents of South America and Africa was presented along with evidence of similar fossils and minerals that were found on both sides of the Atlantic Ocean. It was believed that this would have been impossible if the two separate continents were not at some time joined together.

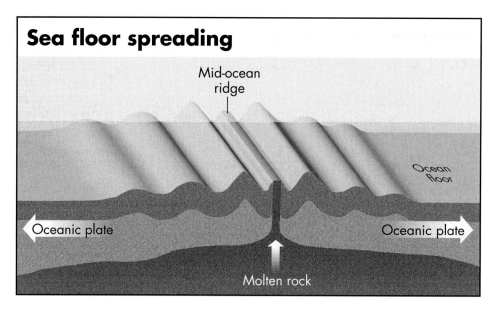

Figure 2-3 The theory of sea floor spreading.
The theory of continental drift was challenged at the time and was not recognized until sophisticated equipment was developed to map the ocean floor using sonic depth recording. Ridges were discovered in the middle of the oceans that rose to a height of 3,000 meters and were 2,000 kilometers wide, larger than the Himalayas. The mapping of the sea floor showed that there is a deep trench that bisects the length of the underwater mountain range, whose depth is more than 2,000 meters. The theory of sea floor spreading proposes that molten magma rises through the trench at these mid ocean ridges and moves away from the ridge in opposing directions. The new material joins the mass of the plates as they move toward the continents. The rock mass grows and spreads enlarging the sea floor, moving until it reaches the continental plates.

These discoveries were the basis for the theory of sea floor spreading, which proposes that molten magma rises through the trench at these midocean ridges and moves away from the ridge in opposing directions (see Figure 2-3). The new material joins the mass of the plates as they move toward the continents. Further studies verified that the age of the rock increases as it moves away from the midoceanic ridge. This data supports the theory that below the earth crust, which is composed of moveable plates and is referred to as the lithosphere, exists a layer of malleable heated rock known as the asthenoshpere which is heated by radioactive sources deep within the earth's mantle. The fluid asthenosphere circulates beneath the lithosphere through conduction, like water that boils in a pan. The conductive force pushes the magma from the core of the earth up through the ridge. The rock mass grows and spreads, enlarging the sea floor and moving it until it reaches the continental plates. When the oceanic plate collides with the continental plate, subduction occurs, forcing the rock mass back downward toward the asthenosphere, where the rock is melted again, thus completing the cycle (see Figure 2-4). The creation of the three types of stone deposits, igneous, sedimentary, and metamorphic, is better described using the concept of mountain building and the rock cycle as supported by the theories of continental drift, plate tectonics, and sea floor spreading. A closer look at the specific process that each of the three stone groups experiences reveals that the characteristics and

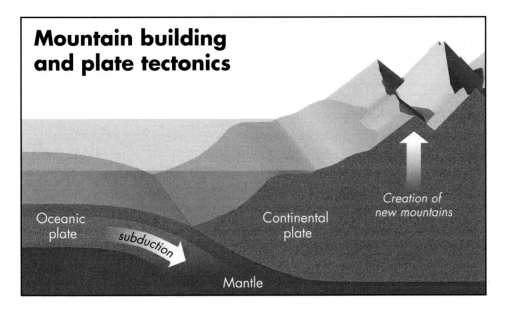

Figure 2-4 Mountain building and plate tectonics.
The related theories of continental drift, plate tectonics, and sea spreading describe the creation of new stone and the reclaiming of existing stone on a global scale. When the oceanic plate collides with the continental plate, subduction occurs, forcing the rock mass downward back toward the asthenosphere, where the rock is melted again. This collision of the oceanic plates with land masses caused uplifts that created mountain ranges, which accounts for the dynamic plate activity along the margin of the continental plates.

composition of individual stones vary because of their formation. With this information, a design and construction team can anticipate the general variation in appearance and the expected performance of a stone type.

The Rock Cycle

A simplified description of the cycle of how the three types of stone are produced uses the example of the rock cycle. (see Figure 2-5). The process begins with hot molten magma rising upward from the earth core to the surface, resulting either from volcanic activity creating pyroclastic ash and lava flows or from the heated magma traveling slowly toward the earth's surface. When this molten material cools and hardens, it can become a stone that is referred to as igneous stone. The literal translation of *igneous* is "of fire" or "fire from fire." Over time, which in geological terms is thousands of millions of years, these igneous deposits can be exposed to other forces of nature, such as wind and rain, which erode the rock. Particles of the igneous matter are then carried away with the winds, water, and ice flowing into rivers and accumulating in lake bottoms and seabeds. These deposits continue to be buried under following layers of sediment and can include the remains of coral and other organisms. These accumulations of eroded materials become consolidated, as a result of the extreme pressure from the weight of overlying material, and form sedimentary stone.

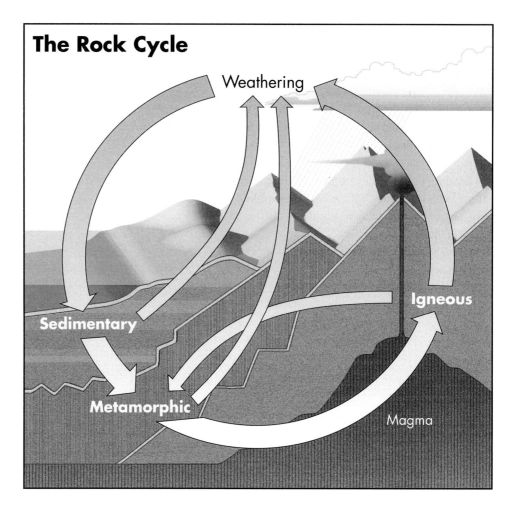

Figure 2-5 The rock cycle.
The rock cycle is a simplified description of how the three types of stone, igneous, sedimentary, and metamorphic, are produced. The process begins with hot molten magma rising upward from the earth's core to the surface, resulting from volcanic activity creating pyroclastic ash and lava flows, traveling slowly toward the earth's surface. When this molten material cools and hardens, it can become a stone that is referred to as igneous stone. Over time, igneous deposits are exposed to forces of nature such as wind and rain, which erode the rock. Particles of the igneous matter are then carried with the winds, water, and ice flowing into rivers and accumulating in lake bottoms and seabeds. These deposits continue to be buried under following layers of sediment, which consolidate as a result of the extreme pressure from the weight of overlying material, and form sedimentary stone. Igneous and sedimentary deposits exposed to great heat and pressure, caused by the continual layering of material over them or the shifting of the earth lithosphere, can experience a metamorphism. Usually, the extreme conditions of a metamorphic event cause a deposit to become plastic, sometimes folding the deposit, which forces the materials of one deposit to commingle with new materials, changing their form and appearance.

Igneous and sedimentary deposits exposed to great heat and pressure, caused by the continual layering of material over them or the shifting of the earth's lithosphere, can experience a metamorphism. Metamorphic stones can originate from either igneous or sedimentary rocks, or both. Usually, the extreme conditions of a metamorphic event cause a deposit to become plastic, sometimes folding the deposit, which forces the materials of one deposit to commingle with new materials, thus changing their form and appearance.

IGNEOUS STONE

Igneous stone is the material at the beginning of the entire stone creation process. Igneous stone begins as hot molten material, or magma, originating deep within the earth's core. As the magma makes its way to the surface, it cools and crystallizes, creating more mass by the joining of adjacent crystals. Igneous stone is classified in three subgroups: intrusive, extrusive, and porphyry stone.

Intrusive igneous stones, also referred to as "plutonic stone," are produced deep within the earth in the form of magma. The magma moves very slowly toward the surface of the earth, cooling and hardening at a slow rate. This allows for the development of individual minerals, growing into larger crystals that form coarse-grain rock. In addition, the more slowly the magma cools, the lighter in color the stone will become.

Batholiths are large intrusions, or the consolidation of several intrusions, of igneous rock that form deep within the earth. Batholiths that form stone deposits can be as large as several square miles in surface area. During batholithic emplacement, the pressure exerted by the overburdening on the almost solidified magma and the final adjustments in the chamber generate stress and directional weaknesses in the rock, creating easier ways of splitting and exposing joints that can be exploited to ease the extraction of building blocks from quarries. Intrusive igneous stone usually becomes solid before reaching the surface of the earth, getting trapped below deposits of other stone. Intrusive stone hardens to form deposits deep below the surface of the earth, which are exposed through erosion of the deposits above or by a metamorphic event that brings them closer to the surface.

Geologists have discovered an enormous granite intrusion that forms the earth's crust below the states of Iowa, Indiana, and Illinois in the midwestern United States. This deposit of granite is buried beneath layers of accumulated sediment that is as much as 1 mile deep. Scientists believe that the magma was unable to penetrate the sedimentary deposits near the earth's surface and spread laterally for hundreds of miles as laccoliths and sills. It may require millions of years of wind and water erosion or the force of a major metamorphic event to expose this deposit. This example of an intrusive deposit differs from intrusive deposits that have been exposed along the margins of the North American continent through upheavals resulting from sea floor spreading and subduction.

Extrusive igneous stones are also created in a molten state, forming closer to the surface of the earth. The deposit is trapped close to the earth surface until volcanic or metamorphic activity creates fractures in the overlying rock. The mass travels to the surface rapidly through fractures in the overlying rock as it forms dikes and lava flows. Mountain building creates volcanoes by bringing material to the surface, which accumulates and grows in size as the volcano develops. Once the material reaches the surface it cools rapidly, further increasing the size of the volcano. Some of the material becomes explosive and is turned to ash as it is expelled from the volcano. The ash can be carried from the volcano for miles, thus providing new material for sedimentary deposits. Because extrusive material cools at a faster rate than intrusive stone, its stones are finer grained and usually darker in color than the slower-moving intrusive stones.

A *porphry* generally has the appearance of a stone produced from volcanic activity; however, this type of deposit is produced by the combination of intrusive and extrusive processes. If a rock deposit develops and cools at a fast rate (extrusive characteristics), then begins to cool more slowly (intrusive characteristics), rock composed of a combination of grain sizes is created; larger crystals are found within finer-grain rock.

Igneous stone produced in any of these three ways will yield material homogeneous in character and produce fabricated stone panels and tile that will be predictable in color and character, as well as consistent in performance from module to module.

The primary minerals of igneous stone are feldspar, quartz, and ferromagnesium minerals. Different combinations of these minerals will yield the various colors of igneous stone; larger proportions of feldspar and quartz will yield lighter colors and are typically referred to as *granites*. An increase of ferromagnesium-type materials will yield darker colors; stones such as basalt are commonly found with this group of characteristics. When varieties of minerals are present in a deposit and the cooling time of the deposit varies, the character of the stone may vary. Such is the case with porphyry, which is characterized by a small granular matrix incorporating larger aggregates.

There are many favorable characteristics in stones of this group. These stones are generally very hard as compared with sedimentary stones, are highly resistant to abrasion, and have greater resistance to acids and staining.

SEDIMENTARY STONE

Sedimentary stones are the products of erosion or weathering of rock deposits, both mechanical and chemical. Mechanical erosion occurs through long exposure of rock to the forces of nature — wind, rain, and ice. In mountainous areas water from rain or melted ice migrates into the fissures and openings in the rock and freezes when the temperature drops. As the water freezes it expands, slowly breaking the rock into smaller and smaller pieces. The mechanical wearing of rock does not change the minerals present in the rock; it only reduces the size of the rock to smaller particles. The breakdown of the rock into smaller particles also exposes more of the rock to further erosion. At a regional scale, the movement of glaciers was responsible for the abrasion of rock surfaces, breaking down the face of the deposits. As the mass of the glaciers grew, they carried the eroded materials and deposited the smaller particles in low-lying areas. Water from mountain and glacier runoff also erodes the disintegrating rock deposits, carrying particles long distances from their points of origin and depositing the larger particles in areas where streams and rivers slow. The finer particles continue with the stream as it grows and makes its way to lower elevations, forming lakes and eventually carrying smaller particles to the seas. Finally, the wind weathering the face of the rock carries fine particles of material and sand in the atmosphere and deposits the eroded rock and sand to form layers of sediment. These deposits often form in low-lying areas and locations where seabeds once existed.

When particles of sediment are transported to bodies of water and deposited, the various particles are sorted by size through natural wave action occurring at the edges of the bodies of water. Greater wave action occurs at the water's edge or shoreline, gathering the larger-sized particles, and finer particles are carried farther away from the shoreline. Material that forms sandstones will deposit close to the shore; finer particles that form shale deposits will occur farther from shore;

and even finer particles that form limestone deposits will occur the greatest distance from shore (see Figure 2-6).

Chemical erosion takes place through oxidation and the chemical reaction that occurs as water carries solutions that break down the rock. In tropical climates where the temperature does not get low enough to cause freezing, it is the oxygen in the air and the acids in the soil from decaying organic matter that destroy the rock deposit. As the rock breaks down to smaller and smaller particles, water distributes the eroded matter to deposit in low-lying areas.

Whether by mechanical or chemical erosion, the layers of sediment continue to build on one another. Deposits composed of finer-grain particles do not allow water to collect because the only voids present are small in size. Pressure resulting from the continual burial by overlying layers compacts the deposit, forcing the water out of any voids that may exist, and allows for the remaining materials to bind. Clays and shales are formed in this manner. Larger particles of sediment allow more water to remain in the void areas, as compared with sediment composed of smaller particles. The remaining sediment, when in contact with various types of calcite, silica, and iron oxides, will bind or cement the deposit together. Minerals such as calcite are formed when precipitated sediment carries chemicals such as magnesium, chloride, sodium, calcium, sulfur, and other chemicals that are soluble in water. Limestone is formed when these types of chemicals precipitate in warm waters and compaction begins within the sediment. Living organisms feed on the minerals in the waters and sediment and add to the deposit as they die and decay. As further compaction of the deposit occurs, the deposit

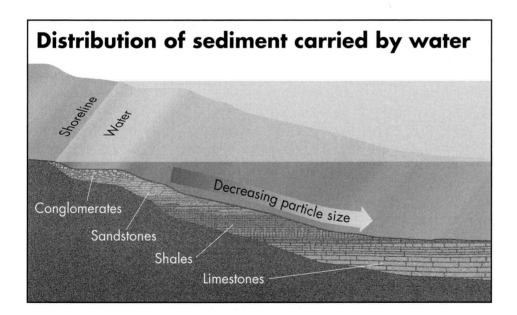

Figure 2-6 Distribution of sediment carried by water.
When particles of sediment are transported to bodies of water and deposited, the various particles are sorted by size through natural wave action occurring at the edges of the bodies of water. Greater wave action occurs at the water's edge or shoreline, gathering the larger-sized particles, and finer particles are carried farther away from the shoreline. Material that forms sandstones will deposit close to the shore; finer particles that form shale deposits will occur farther from shore; and even finer particles that form limestone deposits will occur the greatest distance from shore.

becomes increasingly dense, crystallizing the particles and producing a stone formation that is extremely hard in character. This process is referred to as *lithification,* the creation of stone.

Sedimentary stone can be subdivided into three general groups, based on the type of weathering or chemical reaction that worked to break down the rock:

Detrital deposits, which are composed of particles that have been mechanically disintegrated or ground down and are of varying sizes. Sand, gravel, and silt make up this type of formation; sandstone is a product of detrital deposits.

Chemical formations, which are deposits created through precipitation and evaporation, whereby material is chemically dissolved in a water solution. The common elements in this type of formation are calcium, sodium, magnesium, and potassium; various types of limestone are products of chemical formations.

Organic deposits, which are deposits of organic matter that are also precipitated and that chemically bind with skeletal matter as each layer builds up. When organisms dissolve with these deposits, they produce calcium carbonate, which is the basic element of limestone; organic deposits usually produce shell and coral types of limestone.

The mineral composition of stone types can be recognized within a sedimentary deposit formed by the distribution of various-sized particles within a body of water. The larger particles that form sandstones deposited closer to the shoreline are composed of a greater amount of quartz; farther from shore, the finer particles that form shale are deposited, composed of lesser amounts of quartz than sandstone and increased proportions of clay minerals. The finer particles that form limestone are deposited the farthest distance from shore and are composed primarily of calcite and dolomite. These finer materials whose deposition develops to produce limestone will experience further change as chemical reactions occur during the process of lithification

Calcite, silica, and iron oxides are the materials that cement sedimentary rocks. The presence of iron oxides in sedimentary deposits produce red, orange, and green colorations.

The remains of once living organisms are often found in sedimentary deposits, leaving a record of the period of their deposition. Plant and animal life representing the earth's most recent history have been preserved in layered rock deposits as fossils, which can give us a glimpse of life millions of years ago. One of the most famous discoveries is the fossil of an archaeopteryx (first known bird) on March 3, 1877, in a limestone deposit that was formed during the Jurassic

Minerals Present	Sandstone Composition (%)	Shale Composition (%)	Limestone Composition (%)
Quartz	70	32	4
Feldspar	8	18	2
Clay minerals	9	34	1
Calcite and dolomite	11	8	93
Iron oxides	1	5	—

Period. The archaeopteryx fossil was found by Johann Doerr, a German farmer, in a quarry on his property which he leased to others. This limestone quarry is near Eichstadt, in the Bavaria region of Germany, which is rich in limestone deposits. Johann Doerr's discovery of the archaeopteryx provided evidence to support Darwin's theory of evolution. Soon after his find, Doerr sold the archaeopteryx for 20,000 gold marks to Werner von Siemens, who put the fossil on exhibition at the Museum of Natural History at the Humboldt University in Berlin. Johann Doerr used the proceeds from the sale of the fossil to build his own quarrying and fabrication company. His company, founded in 1877, is still in operation today by his two great-great-grandsons, Johann Neumeyer and Otto Brigl, who are cousins.

METAMORPHIC STONE

Metamorphic stones are created through dynamic geologic activity caused by extreme heat, pressure, or contact with chemical solutions, occurring adjacent to or within a deposit of either igneous or sedimentary stone. The term *metamorphose* is literally defined as "to change form." Metamorphic rocks are created deep within the earth after exposure to extreme heat and pressure during a geologic event that alters the structure of a rock and may even change its mineral composition. These stresses are a result of the mountain building process, the intrusion of magma, or a regional metamorphic event. The change in form of the stone occurs when igneous or sedimentary rock is in a solid state and then experiences the extreme heat or pressure that changes the stone structurally or chemically without melting or reducing it to magma. The kind of metamorphic stone that develops depends on the previous composition of the stone and the temperature and pressure conditions at the time of the metamorphosis; the greater the heat or pressure experienced, the greater the change.

Types of Metamorphic Activity

The three types of metamorphic events are regional metamorphism, contact metamorphism, and a chemical metamorphism that is also referred to as metasomatism. Often the events that occur in each type of metamorphism are similar to those that occur in one of the other categories, such as the burial heat that is created during subduction, which is regional activity, and the heat that is created during the mountain building cycle in a contact metamorphism.

Regional metamorphism occurs when large land forms collide, such as when oceanic plates collide with continental plates during sea floor spreading or when the force of mountain building acts on a large surface area. Mountain building activity is similar to contact metamorphism, differing by its lack of directed force.

Contact metamorphism occurs when directed intrusions make contact with rock deposits and the heat from the intrusion changes the form of the adjacent or country rock deposit (pre-existing rock that is still being formed). The closer the country rock to the source of the intrusion, the greater the change in the rock (see Figure 2-7).

Chemical metamorphism is the change that occurs when chemicals that are carried in water solution or rocks with chemical material make contact with rock deposits, resulting in a chemical reaction that alters the state of the preexisting rock deposit. A chemical metamorphism also occurs when hydrothermal solutions introduce new materials to the deposits. Hydrothermal solutions are created when hot water dissolves minerals and creates a chemical solution. Hydrothermal

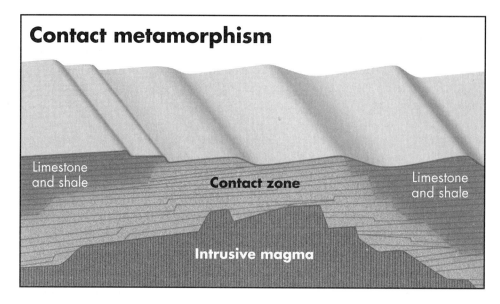

Figure 2-7 Contact metamorphism.
Metamorphic stones are created through dynamic geologic activity caused by extreme heat, pressure, or contact with chemical solutions, occurring adjacent to or within a deposit of either igneous or sedimentary stone. Contact metamorphism occurs when a directed intrusion makes contact with rock deposits and the heat from the intrusion changes the form of the adjacent rock deposit. The closer the rock to the source of the intrusion, the greater the change in the rock. This exposure to extreme heat and pressure alters the structure of a rock and may even change its mineral composition.

activity will speed up a metamorphism, as compared with the activity of a non-heated chemical solution.

Sources of heat that contribute to the metamorphic process are geothermal/burial, contact, and regional sources.

Geothermal or burial heat develops as the temperature rises within the earth as the proximity of the deposit moves closer to the earth's core. This occurs during the recycling stage of the mountain building process and during subduction when the material from the oceanic plate is forced to the core of the earth.

A *contact* heat source, such as magma from an intrusion, initiates a metamorphic event when it comes in direct contact with a rock deposit. This is usually a focused intrusion that has made contact with the surrounding country rock. The intrusion is part of the mountain building process.

Regional heat, such as that generated by large bodies of molten magma below or adjacent to the rock, creates a metamorphism when a rock deposit is exposed to it. This type of activity is similar to an intrusion, but less focused, having an impact on a larger surface area.

The types of pressure that may affect a stone deposit are burial pressure, dynamic pressure, and tectonic pressure.

Burial pressure increases with depth as the accumulation of weight from the layers of the deposit increases. The accumulation of material onto existing layered deposits is part of the mountain building process.

Dynamic pressure is pressure that develops along a fault within the earth, which causes the rock deposits to move and crush. This may occur during earthquakes or when the mountain building process initiates an event that causes the plates along a fault to make contact.

Tectonic pressure develops when large continental formations collide or when plates converge upon each other. This type of dynamic activity occurs during sea floor spreading when the oceanic plate collides with the continental plate or when land masses collide, such as when present-day India collided with the Asian continent to form the Himalayas.

A metamorphism within a rock deposit changes the texture and mineral content of the rock within the deposit. There are two types of changes that occur during a metamorphism: foliation and recrystallization.

Foliation is the folding or layering of metamorphic rock that occurs when pressure is applied from one direction (see Figure 2-8). The minerals that are flatter or platy in character within the stone will align parallel along their axis and elongate. The reorientation of the minerals will be perpendicular to the direction of the force of metamorphic activity. This alignment creates a texture that is a layered cleavage, the characteristic that occurs when slates are formed, or the foliation will produce a stone with a banded character, expressing different colors within the bands as characterized by gneiss and schist. When the pressure applied to the deposit is equal on all sides of the rock, or if the mineral structure of the rock is not flat or platy, the process of foliation will not occur, producing a mineral structure that is nondirectional; these stones are nonfoliated.

Recrystallization is the other type of change that occurs within the metamorphosis of stone. The rearrangement of crystals takes place when smaller crystals collide with larger crystals, merging to become even larger crystals, and existing crystals will change their shape and grow under high pressure. New crystals will develop from the minerals that are present when the existing minerals come in contact with the chemicals of the new minerals. Under the combined forces of heat and pressure, the recrystalization process moves the minerals closer togeth-

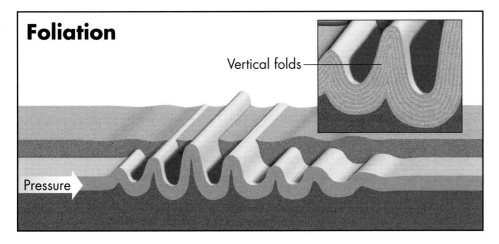

Figure 2-8 Foliation.
Foliation is the folding or layering of metamorphic rock that occurs when pressure is applied from one direction. The minerals that compose this type of rock are flatter or platy in character and will align parallel along their axis and elongate. The reorientation of the minerals will be perpendicular to the direction of the force of metamorphic activity. This alignment creates a texture that is a layered cleavage, which occurs when slates are formed.

er, filling all of the voids and pores of the rock and producing a denser stone with reduced porosity. Many stones that are created in this manner are denser and stronger than sedimentary stone.

The table below gives examples of these types of changes.

Stone Name	Type of Change	Source Stone	Metamorphic Action	Characteristics
Slate	Foliation	Shale and mud	Contact	Splitting or cleaving of the surface; fine-textured structure
Marble	Recrystallization	Limestone	Contact or Chemical	Interlocking, often coarse, calcite crystals, little or no porosity; non-directional alignment of crystals
Quartzite	Recrystallization	Sandstone	Contact	Interlocking, fused quartz grains; little or no porosity; nondirectional alignment of crystals
Schist	Foliation	Fine-grained stone	Regional	Dark and light, fine-banded, wavy texture with layers of aligned materials
Gneiss	Foliation	Coarse-grained stone	Regional	Dark and light, coarse-banded, wavy texture with layers of aligned materials

BUILDING STONE TYPES

A basic understanding of the geology of stone formation is useful when applied to the specific uses of stones in the built environment and the anticipated performance of stone types. The three primary geologic classifications of rock—igneous, sedimentary, and metamorphic—give us clues as to how a stone was created, how it is quarried and processed, and, ultimately, how the stone will perform. Within each geologic classification there are subgroups that are intended to describe in more specific and detailed terms how a stone was formed. Gaining an understanding and appreciation for the creation of one of nature's building materials is challenging, and the subject is easily confused when the forces of international marketing are factored into the equation. A great deal of confusion is created by the marketers of stone products in their effort to create exclusivity of a stone that currently exists or is new to the marketplace. This occurs when a quarrier and supplier incorrectly categorize a stone to better describe how the stone might perform so as to make the stone more marketable. Many marketers of international stones use proprietary names to protect their specification, and eventually their sale, while clouding the real identity of the stones. The negative impact on the industry is obvious: architects and those who specify stone will not have the opportunity to make complete and accurate evaluations of a stone and its performance when its identity is veiled in mystery.

With increasing technology in the quarrying and fabrication of stone and the improvement of the infrastructure of many emerging countries, more new stones are available in the marketplace today than ever before. The following descrip-

Geological Timeline

Era	Period	Epoch	years ago	Events	Sto
Cenozoic	Quaternary	Recent		Modern man. Ice age ends 10,000 years ago.	Alabaster
			—10,000		
		Pleistocene		Human beings. Ice age begins 1.6 million years ago.	Peperino
			—2,500,000		
	Tertiary	Pliocene		Hominids, elephants.	Rosso Le Vista Gr
			—7,000,000		
		Miocene		Ungulates, pinnipeds, marsupials.	Perlato C
			—26,000,000		
		Oligocene		Old and New World primates.	Basaltina
			—38,000,000		
		Eocene		Rodents, whales. Himalayas formed.	Breccia C Chiampe
			—54,000,000		
		Paleocene		Mammals become dominant: Carnivores, early primates.	Beige Ca
			—65,000,000		
Mesozoic	Cretaceous			Mass extinctions at end of Cretaceous: Dinosaurs, ammonites disappear.	Green St Gris Tape
			—135,000,000		
	Jurassic			Giant dinosaurs. Mollusks, echinoderms. First birds. Rocky Mountains formed.	Jet Mist, Jura Beig
			—190,000,000		
	Triassic			First dinosaurs and mammals. Modern corals.	Hualian Jade, Duquesa Gris, Empress Park Green
			—225,000,000		
Paleozoic	Permian			Numerous reptiles. Trilobites. Many invertebrates go extinct.	Blue Pearl, Porphyry, Rubane
			—280,000,000		
	Carboniferous	Pennsylvanian		First reptiles, first flying insects.	Apache Gold, Pink Kershaw, Rose del Salto, Negro Marquina
			—320,000,000		
		Mississippian		Numerous amphibians.	Indiana Buff, Colorado Buff, Red Dragon, Colorado Yule
			—345,000,000		
	Devonian			First amphibians, crabs and insects. Freshwater fish.	Bluestone, Fior di Pesco, Grigio Timau, Sparta Pink, Black St. Laurent, Barre Gray
			—395,000,000		
	Silurian			Brachiopods, crinoids, corals abound. Jawless fish.	Valders Buff, Grey, Dove White; Ajax, Pennsylvania Slate, Macedonian White
			—430,000,000		
	Ordovician			Trilobites, gastropods, bivalves, cephalopods abound.	Creme Fleuri, Kirkstone, White Irina Granite, Golden Buff, Rose de la Clarte
			—500,000,000		
	Cambrian			First trilobites, gastropods, bivalves, echinoderms, brachiopods.	Georgia White, Vermont, Estremoz, Verde Antique, Silver Cloud
			—570,000,000		
Proterozoic - Precambrian				First multicellular animals: Jellyfish, sea pens, worms.	Black Sao Gabriel, Baltic, Cinza Prata, Brown, Dakota Mahogany, Verde Amazonas
			—700,000,000		
Archeozoic				Origin of life. First algal plants: Oxygenation of atmosphere.	
			—3,500,000,000		
Azoic				Formation and cooling of Earth.	
			—4,600,000,000		

Figure 2-8 The geological time line showing the periods when common stone varieties were formed.

tions of the commercially available stone groups include the basic characteristics of stone types and their behavior and assist in the identification of stones to minimize confusion. In chapter 6, "Guidelines for the Selection of Stone," the descriptions of the stone types are expressed in a qualitative format to provide sound guidelines for the proper selection of stone and its application.

Igneous Stones

Igneous stones are subdivided into two sub groups: intrusive stone and extrusive stone. *Intrusive* igneous stones, also referred to as "plutonic stones," originate deep within the earth in the form of magma. The magma moves very slowly toward the surface of the earth, cooling and hardening at a slow rate. This allows for the development of individual minerals into larger crystals that form coarse-grain rock. Intrusive igneous stones are usually lighter in color. *Extrusive* igneous stones also originate in a molten state, but closer to the surface of the earth. The material is trapped close to the earth's surface until volcanic action creates fractures in the overlying rock. The fractures in the rock allow the material to travel to the surface. Through volcanic action, the material is exposed at the earth's surface and cools quickly. Because the extrusive material cools at a faster rate and there is less time for crystals to form, these stones are finer-grained than intrusive stone.

INTRUSIVE OR PLUTONIC STONES

Intrusive igneous stone includes granite, plutonite, and gabbro stone. These stones are then further subdivided, based on their silica content; stone having a higher silica content are classified as granite, and those with lower contents of silica are classified as plutonite and gabbro.

Granites are primarily composed of feldspar and quartz, with smaller quantities of other minerals, such as mica and hornblende The presence of these types of minerals give granite a crystalline form and texture, appearing as aggregates in a uniform matrix material. Because of the igneous origin of granite, these stones have the most uniform and consistent appearance of all of the building stones. The combination of different minerals and the rate of cooling during formation will determine their color and texture. Greater quantities of feldspar and quartz will yield lighter colors; lesser quantities will yield darker colors, such as black granites. The more slowly the granite cools during its formation, the larger the crystals; the faster the cooling period, the smaller the crystals. The common colors of granite are greys, whites, blacks, reds, greens, beiges, and, more rarely, blues.

Gabbro, referred to as plutonite in many European countries, is similar in texture to granite. However, because of a lower silica content, these stones have lesser quantities of the light-colored minerals quartz and feldspar and more dark-colored minerals such as hornblende, pyroxenes, and biotite. The presence of these minerals give gabbro stones their dark grey to black coloring and a relatively finer texture than granite. Stones that are thought to be black granites, from a mineralogical perspective, are classified as gabbro.

Production Finishes

Polished — High gloss, mirrorlike.

Honed — A duller sheen than a polished finish, mattelike.

Sawn—Rough sawn from the block; sometimes shows the coarse blade marks from the gang saw or the circular marks of a disc saw.

Sandblasted—A mechanical finish achieved by sandblasting the face of the stone. The degree of coarseness varies, based on the rate of the blasting and the length of time that the blasting wand is held in place.

Flamed/thermal—A coarse, rough texture. The degree of coarseness depends on the texture of the aggregate or crystal mix.

Water or hydro finish—A texture similar to a flamed finish, although less dramatic and less destructive to the stone than the flaming process.

Bush hammered—A mechanically tooled finish utilizing a chisel-type tool. Many types of directional and nondirectional bush-hammered textures are available.

Split face—A tooled finish achieved by striking the top edge of the stone with a chisel. Split-face finishes can be produced by hand or mechanically.

Tumbled—An antiqued finish achieved by placing small stone modules into a mixing tub with coarse aggregates and water. The tumbling action rounds the edges and corners to give the stone a distressed appearance.

Acid washed—An antiqued finish achieved by applying a diluted acid solution to the face of the stone. The longer the solution is in contact with the stone, the coarser the results. Acid solutions have a particularly aggressive action on calcareous stones.

Uses

Exterior—Facings: adhered veneer, anchored veneer, curtain wall panel systems, and precast panel systems. Paving: thin-set, thick-set, raised paving systems.

Interior—Facings: adhered veneer, anchored veneer. Paving: thin-set, thick-set, raised paving systems. Casework and furniture.

EXTRUSIVE IGNEOUS STONE

Basalt

Extrusive igneous stone is characterized by its fine grain size, which is a result of a rapid cooling and solidification process. The minerals that compose basalt are high in iron and magnesium, with lesser amounts of quartz and feldspar (siliceous minerals). Basalt is formed from volcanic action and lava flows, which contribute to its uniform and consistent appearance. The colors of basalt are generally dark greys and blacks. Deposits are often found in large hexagonal columns (columnar basalt). The columns are the result of fractures formed during the cooling of lava.

Production Finishes

Polished—Some basalt stones can achieve a high-gloss, mirrorlike finish.

Honed—A duller sheen than a polished finish, matte-like.

Sawn—Rough sawn from the block; sometimes shows the coarse blade marks from the gang saw or the circular marks of a disc saw.

Bush hammered — A mechanically tooled finish utilizing a chisel-type tool. Many types of directional and nondirectional bush-hammered textures are available.

Split face — A tooled finish achieved through striking the top edge of the stone with a chisel. Split-face finishes can be produced by hand or mechanically.

Rough from quarry — The texture that is produced by natural erosion and the separation of small blocks from the main deposit.

Uses

Exterior — Can possibly be used in adhered veneer and anchored veneer systems, but because of the limitation in the sizes of blocks and the few fabricators that work with basalt, the primary use for the majority of most basalt stone is in the landscape environment. Basalt can be crushed into uniform shapes and sizes, often used in road building and related construction.

Interior — Facings: adhered veneer and anchored veneer. Paving: thick-set, stair treads, and raised paving systems; few quarriers or fabricators of basalt have the capacity to produce modular thin tile that can be thin set.

Porphyry

Porphyries are characterized by larger crystals or aggregates (formed by slower cooling) within a finer-grained igneous matrix (formed by a faster rate of cooling). The larger crystals are formed as the material cools slowly. When the molten material is brought to the surface rapidly through volcanic action, the larger crystals become surrounded by the fine-grained crystals, referred to as ground mass.

Porhyries are primarily composed of feldspar and contain many other mineral types, depending on the region where the deposit is found. Most porphyries are red and red-orange in color, and some are purple. Historically, the name *porphyry* originated from the Greek word *porphyra,* which means purple. The word *porphyry* is also used to describe characteristics common to igneous stones, rather than a specific stone — larger-grain inclusions found within a contrasting and fine matrix.

Production Finishes

Polished — Some porphyry stones can achieve a high-gloss finish, although their porous nature does not permit a continuous, full-filled gloss finish.

Honed — A duller sheen than a polished finish, matte-like.

Sawn — Rough sawn from the block; sometimes shows the coarse blade marks from the gang saw.

Bush hammered — A mechanically tooled finish utilizing a chisel-type tool. Many types of directional and nondirectional bush-hammered textures are available.

Split face — A tooled finish achieved by striking the top edge of the stone with a chisel. Split-face finishes can be produced by hand or mechanically.

Uses

Exterior — Facings; adhered veneer and anchored veneer. Paving: Thick-set.

Interior — Facings; adhered veneer and anchored veneer. Paving: Thick-set; few quarriers or fabricators of porphries have the capacity to produce modular thin tile that can be thin set.

Sedimentary Stones

LIMESTONE

Limestones are principally composed of calcium carbonate. They can vary dramatically from one type to another in hardness, density, and porosity. The compaction of the deposit and the cementing materials determine the hardness, density, and porosity of a specific limestone. Limestones are generally lighter in color, beige to beige-grey, occasionally highlighted by red, red-orange, or green, depending on the deposit.

The varying composition and characteristics of limestone make it difficult to anticipate the performance of these types of stones as a group. They must be reviewed and compared individually to determine their suitability in specific applications. Limestones are subdivided into three groups: oolitic, calcitic, and dolomitic. These categories are based partly on the manner in which they were formed and, more importantly, by their chemical composition. In addition, the dolomitic and calcitic types of limestone can vary according to the proportion of calcium or magnesium that is present.

> *Limestone:* Stone that is composed of more than 50% calcium carbonate ($CaCO_3$).
>
> > *Oolitic limestone:* Made up of very small spheroidal concretions of calcium carbonate cemented together. At the center of the spheroidal form is a fine grain of sand or other matter, to which the calcium has bonded.
>
> *Dolomite:* Limestone that is composed of more than 50% magnesium carbonate ($CaMg (CO_3)_2$)

Limestone Classification	Minerals Present		Elements Present	
	Calcite %	Dolomite %	Calcium %	Magnesium %
Limestone (Calcite)	90–100	0–10	95–100	0–5
Dolomitic Limestone	50–90	10–50	75–95	5–25
Calcitic Limestone	10–50	50–90	55–75	25–45
Dolomite	0–10	90–100	0–5	45–50

Production Finishes

Polished — Many of the harder types of limestone can achieve a high-gloss, mirrorlike finish.

Honed — Some of the less hard limestones can achieve a high-honed finish, which has a higher degree of reflectivity than a standard honed finish, yet duller than a mirror finish. Standard honed finishes have a duller sheen than a polished finish; matte-like.

Sawn — Rough sawn from the block; sometimes shows the coarse blade marks from the gang saw or the circular marks of a disc saw.

Sandblasted — A mechanical finish achieved by sandblasting the face of the stone. The degree of coarseness varies based on the rate of the blasting and the length of time that the blasting wand is held in place.

Flamed — There are a limited number of limestones that can achieve a flamed finish. It is possible to produce a flamed finish when the limestone is composed of several dissimilar minerals with differing rates of thermal linear expansion. When a limestone is composed of minerals having different rates of thermal linear expansion and the stone is exposed to the focused high heat of an acetylene torch, the minerals with the highest rate of expansion will expand and break from the face of the stone. When exposed to a high heat source for a prolonged period of time, some limestones begin to disintegrate and can be reduced to lime. The flamed texture that a limestone achieves will be flatter than the flamed texture of an igneous stone.

Bush hammered — A mechanically tooled finish utilizing a chisel-type tool. Many types of directional and nondirectional bush-hammered textures are available.

Tumbled — An antiqued finish that is achieved by placing small stone modules into a mixing tub with coarse aggregates and water. The tumbling action rounds the edges and corners to give the stone a distressed appearance.

Acid washed — An antiqued finish achieved by applying a diluted acid solution to the face of the stone. The longer the solution is in contact with the stone, the coarser the results. Acid solutions have particularly aggressive actions on calcareous stones, such as limestone, and are destructive to the face with prolonged contact.

Uses

Exterior — Facings: adhered veneer, anchored veneer, panel systems, and precast panel systems. Paving: thin-set, thick-set, raised paving systems.

Interior — Facings: adhered veneer and anchored veneer. Paving: thin-set and thick-set. Casework and furniture.

TRAVERTINE

Travertine is a crystalline form of calcium carbonate that is developed in layered deposits adjacent to cold and warm mineral springs. The percolating action of the spring water tends to make the travertine formations more porous in character. Some types of travertine can be reasonably hard and have been used in significant buildings since the days of the Romans and Greeks. The holes that are created by the percolating action are typically filled with resin material to make the material more resistant to weathering and wear.

Travertines vary in degrees of hardness, density, and porosity, which makes it difficult to generalize the performance characteristics of travertine. Many are hard and dense enough to be considered for application in building systems; however, each type of travertine should be reviewed independently because of the variance in characteristics.

Production Finishes

Polished — High gloss, mirrorlike.

Honed — A duller sheen than a polished finish, mattelike.

Sawn — Rough sawn from the block; sometimes shows the coarse blade marks from the gang saw or the circular marks of a disc saw.

Split face — A tooled finish achieved by striking the top edge of the stone with a chisel. Split-face finishes can be produced by hand or mechanically.

Tumbled — An antiqued finish achieved by placing small stone modules into a mixing tub with coarse aggregates and water. The tumbling action rounds the edges and corners to give the stone a distressed appearance.

Acid washed — An antiqued finish achieved by applying a diluted acid solution to the face of the stone. The longer the solution is in contact with the stone, the coarser the results. Acid solutions have particularly aggressive actions on calcareous stones.

Uses

Exterior — Facings: adhered veneer, anchored veneer, panel systems, and precast panel systems. Paving: thin-set and thick-set.

Interior — Facings: adhered veneer and anchored veneer. Paving: thin-set and thick-set. Casework and furniture.

SANDSTONE, BLUESTONE, BROWNSTONE, FLAGSTONE, AND QUARTZITIC SANDSTONE

Sandstones are coarse grained and composed almost entirely of siliceous matter or sand, which, chemically, is quartz. The bonding material that cements the grains of sand is typically silica, calcium carbonate, or iron oxide. The compaction of the deposit and the cementing materials determine the hardness, density, and porosity of a specific sandstone. The color of sandstone is affected by the content of iron oxides. The presence of limonite yields yellow, brown, and buff shades. The presence of hematite yields darker browns and reds. The purest of quartz-based sandstones yield whiter colors. The primary component in the composition of sandstones is quartz, which makes sandstone inherently resistant to acid.

Production Finishes

Honed — Some sandstones can achieve a honed finish; however, the finish has a duller sheen than a typical honed finish.

Sawn — Rough sawn from the block; sometimes shows the circular marks of a disc saw.

Natural split face — A natural split-face finish is similar to a mechanically achieved split-face finish, differing only by the natural occurrence of cleaved layers in the sandstone deposit that allows for the sandstone to split. The texture is usually flatter than the mechanically split texture and varies according to the density of the stone within a specific deposit.

Uses

Exterior — Facings: adhered veneer, anchored veneer, and precast panel systems. Paving: thick-set and raised paving systems when the denser varieties are used.

Interior — Facings: adhered veneer and anchored veneer. Paving: Sandstone pavers usually require a thick-set application owing to the inability of most fabricators to produce thin calibrated modules. There are a few types of sandstones, such as bluestone, that are dense enough to withstand the pressure that is required to fabricate thin modules. Casework and furniture.

SOAPSTONE

Soapstones are usually grey green or grey brown in color. The primary components of soapstone are talc and chlorite; the greater the content of chlorite, the more pronounced the green color will be. The talc minerals give soapstone its characteristic slippery feeling. Soapstones are very dense; however, they are also very soft and easily carved.

Production Finishes

Honed — A higher degree of honing is achievable with soapstones; however, a polished finish is not obtainable.

Uses

Soapstones are primarily used for ornamental carving; however, the stone is extremely dense and the mineral composition makes it resistant to acids. Soapstone has been used frequently as countertop material on casework. Historically, soapstone has been the material of choice as a countertop material for chemistry laboratories.

Metamorphic Stones

MARBLE

Marbles are composed primarily of dolomite and calcite. The color of a specific marble is determined by the various other minerals present. The mineral hematite will add red, limonite will add yellow, serpentine will add green, and diopside will add blue. Marbles began as limestone, and the colors, textures, and dramatic veining are produced through the metamorphic activity that the deposit experienced. Many stones are referred to as "marbles" because they can achieve a shine, but a true marble is produced through a metamorphic event.

Production Finishes

Polished — High gloss, mirrorlike.

Honed — A duller sheen than a polished finish, mattelike.

Sawn — Rough sawn from the block; sometimes shows the coarse blade marks from the gang saw or the circular marks of a disc saw.

Sandblasted — A mechanical finish achieved by sandblasting the face of the stone. The degree of coarseness varies according to the rate of the blasting and the length of time that the blasting wand is held in place.

Bush hammered — A mechanically tooled finish utilizing a chisel-type tool. Many types of directional and nondirectional bush-hammered textures are available.

Split face — A tooled finish achieved by striking the top edge of the stone with a chisel. Split-face finishes can be produced by hand or mechanically.

Tumbled — An antiqued finish achieved by placing small stone modules into a mixing tub with coarse aggregates and water. The tumbling action rounds the edges and corners to give the stone a distressed appearance.

Acid washed — A antiqued finish achieved by applying a diluted acid solution to the face of the stone. The longer the solution is in contact with the stone, the coarser the results. Acid solutions have particularly aggressive actions on calcareous stones.

Uses

Exterior — Facings: adhered veneer, anchored veneer, curtain wall and panel systems, and precast panel systems. Paving: thin-set and thick-set. When marbles are used in an exterior environment, caution must be exercised to provide protection from the weather; acids contained in the atmosphere can etch the face of the stone and eventually disintegrate the stone.

Interior — Facings: adhered veneer and anchored veneer. Paving: thin-set and thick-set. Casework and furniture.

SLATE

The primary components of slate are quartz, mica, and chlorite. Many other mineral types are found in slates, such as hematite, graphite, and magnetite, which in varying proportions are responsible for the many varieties of colors. Slate is formed by the metamorphism of shale and clay. The density of slate types is determined by the degree of metamorphic action that occurred during its formation. The consolidation of the shale and clay deposit during metamorphism creates a planar fabric that is referred to as *foliation*. This foliation gives slate its characteristic cleft face. The planar structure is oriented perpendicular to the force of the metamorphosis.

Production Finishes

Honed — Several of the dense varieties of slate can achieve a honed finish.

Sandblasted — A mechanical finish achieved by sandblasting the face of the stone. The degree of coarseness will vary based on the rate of the blasting and the length of time that the blasting wand is held in place.

Natural split face or cleft face — A tooled finish achieved by striking the top edge of the stone with a chisel. Split-face finishes can be produced by hand or mechanically.

Uses

Exterior — Facings: adhered veneer. Paving: thin-set and thick-set. The natural cleaved texture slate makes it inherently slip resistant and suitable for exterior application and wet conditions. Care should be exercised in selecting slates for exterior environments where freeze-thaw conditions are anticipated. The looser varieties of slate will split when water migrates within the cleaved planes during a freeze-thaw cycle. Because of the characteristic cleaved planes of slate, fabrication along the edge to produce slots for anchoring is difficult and may create unsatisfactory results except in only the densest of slate.

Interior — Facings: adhered veneer. Paving: thin-set and thick-set. Casework and furniture. Because of the cleaved characteristics of slate, edges are difficult, if not impossible, to fabricate or detail; bullnose edges and ogee-type detailing are not possible.

QUARTZITE

Quartzite is composed primarily of quartz, with lesser amounts of mica and feldspar. Quartzite is metamorphosed sandstone and may have a planar texture similar to the foliation of slates. The main difference is the mineral composition and the cementing ingredients: slate, clay and shale — as compared with quartzite — quartz and silica. This makes quartzite more compact and denser, and thus a more durable material.

Production Finishes

Honed — Several of the dense varieties of quartzite can achieve a honed finish.

Sandblasted — A mechanical finish achieved by sandblasting the face of the stone. The degree of coarseness varies according to the rate of the blasting and the length of time that the blasting wand is held in place.

Natural split face or cleft face — A tooled finish achieved by striking the top edge of the stone with a chisel. Split-face finishes can be produced by hand or mechanically.

Uses

Exterior — Facings: adhered veneer. Paving: thin-set and thick-set. The natural split-face texture of quartzite makes it inherently slip resistant and suitable for exterior application and wet conditions. The composition of quartz and silica make quartzite inherently resistant to acids and high traffic. Because of the split face texture of quartzite, fabrication along the edge to produce slots for anchoring is difficult and may create unsatisfactory results, except in only the densest of quartzite. Care should be exercised in selecting quartzite for exterior environments where freeze-thaw conditions are anticipated. The looser varieties of quartzite will split when water migrates within the cleaved planes during a freeze-thaw cycle.

Interior — Facings: adhered veneer. Paving: thin-set and thick-set. Casework and furniture. Owing to the split face texture of quartzite, edges are difficult, if not impossible, to fabricate or detail; bullnose edges and ogee-type detailing are not possible. The composition of quartz and silica makes quartzite inherently resistant to acids and high traffic.

SCHIST

Schist stones are the product of the further metamorphism of slate; when schist stones experience another metamorphism, they can become gneiss stones. This explains why schist stones are similar in character to gneiss stones, in that they can both be medium- and coarse-grained and have distinct linear characteristics. In a schist, the grain structure is platy and oriented perpendicular to the force of the metamorphosis but has a more well-defined, banded character than a gneiss.

The pressure and temperature that a schist experiences during its formation is less than the pressure and temperature exerted on a gneiss deposit.

Like gneiss-type stones, schists are also confused with granites. This is because they have a granular crystalline texture similar to that of granites. The differing characteristic is that schist-type stones are foliated. The primary mineral components of a schist are mica, hornblende, and chlorite; the secondary minerals are quartz and feldspar.

Production Finishes

Polished — High gloss, mirrorlike.

Honed — A duller sheen than a polished finish, mattelike.

Sawn — Rough sawn from the block; sometimes shows the coarse blade marks from the gang saw or the circular marks of a disc saw.

Sandblasted — A mechanical finish achieved by sandblasting the face of the stone. The degree of coarseness varies according the rate of the blasting and the length of time that the blasting wand is held in place.

Water or hydro finish — A similar texture as a flamed finish, although less dramatic.

Flamed — Also referred to as "thermal." A coarse, rough texture. The degree of coarseness depends on the texture of the aggregate or crystal mix.

Bush hammered — A mechanically tooled finish utilizing a chisel-type tool. Many types of directional and nondirectional bush-hammered textures are available.

Uses

Exterior — Facings: adhered veneer, anchored veneer, curtain wall and panel systems, and precast panel systems. Paving: thin-set, thick-set, raised paving systems.

Interior — Facings: adhered veneer and anchored veneer. Paving: thin-set, thick-set, raised paving systems. Casework and furniture.

The composition of quartz and hornblende make schist-type stones inherently resistant to acids and high traffic.

GNEISS

Gneiss stones are the product of the further metamorphism of schist stone. This explains the similarity of gneiss stones to schist stones — they are both foliated. The pressure and temperature that gneiss experiences during its formation are greater than the pressure and temperature a schist experiences. During the further metamorphism experienced by gneiss stone, there is greater separation of the minerals into strongly identifiable parallel bands. The bands that characterize gneiss are coarse-grained and show segregation of the light- and dark-colored minerals. Another difference is the mineral composition of gneiss, which is primarily quartz and feldspar. Like schists, gneiss-type stones can be confused with granites owing to the similar color and grain size. Gneiss is distinguished by its strong banding or foliation.

Production Finishes

Polished — High gloss, mirrorlike.

Honed — A duller sheen than a polished finish, mattelike.

Sawn — Rough sawn from the block; sometimes shows the coarse blade marks from the gang saw or the circular marks of a disc saw.

Sandblasted — A mechanical finish achieved by sandblasting the face of the stone. The degree of coarseness varies according to the rate of the blasting and the length of time that the blasting wand is held in place.

Water or hydro finish — A similar texture as a flamed finish, although less dramatic.

Flamed — Also referred to as "thermal." A coarse, rough texture. The degree of coarseness depends on the texture of the aggregate or crystal mix.

Bush hammered — A mechanically tooled finish utilizing a chisel-type tool. Many types of directional and nondirectional bush-hammered textures are available.

Uses

Exterior — Facings: adhered veneer, anchored veneer, curtain wall and panel systems, and precast panel systems. Paving: thin-set and thick-set.

Interior — Facings: adhered veneer and anchored veneer. Paving: thin-set and thick-set. Casework and furniture.

The composition of quartz and feldspar make gneiss inherently resistant to acids and high traffic.

SERPENTINE

Serpentine-type stone is similar in character and formation to marble and is different only in its composition, which is hydrated magnesium silicate. It is called "serpentine" because of its serpent-like bands of color. The primary colors of serpentine are dark green and light green. Many of the green marbles are actually serpentine-type stones. These are very dense stones; however, not all are very hard. The stones that are somewhat soft are difficult to finish to a high gloss.

Production Finishes

Polished — Low gloss.

Honed — A duller sheen than a polished finish, mattelike.

Sawn — Rough sawn from the block; sometimes shows the coarse blade marks from the gang saw or the circular marks of a disc saw.

Sandblasted — A mechanical finish achieved by sandblasting the face of the stone. The degree of coarseness varies according to the rate of the blasting and the length of time that the blasting wand is held in place.

Bush hammered — A mechanically tooled finish utilizing a chisel-type tool. Many types of directional and nondirectional bush-hammered textures are available.

Split face — A tooled finish achieved by striking the top edge of the stone with a chisel. Split-face finishes can be produced by hand or mechanically.

Tumbled—An antiqued finish achieved by placing small stone modules into a mixing tub with coarse aggregates and water. The tumbling action rounds the edges and corners to give the stone a distressed appearance.

Acid washed—A antiqued finish achieved by applying a diluted acid solution to the face of the stone. The longer the solution is in contact with the stone, the coarser the results. Acid solutions have particularly aggressive actions on calcareous stones.

Uses

Exterior—Facings: adhered veneer and anchored veneer. Paving: thin-set and thick-set. When serpentine is used in an exterior environment, caution must be exercised to provide protection from the weather; acids contained in the atmosphere can etch the face of the stone and, over time, prematurely deteriorate the face of the stone.

Interior—Facings: adhered veneer and anchored veneer. Paving: thin-set and thick-set. Casework and furniture.

Stone Fabrication

GEOGRAPHIC LOCATIONS OF STONE PRODUCERS

Deposits of stone are found on all continents throughout the world; their locations are based on the geologic origins of the rock deposits, not political boundaries. According to the theory of continental drift, as discussed in Chapter 2, millions of years ago there was only one continent, Pangea, which was composed of rock deposits that were dispersed throughout the continent. The distribution of these deposits was determined by the creation of rock originating as molten magma from deep within the earth. As the earth evolved and the continent of Pangea separated into several new continents, the deposits of stone located on a specific land mass began to move away from their original locations of deposition. When the shapes of the continents of South America and Africa are examined closely, the possibility of the two continents' originating from one larger continent can be realized. If the stone-producing areas of today's continents are plotted, one can see that large granite deposits are found on the eastern side of South America and on the western side of Africa. Examination of the stone that is produced on both continents shows similarities in its color and structure.

Using the theory of continental drift, it is easily conceived that deposits of rock are distributed throughout the world and that the limitation to the commercial development of these deposits is an economic one. With advances in quarrying and fabrication technology, combined with the improvements in transportation systems, the commercial development and exportation of stone deposits from virtually any area of the world is possible. This is confirmed by the number of new stones that are introduced to the marketplace each year. Many of these stones have been quarried and used in building construction within the region of the

Figure 3-1 Hillside quarry.
Hillside quarry producing Bianco Carrara marble, a metamorphic stone. The quarry is located in the Apuan Alps near Carrara, Italy.

stone deposit, but it is the high technology of global communication and transportation systems that brings marbles from the remote areas of China, Pakistan and India, for example, to the design pallette of architects and designers in the United States.

Because the ancient builders of the Mediterranean region used stone as their material of choice, and because of the durability of stone, the production of stone in this region has continued for thousands of years. The early Egyptians used indigenous limestone and granite when building monuments to honor their kings; the marble quarries of Carrara have been in continuous operation for 2,000 years. Since the time of the Romans, Italy has been the technical center of stone production. This history has provided the experience base on which Italian technology is built, and even today Italian equipment design and production methods are considered to be on the leading edge.

In addition to Italy, most of the countries in Europe, the Mediterranean region, and adjacent areas are stone producers. These include the United Kingdom, Germany, Spain, France, Portugal, Greece, Turkey, Israel, Tunisia, Egypt, and Saudi Arabia. Central and South American stone producers include Mexico, Columbia, Brazil, and Argentina. Both Canada and the United States produce stone for domestic use and export. In recent years stone production in China has increased, as well as in Taiwan, India, and Pakistan. Many other countries are producers of stone, although mostly for domestic use. The countries listed previously are the primary exporters of stone on a worldwide basis.

Types of Quarries

The two most common types of quarries are hillside quarries and open pit quarries. Stone is also excavated by mining, but with less frequency than from hillside and open-pit-type quarries, owing to the difficulty of working underground.

Metamorphic stone is usually found in mountain areas as a product of a metamorphic event, such regional uplift. Metamorphic stones are usually excavated from hillside quarries and sometimes from mines (see Figure 3-1).

Sedimentary stone is found in low-lying areas such as plains, former seabeds, and other areas where the collection of sediment has occurred. Sedimentary stones are usually excavated from open-pit quarries (see Figure 3-2).

Igneous stone deposits can be found in low-lying areas and are quarried in open pits or in hillside terrain, based on the geologic activity at its time of origin.

Stone Deposits

Quarries are excavated in descending levels and are divided into layers, dependent on the location of natural faults or physical changes in the character of the deposit. The natural levels found within a quarry may be horizontal or oriented at an incline following the contour of the deposit; these natural faults are what determine the size of the block. The decision regarding where to cut or drill within a deposit is made by locating the naturally occurring faults in the deposit (see Figures 3-3 and 3-4).

Figure 3-2 Open-pit quarry.
Open-pit quarry producing Jura Beige limestone, a sedimentary stone. The quarry is located in the Bavaria region of Germany.

Figures 3-3 and 3-4 Descending layers of a hillside quarry/descending layers of an open-pit quarry.
Quarries are excavated in descending levels and divided into layers, depending on the location of natural faults or physical changes in the character of the deposit. The natural levels found within a quarry may be horizontal or oriented at an incline following the contour of the deposit; these natural faults are what determine the size of the block.

Figure 3-5 Drilling a guide hole for a wire saw.
Drilling a guide hole through the rock deposit.

Figure 3-6 Guide hole for wire saw.
The saw cut produced by a wire saw looped through the guide hole.

QUARRYING AND FABRICATION OF STONE FROM BLOCKS: LIMESTONE, SANDSTONE, MARBLE, AND GRANITE

Quarrying Methods

The ability to quarry a stone in the form of a block is dependent upon the characteristics of the rock deposit. Desirable deposits are generally large and compact, with fewer occurrences of natural faults and cracks. Limestone, travertine, marble, granite, and some sandstones can be quarried to produce a block that is capable, with further processing, of yielding large slabs.

Blocks of stone are removed from a deposit using one of three primary techniques: removal with wire saws, rock hammer drills, or gallery saws. The use of explosives to quarry stone is limited because of the potential damaging effects it can have on the deposit. When explosives are used, they are generally small charges used in a localized manner to separate a block from the surrounding bench; when large areas of debris are to be cleared, larger charges are sometimes used.

Wire saws — Holes are surveyed and drilled into the deposit, through which a wire travels. The ends of the wire are joined to create a continuous loop, which is fed through a series of pulleys that pull the wire through the holes. Through tension placed on the wire, a helix form is created that keeps the wire in contact with the cutting surface. An abrasive slurry of water mixed with sand is pumped into the hole which, combined with the tension placed on the wire and the speed with which it travels, creates a sawing action. This method of sawing is used for medium to soft stone deposits. With new technology, a diamond-embedded wire is replacing the slurry and wire method and is used for harder stones (see Figures 3-5 through 3-10).

Figure 3-7 Wire saw.
A track-mounted pulley sawing through a marble bench. The pulley is moved back on the track as the wire saws through the deposit.

Figure 3-8 Sawn face of a marble bench.
A wire saw is used to saw the cuts on all sides of a block, including the bottom cut. The integrity of the deposit supports the weight of the sawn bench after the horizontal cut is made.

Figure 3-9 Hydraulic drum.
After all faces of the block are sawn from the bench, an oil-filled hydraulic drum is placed within a recess sawn in the top of the deposit. The oil pressure within the drum is increased, expanding the end of the drum and forcing the block from the deposit from which it was sawn.

Figure 3-10 Inflatable steel air cushions.
These steel mesh cushions are inflated and positioned below the block to lessen the impact of its falling from the bench.

Figure 3-11. Rock hammer drill.
A series of holes are drilled in line spaced close together, forming the outline of the block. The drill is tractor mounted and can be fitted with multiple drills.

Figure 3-12. Fluid-activated wedges.
The hydraulic fluid-activated wedges supported from the tractor will be fitted into the drilled holes. The oil-filled wedges expand as the pressure within the wedges is increased to separate the block from the bench.

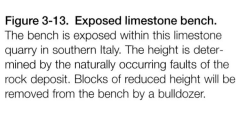

Figure 3-13. Exposed limestone bench.
The bench is exposed within this limestone quarry in southern Italy. The height is determined by the naturally occurring faults of the rock deposit. Blocks of reduced height will be removed from the bench by a bulldozer.

Figure 3-14. Clearing quarry rubble.
Heavy equipment is used to remove quarry debris in preparation for excavating the next bench below the layer currently being worked.

Rock hammer drills — A series of holes are drilled parallel to each other and spaced close together, forming the outline of the cut. Fluid-activated wedges are placed in the holes and pressure is applied, which increases the size of the wedge. As pressure increases, the block breaks free from the layer or bench. Soil and quarry debris are piled beneath the ledge of the block to lessen the impact of the block's falling. This method of cutting is used more often for granite, hard limestones, and other hard stone deposits. Explosives are sometimes used to break the block from the bench. The explosive charges are placed within the holes and ignited, separating the block at a faster rate (see Figures 3-11 through 3-14).

Gallery saws — Gallery saws are the most recent development in block extraction. This type of machine resembles an oversized chain saw and acts in the same manner. The base is stationary and the toothed chain blade is pivoted at the saw base. The saw cuts through the stone the same way a chain saw cuts through timber. Through technological advances, this quarrying technique is improving the efficiency of block removal. This method is used mainly for cutting medium to soft stone (see Figures 3-15 and 3-16).

Figure 3-15. Gallery saw.
A gallery saw travels on parallel tracks supported by vertical hydraulic jacks. The sawn block will be scooped from the quarry deposit by a bulldozer fitted with a wide bucket.

Figure 3-16. Gallery saw working specific areas within the quarry.
Gallery saws are effective for sawing localized areas within a quarry. Specific deposits within the quarry can be excavated when desirable characteristics are found without removing all of the material above, thus saving time.

Figure 3-17. Squaring an irregularly shaped block using a rock hammer drill.

Figure 3-18. Squaring an irregularly shaped block with a wire saw.

Usually, the blocks that are produced are irregular in shape, requiring the squaring of a block within the quarry. The squaring of a block is achieved by drilling parallel holes close together with smaller hand-guided pneumatic rock drills or by utilizing smaller wire saws to remove excess material. Once the blocks have been excavated from the deposit, cranes and derricks are used to load the larger blocks and earth-moving equipment is used to scoop up the smaller blocks, placing them on dump trucks that transport them to the fabrication facility (see Figures 3-17 through 3-20).

Block Processing

The finished products that quarried blocks yield vary according to the size of the blocks, integrity of the stone, and uniformity of block shape. Large monoliths may be used as they are extracted or with little finishing, large squared blocks can produce slabs or be used for monuments, and semisquared or shapeless blocks can be used to produce stone tile.

Once the blocks have been delivered to the fabrication plants, they are examined for their yield and quality of structure. Often a block is sawn on one side with a single-blade block cutter or a stationary wire saw. It is common for the irregular sides of a block to be sawn to produce a more uniformly square block. The more uniform shape makes the further sawing of the block more efficient. It is also beneficial to those selecting blocks, because it permits a view of their color and uniformity. By wetting the exposed sawn face of a block, the color and character can be

Figure 3-19. Loading a block for delivery to the processing plant.

Figure 3-20. Storage of quarried blocks.

observed with reasonable clarity; the appearance is similar to that of a finished slab. The best-quality blocks are selected for slab production. All others are used for the production of tile.

Once the blocks have been reviewed and selected, they are loaded onto large flatbed cars that roll on rails directly to the block-processing equipment. The blocks are moved about the staging yard by large, mobile overhead cranes that also roll on rails. The type of saw used for processing a block is determined by the finished stone product. If the block is to produce slabs, a multiblade gang saw or a stationary wire saw is used; if stone tile is to be produced, a single- or multiblade disc saw is used.

ORIENTATION OF BLOCK SAWING

With most igneous and metamorphic stones, the orientation of the block has no impact on the appearance of the finished stone. The decision regarding how to cut the block is generally based on the most efficient yield, or it may be based on the structural integrity of the block. However, some deposits of metamorphic stones, such as carrara white families, have distinct veining that yields patterns that can be repeated. These patterns are similar in appearance to book matching of wood veneer. In sawing sedimentary stones, other pattern opportunities may be available if the block is oriented as it was removed from the earth, which is called vein cutting, or rotated on its side for sawing, which is called fleuri cutting (see Figure 3-21).

Figure 3-21. Orientation of block sawing.

Vein cut/cross cut—A block sawn from a sedimentary deposit perpendicular to the bed or layer, is termed *vein cut* or *cross cut*. This definition is based on the appearance and the sawing action; sawing through the block exposes the layers of sediment, which appear as veins. Thus the term *vein cut*. *Cross cut* implies the cutting action, crossing the bed. Blocks that are sawn to produce a vein cut will be limited to the height of the bench.

Fleuri cut—A block sawn from a sedimentary deposit parallel to the bed, is referred to as *fleuri* cut. In this case the block is cut through and between the deposited layers, which appear as veins, yielding a mottled, organic, cloudlike character. Sedimentary deposits that are limited in height will yield larger panels when fleuri cut because the usable panel is cut from the width of the block rather than from its height.

Block cuts

Vein

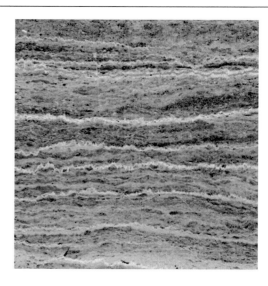

Fleuri

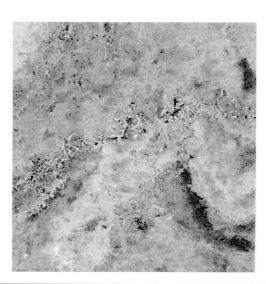

- *Vein cut/cross cut*—When a block from a sedimentary deposit is cut perpendicular to the bed or layer, the block cut is termed *vein cut* or *cross cut*. This definition is based on the appearance and the sawing action; sawing through the block exposes the layers of sediment, which appear as veins. Thus the term *vein cut*. *Cross cut* implies the cutting action, crossing the bed. Stones that have a high contrast in color between layers produce strong directional patterning. A potential disadvantage to blocks that are vein cut is that the size of the panels will be limited in their dimension to the height of the layer or bench.

- *Fleuri cut*—When a block from a sedimentary deposit is cut parallel to the bed, the block is *fleuri cut*. In this case the block is cut through and between the deposited veins, yielding a mottled, organic, cloudlike character. Stones that have a high contrast in color between layers produce dramatic cloud-like patterning, and stones that are more homogenous produce more subtle patterns. In addition, sedimentary deposits that are limited in height yield larger panels when fleuri cut, because the usable panel is cut from the width of the block vs. its height. Another advantage of fleuri cutting is the increased compressive strength of the finished stone. This is because more downward force than horizontal force has been placed on the deposit. Stone that is produced from a fleuri-oriented cut will yield a more compact stone in the stone's thinnest dimension.

SAWING BLOCKS FOR SLABS

Blocks sawn for the production of slabs commonly use three types of saws: gang saws, mono-blade saws, and wire saws. Whether the block is cut for tile or for slabs, further finishing of the stone is required. The tile or slab producer will obtain the quarried blocks and process the block material into finished goods at its facility, rarely at the same location as the quarry.

The blocks that are selected for the production of finished slabs are large and regular in shape. This is because large and regular-shaped blocks can be cut more efficiently and will yield larger panels with greater useable area. Another criterion for blocks used to produce finished slabs is the soundness of the block; blocks that minimize the frequency of cracks and other structural defects should be selected.

Gang saws — A multiblade gang saw is composed of a fixed base and a large, moveable, linear frame with multiple saw blades mounted to it. The frame and blades are reciprocating, parallel to the length of the block, which is set on a flatbed car below. The gang saw frame, to which the blades are attached, is sized to extend beyond both ends of the block below, allowing for a full cut of the block in both directions. The blades are spaced and mechanically fixed to the frame in increments based on the approximate final dimension of the slab; for example, ³/₄ in. (2 cm) thick, ¹/₈ in. (3 cm) thick, 1 in. (4 cm) thick (see Figures 3- 22 and 3-23).

Figures 3-22 and 3-23. Multiblade gang saw.
A multiblade gang saw is used to saw uncalibrated rough slabs of stone from a block. The slabs will receive further processing to receive a final finish and sawing to specific dimensions.

Gang saws utilize either of two types of saw blades; a steel blade using abrasive slurry for the sawing action, or the more recently developed steel blade with diamonds embedded into its edge.

The primary type of gang saw developed for block sawing uses an abrasive slurry, composed of water carrying small steel grit, that is pumped into the path of the reciprocating blades. The steel grit creates friction at the point where the saw blade makes contact with the stone. The abrasive compound is continuously pumped over the block as it is cut. As the blade moves across the steel grit, the grit loses some of its abrasiveness. The saw is equipped to capture the grit and recycle the larger particles, which are mixed with new abrasives. The flow of the recycled abrasive particles as they are mixed with the new particles must be carefully monitored to provide uniform sawing action. This type of saw is most commonly used for sawing marble and limestone blocks. The abrasives used in this process are less costly, but require more sawing time.

The most recent development in gang saws, as mentioned earlier, is the diamond-edged blade. Water is sprayed into the path of the blade to cool it as it saws through the block. This type of gang saw is commonly used for sawing hard stones such as granites. The cost of diamond-embedded blades is higher than that of standard-type blades; however, the time required to saw a block is greatly reduced.

As the blades saw through a block, they may torque slightly because of the variation in tension on the blade, which may have a negative impact on the effectiveness of the abrasive action. This can cause the blade to deflect, producing rough slabs that may vary in thickness from one to another and within the same

Figure 3-24. Contour wire saw. Complex curvilinear dimensional fabrications can be produced with a contour wire saw. Shapes that are curvilinear in plan view, concave or convex forms in vertical elevation, are achieved using the wire loop of the wire saw as a tool for sculpting the surface of a block or thickened slab. Other forms, such as modular panels that are curved in shape, can be produced with a contour wire saw.

slab. It is this variation in slab thickness that precludes stone slabs from use in thin-set floor or wall applications. To achieve a floor installation composed of large modules using noncalibrated slabs, a thick mortar bed installation is necessary.

Wire saws—Less frequently, stationary wire saws are used to cut slabs. Wire saws are used when slabs thicker than 1 ½ in. (4 cm) are desired. A wire saw uses the same technology as the wire saws used in the quarrying process; diamonds are imbedded into the wire cable that creates the sawing action. The cost of using a wire saw for block sawing is higher than that for gang saws because of the high cost of the abrasive wire, and wire saws are used less frequently as a result (see Figure 3-24).

Mono-blade saws—Large blocks that are irregular in shape and are to yield large, squared slabs or are to be processed into tile may be sawn with a mono-blade saw. This saw uses a single reciprocating blade that is fixed in one plane. The block is placed on a flatbed that is able to rotate, allowing the block to have its sides or ends squared. The blade is similar to the blades used in a typical gang saw, but it is taller. The blade may be steel, using abrasive slurry for sawing, or the steel may be imbedded with diamonds. This type of saw is not commonly used for high production owing to the time required to saw a single side. Rather, it is often used to expose the interior of a block to confirm its quality and soundness. The inspection will assist in determining the further processing of the block; if the block is large and free of cracks and other defects, it will be used to produce slabs. If it contains cracks or other defects, it will be used for tile production (see Figures 3-25 through 3-27).

Figure 3-25. Mono-blade saw. Mono-blade saws are used to square irregularly shaped blocks. By exposing one face of the block, the quality or soundness can be determined.

Figures 3-26 and 3-27. Determining the soundness of blocks.

The blocks that are selected for the production of slabs should be large and regular-shaped. This is because large and regular-shaped blocks can be cut more efficiently to yield larger panels with greater useable areas. The best blocks will have a minimal number of cracks or other structural defects, which can be exposed by a mono-blade saw. Figure 3-26 shows the exposed face of a good-quality, sound block with minimal defects. Figure 3-27 shows a block that when sawn exposed two large cracks at the right that run through the block. Consequently, this block will not yield large slabs but will be used to produce tile.

SAWING BLOCKS FOR TILE

The saws used for sawing blocks for stone tile utilize a single diamond-edged disc blade mounted to a bridge that travels the length of the block, which is stationary. This type of saw configuration is similar in appearance to a radial arm saw. The saw blades can be as large as 10 ft in diameter and are precise to 0.5 mm. The development of multiple disc blades has dramatically increased the efficiency of this type of saw, allowing it to saw multiple strips simultaneously. These saws cut strips the length of the block by the approximate width of the finished tile (see Figure 3-28).

Figure 3-28. Single-blade disc saw.
Single-blade disc saws are used for the production of rough strips that will receive further processing to yield tile. The disc saw has been developed to accept multiple disc blades, which increases the efficiency of the sawing process.

Slab Fabrication Process

Rough slabs are placed on an automated conveyor system consisting of metal rollers that span the width of the stone and move the slab through the various stages of finishing. The slab finishing process consists of series of stages incorporating equipment that is linked by rolling conveyors. The side of the slab to be finished is placed up, and the slab begins the finishing process by traveling through a series of horizontal polishing wheels, beginning with coarse abrasives and ending with finer abrasives. The polishing wheels are mounted on a frame that moves from side to side while the slab moves slowly beneath. The polishing wheels are discs approximately 18 in. in diameter and are fitted with multiple abrasive heads. Each of the heads is composed of abrasive grit that polishes the slab from coarse to fine. Each of the polishing discs is driven by an individual cylinder that rotates the disc and applies pressure downward onto the slab. It is the combination of the speed of the rotating disc and the pressure applied to the face of the slab that allows the abrasives to finish the stone (see Figures 3-29 through 3-31).

Figure 3-29. Rough-sawn slabs in preparation for fabrication.
The movable bed at the left is equipped with suction discs and retrieves rough slabs staged at the left. The slabs are transported individually to the beginning of the processing line, where steel rollers convey the slabs through the automated finishing line.

Figure 3-30. Polishing rough-sawn slabs.
A slab is polished by a series of horizontal polishing wheels, beginning with coarse abrasives and ending with finer abrasives. The polishing wheels are mounted on a frame that moves from side to side while the slab moves slowly beneath. Each of the polishing discs is driven by an individual cylinder that rotates the disc and applies pressure downward onto the slab. It is the combination of the speed of the disc rotation and the pressure applied to the face of the slab that allows the abrasives to finish the stone.

Figure 3-31. Polished slabs being inspected at the end of the polishing process.

Tile Fabrication Process

Smaller blocks may be used for the production of tile because the overall size required is less than the size required for slabs. The utilization of smaller blocks maximizes the yield of a quarry. Blocks containing fissures or other flaws may be used for tile production by working around these areas, where slab production would not be possible. However, multiblade disc saws are more effective when using larger and more regularly shaped blocks.

The finishing of stone tile is similar to slab finishing; the primary difference is that finished slabs require additional sawing to the desired dimensions. Tile is finished, cut to the desired size, beveled, and packaged for final installation at one location.

The width of the tile line can be adjusted to accommodate finished widths of up to 24 in. × 24 in., depending on the type of equipment. The strips that are sawn from the rough blocks are typically sawn to double the desired thickness. The strips are the length of the block from which they are sawn (approximately 5 to 6 ft) and are loaded onto rollers that link the equipment and transport the strips through the various finishing and sawing stages. The first stage is splitting the strip into two equal pieces with a horizontally oriented saw. The strips are separated and fed through the first series of stationary polishing wheels, which are used to grind the thickness of the stone to a calibrated dimension. The polishing stages are the same as those in the polishing of slabs, beginning with coarse abrasive discs and working up to finer abrasives. The cylinders that drive the discs are stationary, as compared with the moving discs used for finishing slabs, because the width of the tile is smaller than that of a slab. The speed of the disc rotation, combined with the abrasives of the disc, determine the level of polish of the stone. Upon completion of the finishing process, the strips are sawn with the use of multiple disc saws mounted in tandem, which cut the strips to the desired dimension. The smaller modules are rotated and cut in the opposite direction to produce a square tile module.

To produce a beveled edge on the tile, the sawn tile modules pass through a series of polishing discs that are oriented at an angle to grind off the rough edge, creating a uniform bevel along the top of the four sides.

Abrasives

The abrasives that are used in the polishing process are measured in terms of how coarse they are—the smaller the grit number, the coarser the finish; the higher the grit number, the finer the finish. The grading of abrasives in the stone polishing process is similar to the grading of abrasives in sandpaper for finishing wood. The abrasive particles are sifted through a mesh with a specific number of holes and are measured by the number of holes per inch. For example, an abrasive that is graded 200 grit has particles that pass through a screen of 200 openings per inch. The use of abrasives up to 60 grit is considered grinding, using 120 grit up to 400 or 600 grit is considered a honing, and using 600 grit to 2,000 grit is considered polishing. The finishing process requires an incremental combination of abrasives to achieve the desired level of finish. The effectiveness of the abrasive discs is determined by their speed, the force placed on the stone, and the hardness of the stone. It is more difficult to achieve a high polish in harder stones, and they require more abrasive steps than softer stones. Softer stones may be finished to a high pol-

Figures 3-32 and 3-33. Slabs sawn into strips for tile fabrication.
Smaller irregularly shaped blocks may be utilized for the production of tile, thus maximizing the yield of a quarry. Blocks containing fissures or other flaws may be used for tile production by working around these areas, where slab production would not be possible. The strips are sawn from slabs by multiple disc saws adjusted to the desired width.

Figure 3-35. Calibration process.
The strips are separated and fed through the first series of stationary polishing wheels that are used to grind the thickness of the stone to a calibrated dimension. The polishing stages begin with coarse abrasive discs, working to finer abrasives. The cylinders that drive the discs are stationary, as compared with the moving discs that are used for finishing slabs.

Figure 3-34. Splitting strips to thinner dimensions to prepare for calibration.
The strips are split into two equal pieces by a horizontal-oriented saw.

ish with less effort; however, a softer stone may not achieve the same degree of polish possible in a hard stone. The role of the finishing line manager is to adjust the finishing equipment: balancing the pressure of the heads on the stone, changing the abrasives to suit the stone and desired finishes, and rotating the heads as they wear. Effective management of these components provides a uniform level of stone finish. Consistent monitoring of equipment during the calibrating and finishing process is required to achieve uniform results. The manufacturing team must be competent; any weak link can have a negative impact on the entire process (see Figures 3-32 through 3-40).

Figure 3-36. Calibration and polishing.
The speed of the disc rotation, combined with the abrasives of the disc, determines the level of polish of the stone.

Figure 3-38. Edge beveling.
The sawn tile modules pass through a series of polishing discs that are oriented at an angle, to grind off the rough edge, thus creating a uniform bevel along the top of the four sides. To maintain uniformity of dimension, the pressure applied to the tile edge must be monitored closely.

Figure 3-37. Sawing strips to tile.
The strips are sawn by multiple disc saws mounted in tandem, which saw a strip to the desired dimension. The smaller modules are rotated and cut in the opposite direction to produce a square tile module.

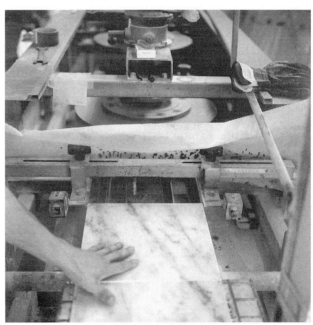

Figure 3-39. Buffing the finished tile.
The final step in the polishing process is to buff the tile to remove any excess grit and fine scratches.

Figure 3-40. Inspection and packaging of the completed tile.
The final step in stone tile production is the selection and inspection of the finished tile. The inspector reviews each tile and separates the tiles by color and character, following a range of variation established at the beginning of the fabrication process.

QUARRYING AND FABRICATION OF CLEAVED STONE DEPOSITS: SLATE AND QUARTZITE

Cleaved or foliated-type rocks are often grouped together and loosely referred to as "slates." This is because of their common characteristic, the ability to be split into thin and sometimes smooth layers. Some of these types of stone are slates and quartzite, which are metamorphic stones, some are sandstones, and even fewer are limestones, which are sedimentary. All of these stones have experienced metamorphism to a greater or lesser extent, which has created a deposit composed of cleaved planes that allow the stone to be split. Most of these types of stone are produced from open-pit quarries, and a few slates that have undergone a more dramatic metamorphism are quarried from hillside quarries.

Generally, the stone deposits that have undergone a metamorphism of lower temperature and pressure are less dense than those that have undergone metamorphism at greater temperature and pressure. The density of these cleaved stones has an impact on how they are quarried. Stones of greater density, such as some of the sandstones and a few slates, can be excavated by means similar to those used in excavating marble, limestone, and granite, allowing the production of blocks and medium-sized slabs. These include natural split face sandstones, bluestones, brownstones and a few North American and South American slates. The stones that are less dense tend to split more easily and cannot produce blocks or slabs of large sizes. Many of these stones are slates that are produced in India, China, and Africa, including the multicolored varieties.

Figure 3-41. Quarrying Solnhofen stone.

Solnhofen stone has the texture and character of stones that are considered to be slate, although actually an extremely dense sedimentary-type limestone. The deposit experienced a metamorphism sometime during its geologic development that caused the minerals to align perpendicular to the force of the metamorphism. This reorientation is what allows the Solnhofen stone to be split into thin layers. Solnhofen Stone is named for the location of the quarries near the village of Solnhofen, Germany.

An anomaly to sedimentary stones is Solnhofen stone, which has the texture and character of stones that are considered to be slate. Solnhofen stone, quarried in the area around the town of Solnhofen, Germany, is an extremely dense sedimentary-type limestone, similar in mineral composition to the Jura limestones quarried within the same area. However, the deposit experienced a metamorphism sometime during its geologic development that caused the minerals to align perpendicular to the force of the metamorphism. This reorientation is what allows the Solnhofen stone to be split into thin layers (see Figure 3-41 on page 58).

Quarrying Methods (Foliated Stones)

Slate and quartzite of low density are easily split along their naturally occurring cleaved planes. The thickness or width of the planes can vary from quarry to quarry and within the same quarry. The cleaved plane is easily recognized, appearing as a linear gap or split between layers of denser stone, and can be separated with pry bars. The height of the bench will vary, which determines the full length of the slab. The cleaved planes will be perpendicular to the bench layers within the quarries and will often be vertical or at acute angles oriented to the surface. This is because slate and quartzite are foliated stones, and during their metamorphism a force imposed on the deposit reoriented the minerals parallel to each other and perpendicular to the force. The newly aligned planes may be oriented vertically, at acute angles, or horizontally within the deposit, differently from sedimentary deposits, which are oriented horizontally, parallel to the bedding plane (see Figures 3-42 and 3-43).

Figure 3-42 and 3-43. Rajah Red Slate Quarry, South/central India.
View of a Rajah Red slate quarry, characterized by cleaved planes perpendicular to the bench layers within the quarries, which can be vertical or at acute angles oriented to the surface. Slate is a foliated stone, exposed to a metamorphic event that imposed a force on the deposit, reorienting the minerals parallel to each other and perpendicular to the force. The newly aligned planes may be oriented vertically, at acute angles, or horizontally within the deposit, differently from sedimentary deposits, which are oriented horizontally, parallel to the bedding plane.

Slate is excavated from its bench in the form of a thickened slab, usually composed of several layers of dense stone separated by the more open cleaved planes. Multiple blunt square-end steel pry bars are driven in a straight line along an open cleave to a depth where the bars can pry the slab away from the bench. A pile of soil and quarry debris is massed at the base of the slab to ease the fall of the slab as it drops to the floor of the quarry. With some slate and quartzite, this process can be achieved quite easily using manual techniques—employing a team of men standing in a row, driving the bars into the bench simultaneously. This opportunity exists because the natural cleaved planes separating the denser planes of stone are open enough to drive the pry bars with relative ease. For deposits where the cleaved planes are denser, this process is accomplished using pneumatic equipment (see Figure 3-44).

Once the thickened slab has been separated from the bench, the fallen slab is hoisted from the quarry by cranes. The size of the slab is determined by the naturally occurring fissures and cracks. If a large fissure is apparent in the slab or if the slab is irregularly shaped, the quarrier will trim the slab into smaller, more regular modules using hammers and chisels. Generally, the size of the slab that is removed is determined by the ability of the equipment or manpower to handle the slab. In many quarries where manpower is abundant, much of this process is executed

Figure 3-44. Excavation of Rajah Red slate slab.
Slate is excavated from its bench in the form of a thickened slab, usually composed of several layers of dense stone separated by the more open cleaved planes. Multiple blunt square-end steel pry bars are driven in a straight line along an open cleave to a depth where the bars can pry the slab away from the bench. A pile of soil and quarry debris is massed at the base of the slab to ease the fall of the slab as it drops to the floor of the quarry.

manually, which limits the size of the slabs, often to the size of what one person can move by himself.

After the slabs have been removed from the quarry, they are staged in an adjacent area where they are grouped by size and readied for further production. Usually, the slabs are transported to a nearby fabrication facility, or they may be split into thinner slabs prior to transporting, depending on the location of the processing facility; thicker slabs will travel greater distances with less damage.

Dense deposits of slate and quartzite, such as those in New England states and in Brazil, are quarried with the use of tractors that pry larger slabs and blocks from the quarry beds. The bedding planes of these deposits are generally oriented horizontally and are compact, able to support the weight of earth-moving equipment. These deposits are capable of producing large slabs and smaller blocks that allow for more automated processing—for example, saws can be used for cutting thin tile. These are the quarries that produce dense slate chalkboards and tops for billiard tables. The dense slates from Brazil and New England are flatter across the cleaved face and are capable of achieving a honed finish with the use of automated slab and tile processing equipment.

Fabrication of Slabs and Tile (Cleaved Stone)

Once the thickened slate and quartzite slabs have been removed from the quarry, the slabs are split into thinner tile. This is done by striking a smaller slab or thin block along its edge with a quick blow from a hammer to a chisel positioned along a natural split. The tile can sometimes be split with one hit, or it may require several strikes of the hammer. The individual tiles that have been split have a natural cleft face on both sides as a result of the splitting. The texture exposed by the splitting will vary upon the density of the slate or quartzite deposit. Some of the stones will split into thin and uniformly smooth surfaces. Others will split into irregular and heavily textured cleft surfaces. This process produces a considerable amount of waste because the cleaved planes occur at random locations, and when split, the resulting thickness may not be of a commercially useful thickness (see Figures 3-45–3-47).

Next, the thin tile sheets are squared by placing them against metal guides or jigs used to maintain a straight edge and sawing the tile with a small disc saw. The disc saws may be moveable, similar to scaled-down bridge saws, or they can be fixed with a moveable platform on which the tile is placed. In either operation, one of the natural split faces of the tile will have to be placed on the platform; the unevenness of the cleft face allows movement or a rocking action of the tile as it is sawn. This movement contributes to the variation in the squareness and edge straightness of this type of tile, making the final product less precise and more rustic.

If the final product is tiles that are to have both sides naturally cleft, the fabrication process is complete and the material is ready for packaging and shipment. Tiles that have a natural cleft on both sides are best suited for thick mortar bed installations, or if carefully hand selected to reduce the variation in thickness, they may be set successfully in a medium mortar bed.

If tiles are to be used in a thin mortar bed installation, additional processing is required. The termed *gauged* is used erroneously by slate producers to describe slate or quartzite tiles that receive additional processing. The term *ground one side* should be used to describe tiles produced in this manner, not *gauged,* which

Figure 3-46. Separating the slab from quarry bed, Mineras Gerais, Brazil.
Once the outline of the slate slabs has been sawn, the quarrymen use pry bars to separate the slab from the bed of the quarry. The slabs are pried open and wood blocks are wedged into the opening to allow for the slab removal. Because of the high density of these slates, the cleaved face is extremely flat.

Figure 3-45. Excavation of a densely compressed slate, Mineras Gerais, Brazil.
The horizontally cleaved planes and densely formed slate of Brazil allows for excavation of slabs using saws similar to concrete cutting saws. Though the overall size of the slabs is determined by the quarrymen, the thickness is based on the naturally occuring cleaved planes.

Figure 3-47. Removing slabs from the quarry bench, Mineras Gerais, Brazil.
A forklift lifts the sawn slabs from the quarry bed. Once the slabs have been removed, they are transported to the processing plant for fabrication. The thickened slabs are sawn into squares and split by machine along their natural cleave. This type of slate is dense enough to withstand the pressure of a standard marble finishing line, which is used to calibrate the slate's thickness.

implies that the product is calibrated. The "gauging" of the tile is most often accomplished by grinding the back side of the tile manually, holding it against a grinding wheel, or by placing the tile on a stationary table and applying a rotating wheel to it. Another method used to reduce the variation in the slate tile thickness is to pass a saw blade set at a fixed height across the face of the tile. The saw blade will remove any material that extends beyond the fixed height of the blade. The density of the stone determines the method for grinding unwanted material from the back of the tile. Slate and quartzite of lower density will break when the pressure applied to the tile is too great. Slates of low density require the care provided by hand-holding the tile face against a grinding stone, or if the density is great enough, a grinding stone attached to a manually operated press can be used to apply additional pressure to the tile face, thus speeding the grinding process. This is why only a few slates and quartzites are capable of receiving a honed finishing treatment. A small number of quartzites from India, Brazil, and Belgium are of the density that can resist the force exerted by a granite tile processing line; only the densest of foliated stone will withstand this pressure.

Whatever processing method is used for the removal of excess material from the tile thickness, if the opposite face is cleft, the unevenness will not allow for the production of a true calibrated dimension.

It is common for slate and quartzite to be packed directly into lined wood crates, but for a small additional cost the tile can be packaged in corrugated paper boxes, which better protect the tile in transit.

SPECIAL STONE FABRICATIONS

Cubic Production

The term *cubic* refers to fabricated stone that is produced from slabs that are greater in thickness than 1½ in. (4 cm), which can be as large as desired, limited only by the size of the block. Cubic work also includes monolithic stone and large-scale stone units that receive little or no additional finishing once the stone has been excavated.

The slabs used for cubic production are sawn from blocks with mono-blade saws and wire saws. Cubic production of stone is relatively more labor intensive because of the inability to utilize automated processing systems ordinarily used by tile and slab producers. The stone selected for cubic use is generally the best quarry selection available; the selection effort is focused on blocks that have minimal occurrences of cracks, dry seams, and voids.

Typical cubic fabrications include copings, lintels, headers, and oversized slab units used for structural and decorative purposes. Cubic fabrications are also used in the restoration of stone buildings that were constructed of stone using masonry-type units for load-bearing walls, feature pieces, and quoining.

Other cubic fabrications include dimensional curvilinear forms, which are produced with the use of a contour wire saw. Complex forms, curvilinear in plain view, concave or convex in vertical elevation, are achieved by using the wire loop of the wire saw as a tool for sculpting the surface of a block or thickened slab. Other forms, such as modular panels that are curved in shape, can be produced using a wire saw. (see Figure 3-24 on page 50).

WATER JET CUTTING

The recent introduction of water jet cutting systems has had a dramatic impact on the production of detail work, such as inlay work and large-scale radius fabrications. Water jet cutting systems are a product of the aerospace industry, where precision metal aircraft parts are produced by focusing high-pressure water capable of cutting metals and other dense materials. Drawings and templates are entered into a program to define the pattern for the cutting of specific pieces and intricate shapes that would be difficult to cut by hand. The cutting action requires that the water jet go completely through the stone that is to be cut. This prevents the water jet from cutting partially through a stone object, thus eliminating opportunities for relief work. However, water jet cutting systems are well suited for the production of large-scale radius pieces, graphic work such as signage, complicated fabrications, and inlay work.

TURNED STONE FABRICATIONS

Columns, balustrades, spheres, and concave shapes are produced with stone lathes that operate on the same principle as wood lathes. Blocks of stone are sawn by reciprocating disc saws or multiblade disc saws, sawing the length of the shape to produce a rough resemblance of the object to be created. The rough stone is mounted onto a lathe, rotating it; then, diamond cutters are positioned to cut the stone piece to the desired shape. Once the form has been turned, finishing of the object is achieved with abrasives applied to the stone as the piece continues to rotate.

PRODUCTION FINISHES AND TEXTURES

Stone that has been quarried requires further processing in anticipation of its final use, whether it is to be fabricated in slab form or as tile, for decorative purposes or for functional requirements. The types of finishes described on the following pages are the most common production finishes, all of which were developed by craftsmen and are of historical origin. Not all stones are capable of achieving all of the finishes described; the ability of a stone to achieve a finish is determined by the texture, structure, hardness, density, and mineral composition of the specific stone. In addition, not all of the finishes are appropriate for all uses; many of the textured finishes are suitable only for use in vertical applications.

The polishing process will close more of the surface, providing a protective barrier. Coarse finish treatments will have less surface protection, and destructive finishes such as flamed textures will be more vulnerable to moisture migration because the surface of the stone has been opened. The rougher textures are achieved by aggressive and destructive means, which reduce the strength of the stone and may require that the thickness of the stone be increased to accommodate the loss of material in processing.

In implementing textural finish treatments, the stone should be rough sawn to allow for the newly created texture to have greater prominence. For example, when a polished stone is flamed, the surface areas that remain intact after the flame has passed will remain polished, surrounded by the coarse texture produced by flaming. The same undesirable texture is created when a polished stone is sandblasted; the remaining polished areas will reflect light from the coarse matte background of the sandblasted surface.

Polished Finish

A polished finish is a mechanically achieved finish produced in the final step in the finishing process with the use of a succession of abrasives, ranging from coarse to fine. Abrasive pads are mounted to a series of rotating discs that polish the face of the stone under pressure. Generally, abrasives from 600 grit to 2,000 grit are considered to yield a polished finish producing varying degrees of reflectivity, depending on the stone. The sheen produced is a reflective high-gloss finish that is flat and smooth, without scratches or circular mechanical markings. A polished finish will close more of the stone surface, creating a surface that will repel moisture.

Not all stones are capable of achieving a high polish; some are capable of reaching only a high honed finish. The stone must have a crystalline mineral structure capable of reflecting light back to the eye. If the stone is composed of flat mineral sections, the light reflection will not be as great and the surface will have a matte appearance. Hardness also has an impact on the polishing process. The harder the stone, the more difficult it is to achieve a polished finish; the softer the stone, the easier it is to achieve. However, hard stones will hold their polish longer under traffic than soft stones.

Stones that are processed to a polished finish will appear darker, and their colors will be richer than those of stones that are finished to a lesser degree of sheen. Stone tiles that receive a polished finish will also be calibrated as a result of the polishing process (see Figure 3-48).

Honed Finish

A honed finish is a mechanically produced finish achieved in the step previous to a polished finish, using the same process employed to produce a polished finish. The reflectivity of a honed finish is less, and the surface will have a duller, or matte, finish, as compared with a polished finish. The abrasives used are coarser than those used for a polished finish; generally, from 120 grit to 400 grit is considered honed. A honed finish is smooth and free of mechanical processing markings when finer grit is used; however, if a coarse abrasive is used without successive finer grit, circular machine markings may remain. The surface of a honed stone will be more open than the surface of a polished stone, yet more closed as compared with stones that have been processed to less than a honed sheen.

Figure 3-48. Polished finish. A polished finish is a mechanically achieved finish produced in the final step in the finishing process with the use of a succession of abrasives, from coarse to fine. The sheen produced is a reflective high-gloss finish that is flat and smooth, without scratches or circular mechanical markings.

Stone that is honed will be lighter than stone with a polished finish, and darker than stone that is finished to lesser degree of sheen. Stone tiles that receive a honed finish will also be calibrated as a result of the honing process (see Figure 3-49).

Sawn Finish

A sawn finish is a textured finish that does not receive processing after the stone has been sawn from the block. Slabs that are sawn with a gang saw generally have a nondirectional surface texture. Stone tiles that are sawn with a disc saw or multi-disc saw will have a texture that consists of circular markings and grooves.

The surface of a sawn finished stone will be open, as compared with a stone with a honed or polished finish, and will be lighter in color. The clarity and character of stone with a sawn finish will be diminished because of the texture produced by the saw blades (see Figure 3-50).

Sandblasted Finish

A sandblasted finish is a mechanical finish achieved by blasting the surface of the stone with sand to create a coarse, sandlike texture. The sandblasted texture can be varied by selecting the grain size of the sand to create relief that is fine, medium, or coarse; a nondirectional texture is produced. The sandblasting process is destructive to the stone and will open its surface, which then does not offer any inherent protection and will require additional maintenance over time. The aggressive action on the surface may require that the stone thickness be increased to accommodate the loss of material resulting from the finishing process.

The texture that is produced will be flat and free of scratches and markings from sawing and will be lighter in color than more finished surfaces. Most, if not all, of the color and natural character of the stone is lost in the sandblasting process. The rough texture produced by sandblasting has nonslip properties and can be advantageous if used in a paving application, although the textures of softer stones will be honed smooth with heavy foot traffic (see Figure 3-51).

Acid Washed Finish

Acid washed finishes are produced by applying acid solutions to the surface of a stone to create a rustic texture. Calcium-based stones, limestones and marbles, are reactive to an acid washed finish; granites and other quartz-based stones are resistive to the finish. Acids are highly destructive, and their effects on a surface will vary, depending on the strength of the acid solution, the amount of time the stone is exposed to the solution, and the calcium composition of the stone. Because of the number of variables that can influence the finish, arriving at a consistent level of treatment from application to application can be a challenge.

Acid washed finishes will appear different from stone to stone; however, the color generally darkens and a satin sheen is produced. The surface of the stone will erode nonuniformly, creating small holes and pits where the acid has been more aggressive, producing a rustic or antiqued texture. The type of acid used is based on the availability of the solution; in the United States the most commonly used acid solution is muriatic (see Figure 3-52).

Figure 3-49. Honed finish.
A honed finish is a mechanically produced finish achieved in the step previous to a polished finish, using the same process employed to produce a polished finish. The reflectivity of a honed finish is less, and the surface will have a duller, or matte finish, as compared with a polished finish. The abrasives used are coarser than those used for a polished finish.

Figure 3-50. Sawn finish.
A sawn finish is a textured finish that does not receive processing after the stone has been sawn from the block. Slabs that are sawn with a gang saw generally have a nondirectional surface texture. Stone tiles that are sawn with a disc saw or multidisc saw will have a texture that consists of circular markings and grooves.

Figure 3-51. Sandblasted finish.
A sandblasted finish is a mechanical finish that is achieved by blasting the surface of the stone with sand to create a coarse, sandlike texture. The sandblasted texture can be varied by selecting the grain size of the sand to create relief that is fine, medium, or coarse; a nondirectional texture is produced.

Figure 3-52. Acid wash finish.
Acid washed finishes are produced by applying acid solutions to the surface of a stone to create a rustic texture. Calcium-based stones, limestones and marbles, are reactive to an acid washed finish; granites and other quartz-based stones are resistive to the finish.

Flamed Finish

A flamed finish, also referred to as a thermal finish, is achieved by passing the flame from an oxy-acetylene torch over the stone slab at a 45-degree angle. The temperature of the torch is 2,800° F, which heats the individual minerals and crystals and expands them until they explode from the surface. The minerals are usually of a larger size than the crystals, but both expand at different rates, encouraging the various materials of the surface to break from the body of the stone. The result of the thermal process is a coarse and irregular surface with slight projections and recessions the approximate size of the crystal structure. Stone composed of a large matrix will create a rougher texture than that with a smaller matrix. The technique of flaming has a traumatic effect on the surface, weakening the stone by causing the loss of a portion of its mass. For this reason, the minimum thickness of a flamed stone is generally ³⁄₄ in. (2 cm), increased to accommodate the loss of material from the process.

Stone that receives a flamed finish is processed in slab form and sawn to smaller dimensional sizes as required. The flaming technique is most successful on large areas, as opposed to edges or angled planes of small dimension. The open areas created by the rapid erosion of the surface expose the pore structure to weathering, allowing moisture-bearing contaminants to migrate through the stone more easily than in a polished finish. The color of the stone lightens and the character is diminished in this process.

Generally, only granites, a few limestones, and other stones that are composed of dissimilar minerals with differing coefficients of thermal expansion can be flamed. A flamed finish cannot successfully be achieved in limestones that are composed of a high percentage of calcium carbonate. The limestones that are capable of achieving a flamed texture will hone smooth over time if they are used as pavers (see Figure 3-53).

Hydro Finish

A hydro finish, or water texture finish, is produced by focusing a source of water under extremely high pressure. The force of the water across the surface of the stone erodes the face, breaking crystals from the surface. The resulting texture is similar to a flamed finish, although not as dramatic and less destructive to the stone. Hydro finishing is not successful on stones other than granites. The clarity of color and character of the granite after receiving hydro treatment are improved, as compared with its appearance after flaming (see Figure 3-54).

Tumbled Finish

A tumbled finish, which is also referred to as tumbled stone or antiqued stone, is produced by placing small stone blocks, water, sand, and small-sized aggregates in an enclosed mixing bin and agitating for a desired length of time. The stone blocks are usually not larger than 15 in. × 15 in. by twice the desired thickness and are sawn to half the thickness after the tumbling process. The tumbling rusticates the stone faces, edges, and corners, giving the stone an aged appearance. Most stones can be tumbled, although those that are stronger will better withstand the aggressiveness of the process. The tumbling process can be augmented with the introduction of mild acids to the stone mix, which erodes the surface slightly more and creates a sheen on its surface (see Figures 3-55 and 3-56).

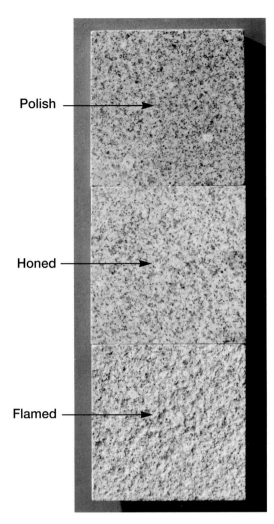

Polish

Honed

Flamed

Figure 3-53. Flamed (thermal) finish.
A flamed finish, also referred to as a thermal finish, is achieved by passing the flame from an oxyacetylene torch over a stone slab at a 45-degree angle. The result of the thermal process is a coarse and irregular surface with slight projections and recessions the approximate size of the crystal structure.

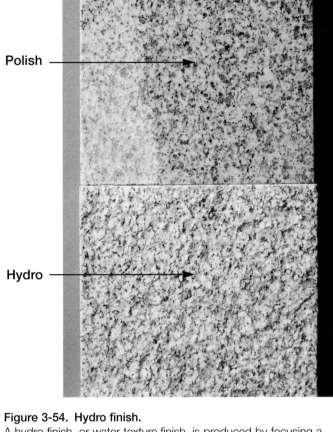

Polish

Hydro

Figure 3-54. Hydro finish.
A hydro finish, or water texture finish, is produced by focusing a source of water under extremely high pressure. The resulting texture is similar to a flamed finish, although not as dramatic and less destructive to the stone.

Figures 3-55 and 3-56. Tumbled finish.
A tumbled finish, which is also referred to as tumbled stone or antiqued stone, is produced by placing small stone blocks, water, sand, and small aggregates in an enclosed mixing bin and agitating for a desired length of time. The tumbling rusticates the stone face, edges and corners giving the stone an aged appearance. After the stone blocks are tumbled, they are sawn into two tiles; the rusticated face of the of the block becomes the finished face and the sawn face becomes the tile back.

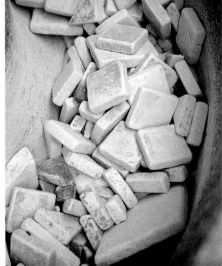

Cleft Face Finish

A cleft finish, also referred to as a cleaved finish, is a natural texture that is produced by splitting or separating stones that posses natural cleaved planes. Foliated stones such as slate and quartzite are capable of yielding a natural cleft finish and will split in only one direction. The color after splitting is not disturbed and represents the true color of the stone. The amount of texture will vary from stone to stone and is determined by the density of the stone; dense stones will cleave in flat planes, and less dense stones will cleave with greater irregularity.

Foliated stones are split manually by striking a chisel or wedge with a hammer placed at the edge of the stone block or slab. The stone will separate along the natural cleavage plane, creating a rough cleft texture on both split faces (see Figure 3-57).

Bush Hammered Finish

Bush hammered finishes are textures that were traditionally produced manually by striking the stone surface with a hammer fitted with multiple heads composed of projecting pyramidal teeth. When the hammer struck the stone surface, a coarse texture was produced. Hand-held pneumatic hammers and automated finishing equipment fitted with multiple chisel heads are used in modern production. The process can be varied to create a nondirectional pattern of fine, medium, or heavy texturing or a directional pattern. Bush hammered textures can be applied to most stones, most successfully in dense materials. When the process is manually performed, the texture is affected by the force of the hammer blow and the number of times the hammer strikes the surface.

Figure 3-57. Cleft face finish.
A cleft finish, also referred to as a cleaved finish, is a natural texture produced by splitting or separating stones that posses natural cleaved planes. The amount of texture will vary from stone to stone and is determined by the density of the stone; dense stones will cleave in flat planes, and less dense stones will cleave with greater irregularity.

Figure 3-58 Bush hammered finish.
Bush hammered finishes are textures that were traditionally produced manually by striking the stone surface with a hammer fitted with multiple heads composed of projecting pyramidal teeth. When the hammer struck the stone surface, a coarse texture was produced.

Figure 3-59 and 3-60. Tooled finish.
Tooled finishes are similar to bush hammered finishes, differing mainly in the character of their texture. Tooled finishes are typically directional, and bush hammered finishes are nondirectional; tooled finishes are more often dramatic in the depth of texture produced, and bush hammered textures are not as coarse in appearance.

Bush hammering the surface of a stone lightens the color dramatically and eradicates the character of the stone. Because of this, stones that are compact yet soft, and lower in cost, are better suited to receive this texture. If the finish is to be achieved through mechanical means, the stone will require greater strength to withstand the increased pressure applied by the disc-mounted heads. The stone to receive such hammering should be of a thickness that can absorb the aggressive shock from the bush hammering apparatus (see Figure 3-58).

Tooled Finish

Tooled finishes are similar to bush hammered finishes, differing mainly in the character of their texture. Tooled finishes are typically directional, and bush hammered finishes are nondirectional; tooled finishes are more often dramatic in the depth of texture produced, and bush hammered textures are not as coarse in appearance. The origin of tooled finishes is the same as for bush hammered finishes; they were traditionally produced by picks and hammers fitted with spikes or pyramids that created textures by striking the stone. Mechanical systems have been developed to create tooled textures increasing production capability, yet the hand-dressed textures have more character resulting from the irregularity of the manual method.

Mechanical tooled textures can achieve a linear striated pattern when the stone is pushed through a stationary rotating head mounted to a press. Heads fitted with dense spike patterns will produce lines spaced closely together, and heads with an open pattern of spikes produce wider line patterns.

The surface of the stone should be flat and rough sawn to contrast with the texture of the tooling that is created. Most of a stone's character is diminished when the surface is tooled. The tooling process is more successful when applied to softer stones that allow the spikes to dig into the stone (see Figures 3-59 and 3-60).

71

Split Face Texture

A split-face finish can be produced manually with a hammer and chisel, although power-driven chisels or, on a larger scale, guillotines are more often used when greater production quantities are required. The process used for split-face production is similar to that for cleft finished stone — the texture is created through the separation of the stone. The difference is that the stone does not have to be foliated to achieve a split face, and most stones are capable of splitting. Stones with predictable weaker planes, natural faults and cracks, or in which natural mineral separation occurs, are more successfully split. When a guillotine is used, thick sections can be split; the term *snapped* is often used to describe the process. The sizes that are produced by using a guillotine can be as thick as 3 ft - 0 in. and are suitable for masonry-type units. Smaller power-driven wedges mounted to a press are used for smaller dimensional splitting and are capable of splitting up to approximately 4 in. in thickness. Sandstone, bluestone, brownstone, quartzite, and granites can be reliably used to produce a split-face texture.

The surface that is produced will vary according to the stone and can range from a relatively flat-textured face to a dramatically pronounced texture. The degree of coarseness can range from a heavily textured flamed finish, approaching the coarseness of a pitched face. The color of the resulting finish is lighter and the clarity of the stone character is lost when the stone is split; however, the dimensional texture that is created can be dramatic, producing interesting shadow effects (see Figure 3-61).

Figure 3-61. Split face finish. A split-face finish can be produced manually with a hammer and chisel, although power-driven chisels or, on a larger scale, guillotines are more often used when greater production quantities are required. The process used for split-face production is similar to that for cleft finished stone—the texture is created through the separation of the stone.

Pitched Face Texture

A pitched face, also referred to as a chiseled finish, is a manually produced texture created by using power-driven carving wedges and chisels. This process produces a texture with the greatest dimensional relief of all the decorative finishes, breaking off large chips and splinters from the surface of the stone. A pitched face finish is most successful when applied to dense, compact stones such as granite and limestone and when applied to large areas. The thickness of the stone module must be great enough to accept the aggressive tooling of the pitching process. Pitch face textures are commonly fabricated on stone modules that are to be used as masonry units.

Large-scale curves and angles are achievable in pitched face textures when the stone units are of a sizable area. The color of the stone after pitching will be lighter, and the overall character will be reduced (similar to the effects in split-face finishing; (see Figure 3-61).

4

Installation Methods

SAND BED INSTALLATIONS

The first walking surfaces of villages and towns were composed of beaten earth, which was improved by burying large cobblestones in soil or sand. The early cobblestones were found in nature and were generally smooth and rounded, coming from streams and riverbeds or gravel deposits. They were hand-selected for size and shape, requiring no further work prior to setting. Later, as hand stone finishing work became more sophisticated, regularly shaped paving stones and cubed stones were used as materials for paving streets.

Today sand bed installations are generally selected for exterior applications because of the increased depth required for the setting bed. Areas in which sand bed installations are commonly used include driveways, plazas, walkways, and patios. In Europe it is very common for sand bed installations to be used for roadways, incorporating stone cubes or cobblestones as the paving material. Sand bed installations are ideally suited for rustic, roughly finished, split-face, ungauged stones such as quartzites, slates, sandstones, and flagged stones because the difference in thickness between the stone modules can be absorbed by the setting bed.

The flexibility of a sand bed is also a benefit in exterior paving in freeze-thaw-sensitive locations, allowing for movement of the subsurface foundation material during periods of freezing temperatures. However, if the foundation bed and the following sand setting bed are not adequately compressed, or if extreme tempera-

Figure 4-1. Preparation of the setting bed.
The earthen base is prepared by grading to the appropriate depth, which is determined by the thickness of the paver stone and the setting bed.

tures in a freeze-thaw cycle are experienced, some settling or movement of the paving stone may occur, requiring maintenance and resetting. If stone pavers have been set in a sand bed without the incorporation of cement, the repositioning of the pavers is easily achieved.

Stone Modules

Nearly any shape or size and many types of stone are suitable for use in an exterior sand bed installation, provided that the climate is mild. If freezing temperatures are to be experienced, only materials that are considered to be freeze-thaw stable should be selected, so as to avoid surface damage or breaking of the stone; the volume of water will expand to 8% of its size when it freezes. Stones that have a low rate of water absorption are "vitreous," with a rate of absorption between 0.5% and 3% are considered suitable.

The finish on the face of the stone should be slip resistant, such as created by natural splitting to produce a cleft face, a flamed finish if achievable, bush hammered, sandblasted, or sawn; honed or polished finishes should not be used in exterior installations. The Americans with Disabilities Act Accesibility Guidelines (ADAAG) recommend that the coefficient of static friction be .06 for flat walking surfaces and 0.8 for inclined walking surfaces.

Paver tile: Paving modules may be of any size or shape and can be gauged or ungauged. The term *gauged* refers to the uniformity of thickness that is achieved through calibration of the stone during processing. Stone that is ground at the back, or sawn on the back perpendicular to the tile face, is not truly gauged. However, as previously described, ungauged pavers are perfectly suited for a sand bed installation because of the flexibility provided by the setting bed.

Figure 4-2. Limestone paver modules.
Limestone pavers 20 cm (8 in.) thick are staged prior to setting in the sand bedding layer. The increased thickness of the pavers will accommodate the load of vehicular traffic.

Paver tiles may be sawn from blocks or slabs or split by hand directly from the quarry bedding planes. Stone tiles generally receive further processing to achieve regular modules, which are usually rectilinear in shape. For this purpose, disc saws are used for sawing gauged stone or stone of similar thickness, such as slates, limestones, and granites, a small-scale guillotine for thicker and less regular thicknesses, such as porphyries and quartzite, and hand-held tile crimpers for thin dense slates and Solnhofen limestones.

In more rustic types of ungauged hand-split stones, the variation in thickness can be from ¾ in. to 2 in. (2 cm to 5 cm); the length of the paver tile will vary, but is at least the width in dimension, usually based on increments of 2 in. (5 cm) starting at 4 in. (see Figure 4-2).

Flagged stone (also referred to as flagging or crazy patterned stone): This type of stone is generally sedimentary in formation, allowing for slabs or stone pieces to be pried out of the quarry bedding plane with front end loaders for large pieces, or pry bars for smaller-sized flagstone. The finish available for flagged stone is a natural quarry rough finish or a split-face finish. This type of stone module is sorted at the quarry by thickness and size into three dimensional categories, noted below.

Cubes: Stone cubes are produced primarily for use as street paving and for plazas. The thickness and, consequently, the overall size of the cube increase as required to accommodate the increased loads from pedestrian and vehicular traffic. Stone paving cubes are generally produced from large slabs of varying thicknesses of porphyry, granite, or other material of volcanic origin. The slabs are reduced to smaller sizes and are hand-split into cubes with the use of pneumatic stationary presses similar to a guillotine. Standard stone cubes range in size from the smallest, at approximately 2 in. × 2 in. × 2 in., to the largest at 8 in. × 8 in. × 8in., increasing in 2 in. increments. The smaller-sized cubes allow for the installation of complex geometric and circular patterns, as found in the plazas of cities throughout Europe.

Preparation of the Setting Bed

Because of the varied types of soil mix that make up an earthen base, when utilizing a sand bed installation for large-scale projects, it is important to consult with a geologist or soils engineer for determining the appropriateness of the site and for recommendations on the sizing of the new fill or foundation layer. Soil that makes up an earthen base that is composed of rocky material, compact gravel, or sand and dry clay is considered to be a good base to build on because it can be compacted easily to form a solid base. Soil mixes of sand with a high proportion of clay and wet clay are considered to be a medium choice, inasmuch as there will be an

Type	Diagonal Dimension		Thickness
Standard Dimension	Minimum: 8 in.	Average: 8 in.	¾–2 in.
Thin Dimension	Minimum: 8 in.	Average: 8 in.	⅜–1⅛ in.
Large Dimension	Minimum: 16 in.	Average: 16 in.	1⅛–2⅝ in.

opportunity for the clay materials to expand with the introduction of water and contract as the soil dries. This instability will cause the stone to move within the setting bed over time. When the soil mix is wet and marshy or has a high content of organic material, the probability of extreme movement and settling is likely even with the introduction of corrective fill, because the site will tend to compact and continue to settle with the additional load from the fill and stone. The more compact the earthen base the setting bed is placed on, the greater chances of a long-term successful final installation.

A setting bed that is prepared and graded onto an earthen base is divided into two parts: (1) the compacted foundation layer and (2) the bedding layer that the stone will be set into. Both layers are composed of new material and are placed on a natural earthen base that has been excavated and graded to the desired depth.

The *foundation layer* is intended to form an incompressible layer on which the bedding layer is placed. The most common materials for the foundation layer are crushed and sorted aggregates, beginning with larger stones placed directly on the earthen base and building up with successive layers of smaller and smaller aggregate. A mixture of gravel, clay, cement, and lime with various sized stone aggregates also constitutes a stabilized layer. The angular faces of the crushed rock promote a stable and compact bed through the mechanical resistance produced by the compaction of the faceted aggregate. When the height of the foundation layer has been established, the aggregate is compacted in place using a weighted compactor with a vibrating base, followed by a weighted roller. For smaller areas hand-pulled weighted rollers are used, and for larger areas, road bed rollers are used. More aggregate is added to make up the difference in height from the compaction, as required.

The second type of foundation layer is a concrete slab with welded wire reinforcing mesh positioned within the bed. The additional stability the concrete slab provides can overcome a less stable earthen base and increase the speed of installation.

The thickness of the foundation layer will vary, based on the thickness of the stone that is to be used and the load that the paving system is to carry. Generally, the thickness can be estimated at two times the thickness of the bedding layer (see Figures 4-1 and 4-3).

The *bedding layer* is the setting material in which the stone is set. The traditional method uses a washed sand of a fairly large grain for increased mechanical resistance. The sand should be free of soil that could be washed away with migrating water after installation, which is the cause of sagging and settling of the final installation. The use of sand from the ocean should also be avoided, as the salts that are present may cause efflorescence to appear on the stone. In addition, fine sand and sand containing lime should not be used in the bedding mixture, because they will not produce a mechanical resistance between the individual particles of sand and the stone materials.

Cement can be added to a sand bed as another means of producing a bedding layer. A small amount of cement should be combined with sand in a mixer, in the proportion of 1 liter of cement per cubic meter of sand (1.05 quarts dry cement per 1.3 cubic yards sand), to produce a uniform blend of the two materials. The addition of the cement will create a more rigid bedding layer that will hydrate and cure when water is sprayed onto the pavers upon completion of the installation. The final installation is not as elastic as one with a pure sand bedding layer; however, the addition of the cement creates a more compact bedding layer.

Figure 4-3. Preparation of the setting bed.
Because of the varied types of soil mix that make up an earthen base, when utilizing a sand bed installation for large-scale projects, it is important to consult with a geologist or soils engineer for determining the appropriateness of the site and for recommendations on the sizing of the new fill or foundation layer. Soil that makes up an earthen base that is composed of rocky material, compact gravel, or sand and dry clay is considered to be a good base to build on because it can be compacted easily to form a solid base.

Once the bedding fill has been spread and the grade established, the bedding layer is compacted as described for the foundation layer. More fill is added to regain the grade that has been compacted. Care should be exercised to avoid creating a bedding layer that is too deep, which can be vulnerable to later sagging of the paving. The thickness of the bedding layer will depend on the stone modules that are used and the anticipated load; however, its thickness should be less than the thickness of the foundation layer. Generally, for cube pavers the thickness of the bedding layer is no greater than the thickness of the stone modules and no less than 60 % of the stone thickness, but not less than ¾ in. to 1 in. For stone pavers that are thinner than stone cubes, the thickness of the bedding layer is twice the thickness of the stone modules and no less than the stone thickness.

Installation

To begin the installation of the stone modules, the finished grade or height must be established. Datum points such as grade stakes, metal spikes, a stone module, or a metal screed are used to maintain the finished grade. The grade may vary, sloping in one or more directions to accommodate the drainage of the site. Metal screeds or edging similar to terrazzo strips are often used to establish the end of the paving, in the absence of a wall or other architectural element, and are beneficial as a guide for grading.

The stone pavers are set directly into the bedding layer by twisting slightly and tamping the top of the stone into the desired alignment. If the bedding layer is a sand and cement mixture, water is sprinkled over the setting bed to begin the hydration process. If a thicker stone is set, the setting bed can be adjusted to accommodate the increased thickness; if the stone is thinner than the adjacent stone, the bed can be backfilled to achieve the required height. A straightedge is used to maintain alignment across the face of the pavers, using the datum guides at one end of the straightedge with the opposite end set on another datum point or on the finished stone as the pavers are set.

After the pavers are set in place and tamped for a snug fit, the joints can be filled with sand or a sand and cement mixture. The joint filler is poured onto the stone surface and spread over the stone with a stiff broom, working the sand into the joint spaces. Wider joint spaces between pavers are vulnerable to washout and require frequent sand refilling immediately after paver installation, as well as ongoing maintenance. Narrower joints, or the use of cement in the sand mixture, will reduce the frequency of refilling; however, pavers with sand as a joint filler are not as permanent as grouted pavers, which require a mortar bed.

In installing flagged or crazy pattern stones, additional care and effort are required for matching the irregular edges of the different pieces, a challenge similar to fitting the pieces of a jigsaw puzzle together. Wider joints between the stones allow for an easier match of the stone edges, although this increases the vulnerability of the joint material to washout. Narrower joints require that the installer chisel the pieces along the edges with a mason's hammer to create a snug fit between the flagged stones. Installation begins by placing the larger stone pieces first, and distributing them randomly across the area to be paved. The heights are set using the datum points and a straightedge and tapping the stone into place. The installer then places smaller pieces within the field of larger pieces, choosing a close edge match where possible and chiseling the edges where necessary for a snug fit. Once all of the pavers have been set, the joints are filled in the manner previously described (see Figures 4-4 and 4-5).

Advantages of Sand Bed Installation

- Sand beds provide an opportunity to use stone of varying thickness; the variation is absorbed within the sand setting bed.
- A sand setting bed installation is flexible, which allows for movement during freeze-thaw cycles.
- The setting bed is more forgiving without the use of cement in the sand mixture, allowing for the repositioning of the stone modules during installation.
- The sand joints between modules and the sand setting bed allow for drainage of the paved surface.
- Repositioning, maintenance, and replacement of damaged stone pieces are easily achieved after the initial installation.
- Material costs are reduced, owing to the minimal processing requirements; however, larger and thicker stones weigh more than thinner stones and require a greater allowance for freight costs.
- There is increased elasticity of the entire paving system, which will provide for uniform absorption of the load of traffic.

Figure 4-4. Installing limestone pavers in sand setting bed.
The stone pavers are set directly into the bedding layer by twisting slightly and tamping the top of the stone into the desired alignment. The increased thickness of the stone requires tamping into place with a steel rod.

Figure 4-5. Completed limestone pavers.
Sand bed installations are generally selected for exterior applications because of the increased depth required for the setting bed. Areas in which sand bed installations are commonly used include driveways, plazas, walkways, and patios. These locally quarried limestone pavers have been set in a sand bed for use as a roadway that supports car and truck traffic. The flexibility of a sand bed is a benefit in exterior paving in freeze-thaw-sensitive locations, allowing for movement of the subsurface foundation material during periods of freezing temperatures. If the stone pavers have been set in a sand bed without the incorporation of cement, the repositioning of the pavers is easily achieved.

Disadvantages of Sand Bed Installation

- There are limitations in available finishes of the stone type; they are generally more rustic in appearance.

- The additional stone thickness requires a thicker setting bed, which limits the use of sand beds to exterior applications.

- The setting bed may settle if not properly compacted and is vulnerable to the shifting and movement of freeze-thaw cycles, requiring an ongoing maintenance program to reposition the stone modules as they continue to shift over time.

- There are slightly increased installation costs, owing to the more artistic efforts that are required of the installer.

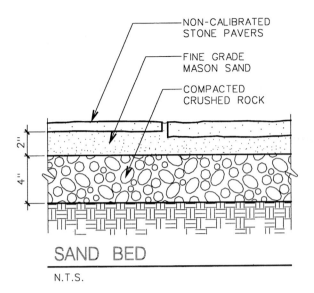

Figure 4-6. Detail of noncalibrated stone pavers set in sand bed.
The depth of the sand bed has been adjusted to accommodate the irregularity of thickness in the paver stones. The pavers here are thin and intended for pedestrian traffic.

MORTAR BED INSTALLATIONS (FLOOR APPLICATIONS)

A mortar bed installation is also referred to as a thick bed or a mud set installation. The terms *mortar bed, mud set,* and *thick set* are used synonymously and are defined as installation methods that utilize a thick mortar bed with a mortar system that is dryer in consistency, or mudlike. The thickness of the setting bed can be from ¾ in. to 2 in. This type of installation is required when stone modules are of irregular thickness from module to module or when the thickness varies within the same module, from one end to the other.

The thick-set installation method is the predecessor of the thin-set tile system and was used exclusively prior to the development of thin tile fabrication. Before thin tiles were available, stone modules were not calibrated; all stone modules were cut from slabs that varied in thickness. Consequently, the variation in thickness had to be made up in the setting bed. Moreover, most earlier floors were ground and polished in place; this required thicker stone modules, which could be successfully set in place only with a mortar bed installation.

Another benefit of using a thick-set installation is evident when a narrow joint is desired. Grout-filled joints are used to help align the edge of the stone module; misalignment is referred to as *lippage*. If a narrow joint width of ¹⁄₁₆ in. or less is used, it is difficult to avoid lippage conditions unless the floor can be finished in place, which is achievable with a thick setting bed.

Thick setting bed installations are also beneficial in installing large-sized modules, because the thicker setting bed will level irregular substrate conditions, allowing larger modules to span the highs and lows of the subfloor. Mortar beds that are composed of a high percentage of sand and set in thicker sections are more durable and capable of bearing increased traffic and heavier loads.

Stone Modules

A thick setting bed will allow for the installation of almost any type of stone, including rustic ungauged materials like quartzite and slate, large-sized prefinished modules with beveled edges, and unfinished stone that is finished in place.

Thick setting beds are ideal for installations of ungauged quartzite and slate that have been cut into tiles or irregularly shaped stones that are installed in a flagged or "crazy" pattern. It is common for these types of stone to vary in thickness from $\frac{3}{8}$ in. to 1 in., which would be impossible to install if a thin-set system were used.

Fabricating equipment that is capable of producing calibrated stone tile has been available for only approximately 30 years. Prior to the development of machinery that produces thin prefinished tile, most stone floors were finished in place. The stone modules used would vary in thickness, and flatness in the finished floor would be resolved through the thicker setting bed absorbing the variation at the underside of the stone, with near perfect leveling achieved as the stone floor was ground and polished in place.

Large-sized prefinished and calibrated stone tiles are also used in a thick-set system. The thicker setting bed will level irregular substrate highs and lows, which a larger module could not allow if a thin-set system were used. The high and low spots of a substrate make lippage conditions nearly impossible to avoid when thin-setting a stone tile.

Floor Preparation

Prior to installing a mortar bed, the subfloor should be covered with a sheet-type membrane, referred to as a *curing membrane*. The purpose of the membrane is to prevent the sub-floor from absorbing moisture from the mortar bed (moisture is required for the proper curing of the mortar bed). Common materials used as a curing membrane include 6 mil plastic film and 15 lb tar paper. The separation between the subfloor and the mortar bed created by the curing membrane allows the setting bed and stone floor to float independently of the structural slab or subfloor, thus reducing the potential for cracking of the finished floor. The Marble Institute of America (MIA) recommends that the maximum deflection of the substrate be no greater than 1 / 720 when using mortar bed systems.

A wire mesh, which is used to reinforce the mortar bed, should be set roughly in the center of the mortar bed. A small amount of mortar is shoveled into place to provide support for the reinforcing wire mesh.

A metal or wood form used at changes in elevation, and float strips used in the field area of the mortar bed, establish the final height of the mortar bed. The forms and the float strips also assist in leveling the mortar bed by providing a support base for a straightedge, which is used to screed off excess mortar while leveling the surface. The straightedge, which can be wood or metal, is pulled across the top of the mortar with a side-to-side sawing motion. The excess mortar is pulled along to level the mortar bed and exposes low areas in the bed. Additional mortar is added to the low areas, and a wood float is used to trowel the surface flat (see Figures 4-7 through 4-9).

Figure 4-7. Building the mortar bed.
The traditional mortar mixture used in a mortar bed or thick-set installation consists of one part portland cement, three to five parts sand, and one part water. The greater the quantity of sand and the closer together the grains of sand in the mixture, the greater the strength of the floor when the setting bed is cured. This combination yields a texture that is dry and crumbly with higher percentages of sand, and a more plastic texture when the quantity of sand is reduced.

Figure 4-8. Floating the mortar bed.
A wood form is used at changes in elevation of the stair treads to establish the final height of the mortar bed. The forms assist in the leveling of the mortar bed by providing a support base for a straightedge, which is used to screed off excess mortar while leveling the surface. The straightedge is pulled across the top of the mortar with a side to side sawing motion. The stone setters are using a wood float to trowel the mortar bed surface flat.

Figure 4-9. Removing the mortar bed forms.
After the mortar bed has set up and is ready to receive stone, the forms are removed.

Mortar

The traditional mortar mixture used in a mortar bed or thick-set installation consists of one part portland cement, three to five parts sand, and one part water. The quantity of sand used in the mortar mix is determined by the final use of the floor and environmental factors such as temperature and humidity. The greater the quantity of sand and, consequently, the closer together the grains of sand in the mixture, the greater the strength of the floor when the setting bed is cured. This combination yields a texture that is dry and crumbly with higher percentages of

Observing variation in Calacatta blocks.
A quarry man explaining the anticipated variation of Calacatta blocks to an architect who has specified the marble
for use as an interior paving and veneer. The wire-sawn exposed face of the bench within the quarry allows for the
observation of color and character of the marble.

The Kirkstone Quarries.
The Kirkstone Quarries, located in the Lake District of the United Kingdom, produce a stone prized for its beauty and strength that is unique in its geologic formation from all other stone types. Although many stone deposits experience multiple geologic events, the final deposition of Kirkstone possesses characteristics of each of the geologic types. The primary mineral composition of Kirkstone is silica, derived from its igneous beginnings. Additionally, the deposit is foliated perpendicular to the sedimentary bedding plane similar in formation to slate, providing the opportunity for the stone to split along its cleaved plane. The density of the stone produced from the re-crystallization of the deposit at the time of its final metamorphism allows for the stone to be polished to a low luster or honed finish.

Bianco Carrara marble quarry.
Quarry men inspecting blocks prior to separation from the quarry bench within a Bianco Carrara marble quarry near Colonata Italy. The quarries of Carrara have been in continuous operation for over 2000 years, producing the white-colored marble "Statuario" that was sought by Michaelangelo and many sculptors to follow.

Trulli stone houses.
Following an ancient plan for the building of homes, the Trulli stone houses of the Puglia region of Italy use indigenous limestones quarried by hand which are set into place in a dry stack manner. The stones are sized and fitted to their location within the wall and roof structure of the homes, relying on the careful placement of each stone and gravity to achieve integrity of structure. The stone walls are often plastered with cement made from the same limestone.

The tower of Trani Cathedral.
The tower of the cathedral of Trani is built of local limestone which is sawn into masonry units to form the church exterior, and then hand-carved to create copings, cornice pieces, and decorative embellishments.

Trani Cathedral (details).
Details of the main entry and a secondary entry to the Trani Cathedral adorned with local, hand-carved limestone. The cathedral dates to the early 1200s and has survived beautifully, despite its proximity to the Adriatic Sea, which is only a few steps away.

Carved limestone entryway.
Decorative carved limestone blocks in a quoined expression form the entry to a private residence built within walls of rubble stone whose plaster has worn long ago.

Greek Revival pediment (detail).
Pediment composed of carved limestone and sandstone blocks of massive proportion to form the building's facade and structure.

Flattened arch (detail).
A flattened arch built of carved blocks within a vestibule. Because of its exaggerated mass, the design is both structural and decorative.

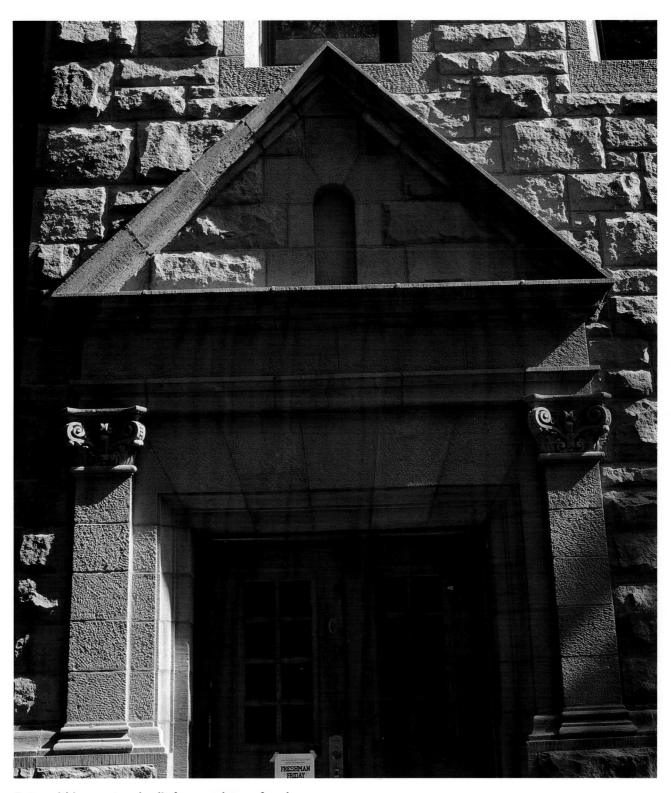

Entry within a restored split-face sandstone facade.
A restored facade composed of a carved sandstone gable and pilaster entry set within a pitch face sandstone wall.
The dimensions of the sandstone are massive, allowing the pitched-face treatment of the blocks and creating dramatic textural relief.

Split-face sandstone exterior.
Details of split-face sandstone exterior and arch on a restored building facade.

Washington Mutual Tower.
Flamed and polished granite are integrated with a curtain wall system that form the exterior of the Washington Mutual Tower, Seattle, Washington (at left). Architect: Kohn, Pederson, Fox Architects; New York.

Douai Abbey Church.
The restored Douai Abbey Church with new Kirkstone Silver Green and Sea Green pavers. The walls, columns, pointed arches and groin vaults are indigenous limestone, carefully restored. Architect: Michael Blee Design, United Kingdom.

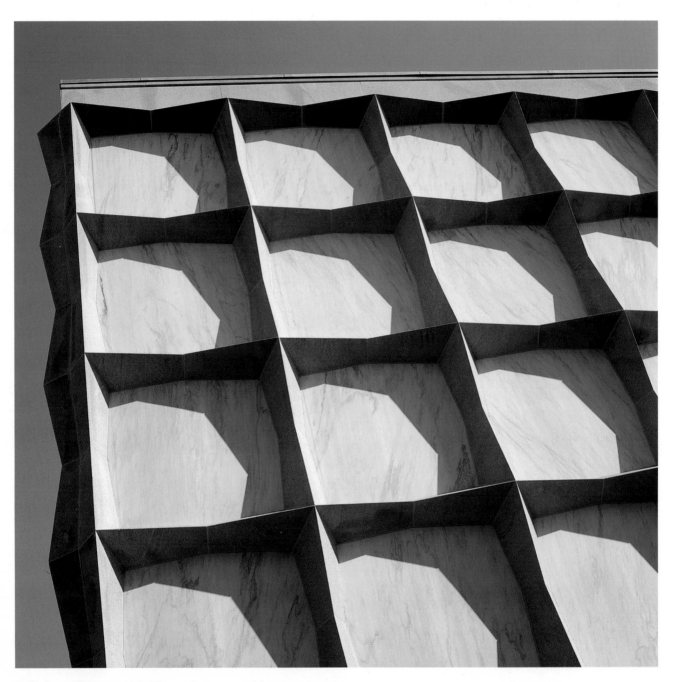

Curtain wall frame with Bianco Carrara marble.
Bianco Carrara marble has been fitted within a curtain wall frame that conceals the joints between the stone veneer panels, allowing for movement of the stone within the building facade.

U.S. Bank Center, Seattle, Washington.
Flamed Sardinia-grey granite pavers, treads, and risers with polished granite installed in the rotunda and building lobby of the U.S. Bank Center in Seattle, Washington. The architects used the paver and veneer modules (many as large as 36" x 36" installed in a 2" deep mortar bed) to reinforce the sense of elegance and grandeur. Architect: Callison Architecture; Seattle, Washington.

Limestone entryway.
Indiana limestone veneer is used at the entry focal point, building wainscot, coping, and cornice of this department store to create a sense of permanence and strength, enabling the building to blend with the regional vernacular. Architect: Callison Architecture; Seattle, Washington.

Use of traditional and non-traditional marbles in lobby space.
Traditional marbles, Calacatta Moonlight, Rosso Levanto, and Black Absolute granite compliment the spirit of elegance in this lobby space. Architect: Callison Architecture; Seattle, Washington.

Valley Fair Shopping Center, San Jose, California.
The architects selected several limestones of subtle
color variation, bordered by a contrasting accent
stone at the storefront tenant line to create a retail
street scene in the renovation of the Valley Fair
Shopping Center, in San Jose, California. Indian
sandstone was used to integrate existing columns
and contrasting limestones with new patterns at the
center of the court area to give prominence to the
retailers that border on the space. Architect: Callison
Architecture; Seattle, Washington.

Use of Italian limestone and American bluestone.
Various Italian limestones and American bluestone are incorporated in a contemporary composition recalling the traditional spirit of Roman gardens and villas. Architect: Callison Architecture; Seattle, Washington.

Nordstrom, Mall of America.
Red Imperial granite, Black Absolute granite, and Sea Green Kirkstone form an articulate geometric pattern within a field of Botticino marble to announce arrival at this elevator lobby. Architect: Callison Architecture; Seattle, Washington.

Vein-cut, polished limestone.
Vein-cut, polished limestone is installed on the columns, tub, and bathroom floor of this luxurious hotel suite.

Tumbled limestone pavers.
Rustic tumbled limestone pavers create a sense of refinement as installed at this entry office vestibule.

Sea Green Kirkstone.
Sea Green Kirkstone, a metamorphosed quartzitic sandstone, was selected because of its extreme durability for this bar counter-top application. Because of its mineral composition, Kirkstone is inherently resistant to citric acids and staining, comparable to granite, making it the material of choice for high wear environments.

Indian multi-colored slate.
Rustic in character, this Indian multi-colored slate is successfully installed in a mortar bed as an adhered veneer.

Non-traditional use of marble.
A unique application of this Spanish marble used to form a light fixture, projecting out from the marble veneer wall.

Kirkstone lavatory counter.
Stone is a practical material for use as counters and work surfaces. Stone types that are composed of calcium should be limited to low use areas as they are more vulnerable to acid etching and wear from abrasion. This lavatory counter utilizes Kirkstone as its surface material which possesses wear characteristics similar to durable stones such as granite.

Split-face sandstone used in private residence.
Indigenous split-face sandstone is used as the exterior facing of
this home to capture the ruggedness of the Utah surroundings.
The sandstone was brought into the home's interior and combined
with a limestone that softens the rugged character of the split-
face stone columns.

Split-face stone stairway.
Natural split-face Kirkstone integrates beautifully with the natural landscape to form the treads and risers of this garden walkway.

sand, and a more plastic texture when the quantity of sand is reduced. Other materials such as lime and latex or acrylic additives can be mixed with the mortar to achieve different results, such as increased plasticity, which will make the mortar more spreadable.

The traditional mortar bed, which has been used since ancient times, is a three-part system. The first coat or base coat of mortar, which imbeds the reinforcing mesh, is applied over the curing membrane. This coat is slightly coarser because of the addition of greater amounts of sand. A thinner second coat is troweled onto the base coat and is used to level the mortar bed. The final coat of mortar contains a higher percentage of cement mixed with water to create a pastelike texture. This coat acts as the bond coat between the stone and the mortar bed.

More recently, a one-step mortar mix has been used to increase the speed of the installation process. A curing membrane and reinforcing mesh are also used; however, the mix is shoveled into place at one time, rather than in separate steps using differing textures of the mortar. A bed prepared by the one-coat method can receive stone while it is still wet or can be allowed to set up and partially cure.

Installation

Setting stone into the mortar mix when it is still plastic is referred to as a fresh set, and allowing the mortar bed to partially set before beginning installation is referred to as thin set.

Fresh-set installations allow for the immediate installation of the stone module into a plastic mortar bed. After the mortar bed has been screeded to the desired plane, the stone modules can be set into the bed once the stone has been back buttered. The back butter mortar coat is a mixture high in portland cement and has the consistency of a sticky paste. The back butter process increases the bond between the stone and the mortar bed. Back buttering is achieved in two steps.

The first step is to *flash* a layer of mortar onto the back of the stone. The flash coat is a thin layer of mortar that is troweled hard onto the back of the stone, imbedding mortar into the recesses of the stone back.

A thicker second coat of the same mortar mix is troweled onto the back of the stone on top of the flash coat. This thicker layer of mortar is the bond coat.

The stone is then set in place with a slight twisting motion, when possible, and tamped to its true and level position. Because the fresh set mortar has not yet set up, the mortar bed is workable and can be easily manipulated to achieve proper alignment of the stone. As the stone is set in place, the grouting of the joint spaces can be performed. Grouting at this time allows for the grout mixture to cure at the same rate simultaneously with the mortar bed.

Thin-set installations are executed after the mortar bed has partially set — usually after 24 hours, which is when the greatest amount of shrinkage takes place. When the mortar bed is firm and ready to receive the stone, the stone modules are back buttered as in the fresh set method, with a thick layer of cement paste. The stone is then tamped into a true and level plane on the mortar bed. The bonding of the stone with the setting bed occurs as the wet paste of cement that is buttered onto the back of the stone reacts with the cement in the mortar bed. The joints are grouted in the same manner as in other tile installations. If a butt joint or minimal-width grout joint is desired, the face of the stone will require grinding and polishing of any misaligned edges (see Figures 4-10 through 4-19).

Figure 4-10. Preparing the vertical surface to receive the riser.
Nonbonded areas of excess mortar are removed, and the vertical surface is prepared to receive the riser. Mortar has been applied to the back of the riser to bond with the cured mortar bed.

Figure 4-11. Setting the riser in place.
The riser shown is 3 cm thick (1⅛ in.) and requires the careful attention of two stone setters to achieve proper placement.

Figure 4-14. Troweling a thin coat of mortar to the cured mortar bed.
A thinner coat is troweled onto the base coat and is used to level the mortar bed. The final coat of mortar contains a higher percentage of cement mixed with water to create a pastelike texture. This coat acts as the bond coat between the stone and the mortar bed.

Figure 4-15. Preparing the tread for installation.
The back of the tread is moistened with water prior to an application of mortar, referred to as back buttering. The back butter process is composed of two steps. The first is to *flash* a layer of mortar onto the back of the stone. The flash coat is a thin layer of mortar that is troweled hard onto the back of the stone, imbedding mortar into the recesses of the stone back. The thicker second coat of the same mortar mix is then troweled onto the back of the stone on top of the flash coat. This thicker layer of mortar is the bond coat.

Figure 4-16. Installing the back-buttered tread.
The back butter mortar coat is a mixture high in portland cement and has the consistency of a sticky paste. The back butter process increases the bond between the stone and the mortar bed.

Figure 4-12. Final positioning of the riser.
The craftsman makes final adjustments to the placement by tapping the riser into alignment.

Figure 4-13. Truing the mortar bed in preparation for the installation of the tread.
The stone setter confirms the level plane of the mortar bed using a bullet level prior to installing the tread.

Figures 4-17 and 4-18. Setting the tread in place.
The stone is then set in place with a slight twisting motion and tamped to its true and level position. Because the fresh-set mortar has not set up, the mortar bed is workable and can be easily manipulated to achieve proper alignment of the stone.

Figure 4-19. Detail view of the tread nosing.
Three parallel grooves are sawn near the edge of the nosing and filled with preformed carborundum strips for improved slip resistence. The vertical leading edge of the tread is sawn back to reduce the tripping hazard.

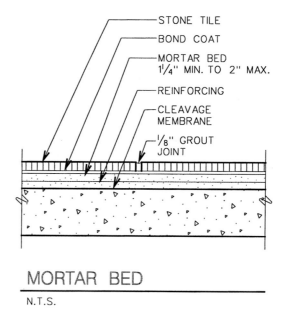

STONE TILE
BOND COAT
MORTAR BED
1¼" MIN. TO 2" MAX.
REINFORCING
CLEAVAGE
MEMBRANE
⅛" GROUT
JOINT

MORTAR BED

N.T.S.

Figure 4-20. Detail of a stone module set in a mortar bed system.

Advantages of Mortar Bed Installation

- Offers increased design opportunities owing to larger sizes of stone modules available.
- Makes possible the use of stone of irregular thickness and size.
- Offers an opportunity to achieve no joint or minimal-width joints between stone modules.
- Can be used when a sloped floor is required, such as in a toilet room.
- Can take greater loads.
- Allows multiple plane work that requires leveling and plumbing of the setting bed, such as in stairs.

Disadvantages of Mortar Bed Installation

- Finished-in-place installations require water in the finishing process and create sludge as a by-product, which requires additional protection of adjacent areas and increased cleanup.
- Additional thickness is required, which may not be available in remodel conditions, or may require modification to the building structure to accommodate depressed areas to receive the thicker setting bed.
- Greater costs of materials and installation are incurred.

THIN–SET INSTALLATIONS (THIN– AND MEDIUM–BED FLOOR APPLICATIONS)

Installing thin stone tile in a thin mortar bed system is an installation method that has been practiced only for the past 30 years, made possible with the development of fabricating equipment capable of producing thin stone modules. Thin tile fabrication technology has had a greater impact on the stone industry than any other development in the past 100 years, as it has made stone available to nearly any project budget. Previous to thin tile production all stone flooring was set in a full mortar bed, which required a minimum depth of 2 in. and necessitated the finishing of the stone in place. Consequently, the cost of installing stone in a mortar bed was very high, making the use of stone for flooring available only for monumental-sized projects or for the wealthy.

The Tile Council of America (TCA) defines the process thus: "The term *thinset* is used to describe the method of installing tile with a bonding material usually $3/32"–1/8"$ in thickness. In some geographical areas the term *thinset* may be used interchangeably for dry set portland cement mortar."

The prefinished tile is adhered directly to the substrate with a cementitious mortar adhesive. This type of system requires tile modules relatively small in size, from a 1 in. mosaic to 24 in. × 24 in., which is usually considered the maximum size for thin-set installation; a tile module of 12 in. × 12 in. is the most common. A thin-set system requires that the tile be calibrated or gauged to a uniform thickness. Setting beds of up to $5/8$ in. can be achieved utilizing specialized mortar formulas that are designed to resist shrinkage and cure properly in thick sections. One-coat mortar systems that are formulated in this manner are referred to as *medium-set* or *medium-bed* systems. Thin-set tile systems and medium-bed systems can be used in both interior and exterior applications.

The substrate for thin-set stone tile must be dimensionally stable, with a minimum of deflection, to obtain the best results. The substrate may be a concrete slab or a concrete backer board. Thin tile can be installed over other substrate materials such as metal, gypsum wallboard, plywood, existing ceramic tile, existing terrazzo flooring, and other stable substrates. The mortar requirements for different substrates may vary and should be confirmed with the specific mortar manufacturer for compatibility of the specific application; refer to "Mortars, Setting Materials, and Grout Systems" on p. 133 for more information.

Stone Modules

The standard size of stone tile is 12 in. × 12 in. × $3/8$ in. thick, and it is available up to a size of 24 in. × 24 in. × $3/8$ in., based on the equipment available at the fabricator's plant. From an installation perspective, the 24 in. × 24 in. tile should be considered the maximum size that can be thin set. As the tile size increases, the degree of installation difficulty increases: aligning tile edges and corners becomes difficult because of the imperfections in the subfloor, and the subfloor must be flatter, requiring a higher level of perfection.

Because the fabricating equipment is adjustable, in theory, any tile size should be available smaller than 24 in. × 24 in.; however, there are other factors to review in considering nonstandard sizes. The main consideration is the quantity required for the project. If the quantity is small, it will be difficult to persuade a fabricator to shut down the fabrication line, recalibrate the equipment for the new size, run the material, and reset the equipment. If a fabricator is found who will do this, it will be costly. Stone tile fabricators want to produce one size in as large quantities as possible to reduce waste and increase efficiency. If a project requires multiple sizes in the same stone and the different sizes are to be installed together, the fabricator in most cases will fabricate each size consecutively — not simultaneously.

Additional time should be planned to accommodate this process. Another concern in selecting stone tile sizes is the shape of the tile. Square tile can be beveled with the use of automated equipment; for rectangular or other shapes that are not square, at least half of the sides will require hand-beveling, which will increase the cost of the tile.

Standard sizes are based on metric dimensions:

Standard Metric Size	Nominal U.S. Equivalent	Actual U.S. Equivalent
30 cm × 30 cm	12 in. × 12 in.	$11^{13}/_{16}$ in. × $11^{13}/_{16}$ in.
30.5 cm × 30.5 cm	12 in. × 12 in.	12 in. × 12 in.
40 cm × 40 cm	16 in. × 16 in.	$15^3/_4$ in. × $15^3/_4$ in.
60 cm × 60 cm	24 in. × 24 in.	$23^5/_8$ in. × $23^5/_8$ in.

Floor Preparation

A proper floor installation begins with examination and preparation of the substrate. To achieve a successful installation, the substrate must be sound and stable. Several informal test methods have been developed by tile and stone consultants to determine the soundness of a substrate. One method is to slowly drag a long length of metal chain in a serpentine pattern over the substrate. The noise created by the chain will ring consistently when it is dragged over areas that are sound and will reverberate a hollow tone over areas that are not. A steel rod can also be used to tap gently on the substrate to locate hollow or loose areas of the subfloor.

Prior to the tile installation, the substrate should be fully cured and the stone tile and substrate should be clean and free of debris. The subfloor should be cleaned with aggressive cleaners; the use of acids or high alkaline detergents should be avoided if possible. Care should be exercised in using acids, so as to prevent future contamination or damage of products that will be used in the installation process. If acid solutions are used, the surfaces should be thoroughly cleaned of all residue and neutralized. Sealed concrete subfloors can be prepared by scarifying the surface, using mechanical methods such as sandblasting, bead blasting, or blast tracking, to erode the top surface containing the sealer. Bead blasting and blast tracking are types of sandblasting that use metal spheres to roughen the subfloor. The metal beads are vacuumed simultaneously to the blasting and recirculated with new spheres. Any of these methods can be employed to provide a tooth or texture on the substrate, which allows for better bonding of the tile to the subfloor.

It is often necessary to level the slab, which can be achieved in various ways, depending on the condition of the slab and the requirements of the final installation. Many proprietary cementitious mortar mixes are available that have been designed specifically as underlayment. The underlayment is poured in a slurry and screeded, then floated, to achieve the desired surface. A final surface plane that is true to approximately $^1/_8$ in. in 10 ft 0 in. is usually satisfactory. The requirement "$^1/_8$ in. in 10 ft" is defined as no high spots or low spots greater than $^1/_8$ in., no ridges or sudden changes in plane, and no more than one high or low spot along any 10 ft line, as determined by a 10 ft long straightedge placed across the floor. Similar mixes are also used in areas sloping to drains, to create a transition between differing elevations, or in areas around obstacles that necessitate truing. There are limitations to the use of these types of fill; they may require the use of a mortar bed if the subfloor conditions are severe.

Exterior-grade plywood can provide a rigid subsurface for floor tile installations and is lower in cost than concrete backer board. Plywood was widely used prior to the introduction of concrete backer board; however, because of the possibility of plywood delaminating when exposed to prolonged contact with moisture, caution should be exercised in using plywood as a subsurface for floor tile in a wet environment.

Crack Isolation Membrane

Where there is concern about cracks within an existing slab, or the potential of cracks in a new slab because of shrinkage or normal dynamic movement at construction and control joints, the use of a crack isolation membrane is recommended. The purpose of a crack isolation membrane, or slip sheet, as it is sometimes called, is to introduce a slip plane between the substrate and the stone tile. This membrane allows for slight lateral movement in the substrate by moving with the slab on the underside while maintaining a bond to the tile above. The crack isolation membrane disperses the dynamic movement away from the crack in the substrate and allows for the movement to occur in the nearest adjacent grout joint or sealant joint, rather than telegraphing directly through the stone. Crack isolation can be achieved by using one of two products: a sheet-type or an embedded system.

A sheet membrane is composed of layers of flexible polymer mesh that are laminated together with a durable rubberlike layer. The overall thickness of the membrane sheet is approximately 1/16 in. The isolation sheet is adhered directly to the substrate and rolled smooth. The stone tile is installed directly to the isolation membrane like any other substrate. Manufacturers of the sheet-type crack isolation membrane contend that their system is easier to install and, consequently, lower in cost.

The embedded system is composed of three parts. The first part is a cementitious bed with elastomeric properties that is troweled to the subfloor, followed by a flexible fabric-type mesh that is placed directly into the thin bed. Once the system sets up, the stone is thin-set over the embedded membrane with the final layer of thin-set adhesive. Although the embedded system sounds labor-intensive, its manufacturers state that this system is competitive with other isolation products and is more adaptable to unusual or complex conditions.

Both systems have had long, successful histories, and the application of either type can add value to a finished floor. Note that these systems are intended for application with small cracks up to $1/8$ in. in width and with cracks that may experience only slight lateral movement. Nothing will prevent cracking of a stone tile floor when the anticipated slab movement is vertical or if the substrate is not sound.

When moisture protection is desired, waterproof membranes may be used to create a barrier between the stone installation and the subsurface. This is usually achieved through the use of sheet products that are also used for crack isolation. The origin of crack isolation membranes is based in the development of waterproof barriers. The sheet membranes are adhered to the subfloor, and the stone is adhered directly to the waterproof membrane.

Mortar Systems

There are a variety of mortar formulas available that can be selected for specific applications as the installation demands. The primary mortar systems are as follows:

1. *Thin-set mortar.* This is a term applied to general mortar systems that are used as a bond coat for setting thin, flat stone units. The components of thin-set mortar systems are sand, portland cement, and water. Thin-set mortar mixes are available in premixed packages or can be mixed on-site. In certain geographical areas, the term thin-set is used interchangeably with dry-set portland cement mortar. Additives can be mixed with the basic mortar system to enhance its properties for specific installation requirements.

2. *Latex modified portland cement mortar.* Latex mortar systems are portland cement mortar systems that contain latex additives to improve the elasticity of the setting bed, allowing the final stone installation greater flexibility to the occasional lateral movement of the subsurface. The addition of latex to the mortar mix will improve adhesion, provide higher bond strength, reduce water absorption, and produce greater resistance to shock and impact. Latex additives can be mixed with thin-set, medium-set, and other mortar bed systems.

3. *Rapid-set thin-set mortar.* Rapid-set thin- or medium-bed mortar systems are fast-setting cementitious mortar systems, some of which are latex or polymer modified, that are used to expedite the setting and curing process of a mortar bed.

4. *Medium-bed mortar.* The components of a medium-bed mortar system are the same as those of a dry-set mortar system, adapted to achieve greater thickness. To accomplish the increased setting bed thickness, a coarser grade of sand is used with the mix of cement. Medium-bed mortar systems are specially formulated to reduce shrinkage and cracking when troweled in thick sections, as compared with thin-set systems. If a medium bed is required, thin-bed systems should not be used.

5. *100% solids epoxy mortar.* One hundred percent solids epoxy mortars are thermosetting, contain no water, and are capable of generating extremely high bond strength and providing exceptional performance. The mortar system consists of two components, resins and a reactive hardener or curing agent. Epoxy mortar systems are commonly used with water-sensitive stone, such as green marble, or large units of agglomerate stone. They are also used with nonconventional substrates such as steel, glass, and plywood.

There are many other formulas available with similar opportunities for thin bed and medium bed application. (See "Mortars, Setting Materials, and Grout Systems" on page 133 for more information on mortar systems.)

Once the tile has been set in place and has cured, the grouting process can begin. The time required before grouting can occur will vary, based on the type of mortar mix that is specified. Grout systems vary as much as mortar systems and can be tailored for the specific requirements of an application. For example, epoxy solids can be integrated into a grout system to eliminate the staining of the grout. This can be particularly useful in a food serving environment. The manufacturer of the mortar will have recommendations for determining the time required for the setting bed to cure enough to receive grout and foot traffic. (See "Mortars, Setting Materials, and Grout Systems" on page 133 for more information on grout systems.)

Installation

Thresholds and metal termination screeds are sometimes set in place prior to beginning the tile installation. They are useful as starting points in laying out tile coursing and determining the finished elevation. Metal screeds offer the additional benefit of protection from chipping along the edge of the tile as it terminates the stone field or creates a transition to other materials, such as carpet. Metal screeds are extruded metal configured in an L shape and are fabricated off-site. They are installed with the short side, or horizontal leg, of the L oriented to the underside of the last course of tile.

When installation begins, the stone tile is dampened prior to the application of mortar, so as to reduce the absorption of water from the mortar, which could cause excessive suction and improper hydration of the mortar. A layer of mortar is troweled onto the subfloor with a notched trowel. The size of the notched trowel is determined by the thickness and type of mortar that is used; thin-set mortars require a smaller notch than medium-bed mortar systems. The size of the area is limited to the area that the craftsman can install before the mortar sets up.

Back buttering, as discussed earlier, refers to the troweling of mortar onto the back of the stone tile. Many believe that applying this mortar coat to the tile back will complement the layer of mortar applied to the substrate, and thereby increase the coverage or bond between the tile and subfloor to nearly 100%. Most failures of thin-set stone tile are due to an incomplete bond between the tile and the substrate. When a crack occurs along the edge or at the corner of a tile, it is usually because there is a void in the mortar bed below the installed tile. It is common practice for the architectural specifications to require that a stone tile be removed at random and examined for the coverage of the mortar on the back of the tile. If there are areas where coverage is incomplete, the installer is notified to allow for the development of corrective measures. Weight directed through a small area, such as the heel of a woman's shoe, could break a tile if there is a void in the mortar bed directly below the point of contact. Imagine what a loaded pallet jack with steel rollers will do! This is a point of sensitivity for many in the tile industry: to back butter or not back butter? There are two distinct camps, and both positions have merit. Many installations, using both systems, have been reviewed, and both good results and unsuccessful results have been observed. The main concern from an owner's perspective is cost. Why should an owner pay more for this additional attention when the coverage should be adequate using the traditional method? It is tough to argue the point, particularly when a failure can occur with either system if the stone is not properly set. Certainly, any insurance that can produce good results is worthy of review and purchase if the budget will allow.

Once the setting mortar has been troweled to the substrate and the stone tile has been back buttered, the tile is set in place. The installer pushes the tile firmly into place with a slight twisting motion. Gently tapping the tile into place with a

Figure 4-21. Application of thin-set mortar to substrate.
Where there is concern about cracks within an existing slab, a crack isolation membrane is recommended. This membrane allows for slight lateral movement in the substrate by moving with the slab on the underside while maintaining a bond to the tile above. The isolation membrane is adhered directly to the substrate and rolled smooth. A coat of mortar is troweled onto the subfloor with a notched trowel. The size of the area is limited to the area that the craftsman can install before the mortar sets up. The stone tile is installed directly into the setting bed, which is bonded to the isolation membrane.

Figure 4-22. Back buttering the stone tile prior to installation.
The stone tile is dampened prior to the application of mortar, to reduce absorption of water from the mortar, so as to prevent excessive suction and improper hydration of the mortar. Often, the architect will specify that a mortar coat be troweled onto the back of the stone tile, a process called back buttering. It is believed that this mortar coat will complement the layer applied to the substrate to increase the opportunity to achieve near 100% coverage or bond between the tile and subfloor.

Figure 4-23. Setting the stone tile.
Once the setting mortar has been troweled to the substrate and the stone tile has been back buttered, the tile is set in place. The installer pushes the tile firmly into place with a slight twisting motion. Gently tapping the tile into place with a wood block or rubber mallet, the tile setter aligns the edges and corners of each tile with the adjacent tiles.

wood block or rubber mallet, the tile setter aligns the edges and corners of each tile with the adjacent tiles. Aligning the stone tile edges requires particular attention. Misalignment or lippage of approximately $1/16$ in. is generally accepted in the industry. When lippage greater than $1/16$ in. occurs, a tripping hazard may be created (see Figures 4-21 through 4-25).

Plastic spacers are sometimes placed between the tile modules to maintain uniformity of joint width. The spacers are removed prior to the grouting of the joints, and excess mortar between the tiles is removed to allow for grouting. The joints should be raked to a depth of $1/4$ in. to accept the grout. Joints that are to receive a sealant should be raked the full depth.

The grout mixture is applied to the joint space between the tile modules in a slurry. This mixture contains fine sand aggregate for joint widths greater than $1/8$ in.; unsanded grout is used for joints of $1/8$ in. and smaller. The grout mixture is spread over the joint and worked into place with a squeegee or similar tool to force the grout down deep into the joint cavity. For large areas the grout may be worked into place with a floor-polishing machine retrofitted with soft rubber blades. This method can dramatically cut grouting time; however, the operator must be aware of the curing characteristics of the grout mixture to ensure that the work is completed before the grout begins to set and must be careful not to overwork individual locations, which can result in surface scratching. (See "Mortars, Setting Materials, and

Figure 4-24. Aligning the edges of adjacent stone tile

To prevent the occurrence of lippage the craftsman is aligning the edges and the faces of adjacent tiles. When lippage greater than $\frac{1}{16}$ in. occurs, a tripping hazard may be created.

Figure 4-25. Checking the surface of adjacent tile for level.

The installer checks the surface of the most recently installed stone for trueness of plane.

Grout Systems" on page 133 for more information on grout joint widths and materials used as joint fillers.) Once the grout has been worked into place, a sponge is used to tool the top of the grouted joint concave. The top of the finished joint should align with the bottom of the bevel, if the tile has a bevel; if the tile has a square edge, the joint should be filled just slightly below the top of the tile.

Narrower joints have always been popular — the smaller the better from an aesthetic point of view. Typically, wider joints are associated with ceramic tile and narrow joints can evoke the character of a monolithic slab. A standard joint width for use with thin calibrated stone tile is $\frac{1}{8}$ in., which may be reduced to $\frac{1}{16}$ in. if a nonsanded grout is used and the subfloor is flat and true. If narrow joints are desired in a thin-set application, a joint width of $\frac{1}{16}$ in. is the minimum. *Do not butt joint stone tile.* This will no doubt lead to a failure when the stone floor gets wet, causing the setting bed to deteriorate. An unfilled joint will also be a collection place for dirt, debris, and germs. Narrow joints are difficult to achieve, and if the subfloor is not perfect, the installation of tile with narrow joints will result in additional costs.

Another area of concern in grouting is the staining of light-colored tiles. If a light-colored stone tile is selected, the color of the grout should not be too dark, as it may possibly stain the face or edges of the tile. When the edges of the tile absorb pigment from the grout, it is referred to as "windowpaning." A grout release may be used to prevent it from being absorbed along the edges; however, this may result in failure of the bond between the grout and the stone if not properly executed. The longer the grout sits on the surface of the tile, the greater the chance of the fissures, or openings, on the tile to absorb the grout permanently. The challenge is to select a color that will achieve a balance between one that may stain the face of the tile (too dark) and a color that is too light, which will eventually darken as a result of staining from foot traffic. An installation mock-up executed prior to beginning tile installation is a valuable tool for testing the absorption of color from the grout.

Advantages of Thin-Set Stone Installation

- Lower material and installation costs are incurred, as compared with mortar bed installations.

- A thin-set stone tile system is lighter in weight, requiring less floor structure.

- Thin-set installations are well suited for remodel work because of the reduced depth of the mortar system, allowing for easier transitions between floor finish types.

- Smaller tile modules can easily accommodate the contour of a slightly irregular floor without creating conditions of lippage.

Disadvantages of Thin-Set Stone Installation

- The stone tile modules must be uniformly thin. This requires that the stone tile be calibrated, gauged, ground, or hand-selected to achieve a consistent thickness. Stones that are heavily cleaved, such as slate and quartzite, are inherently inconsistent in thickness and will require grinding on the back side to yield a more uniform thickness. Some slates that have a naturally occuring flat cleaved texture may require only hand-selection.

- The size of the tile is limited; 24 in. × 24 in. is generally the largest-sized module that can be fabricated on stone tile factory lines.

- The larger the tile module, the more difficult it is to follow the contour of an irregular substrate. In today's buildings, where lighter-weight steel and concrete systems are used, it is rare that a tile installer will encounter a concrete substrate that is flat to 1/8 in. in 10 ft. More often the subfloor will roll up and down between the structural beams. This makes it difficult to align the edges of each tile without lippage. Smaller modules will follow the imperfect surface more readily.

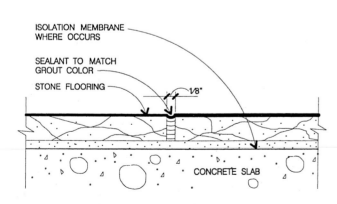

Figure 4-26. Detail showing thin-set stone tile.
Detail of thin-set stone tile shown where an expansion joint occurs. Joints filled with expansion material work best when located over a crack isolation membrane.

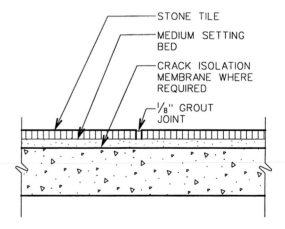

Figure 4-27. Detail showing medium-bed stone tile installation.
The configuration of a medium bed is similar to a thin mortar bed installation, although the formulation of the medium bed accommodates the increased mortar depth, allowing for proper curing.

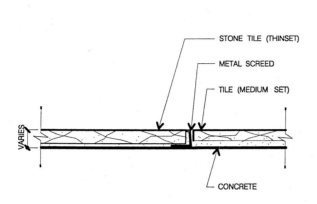

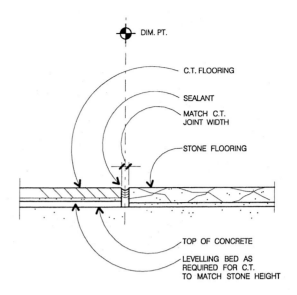

Figure 4-28. Transition detail showing a thin-set installation adjacent to a medium-bed installation. The use of two setting bed thicknesses allows for the installation of two stones with differing thicknesses. The separation of the thin mortar bed from the medium bed is achieved with a metal screed.

Figure 4-29. Transition detail showing thinner ceramic tile installed adjacent to a thicker stone tile. The thinner ceramic tile is set over a thicker mortar bed to meet the height of the adjacent stone tile.

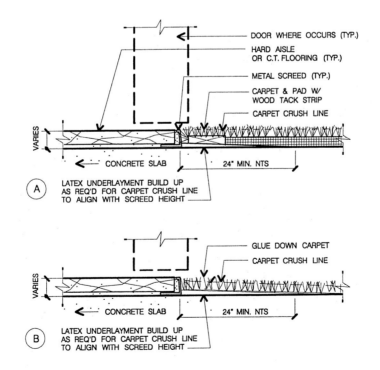

Figure 4-30. Transition detail showing thin-set stone tile adjacent to direct glue-down carpet and carpet over pad.

ADHERED STONE VENEER (THIN-SET AND MORTAR BED WALL APPLICATION)

Adhered stone veneer is a system in which individual stone veneer units, or tiles, are adhered directly to a subsurface to form a finished wall surface. The application of stone tile to a vertical surface is similar to the installation of tile to a horizontal surface; however, installing tile vertically has the additional challenge created by the forces of gravity. Whereas a horizontal application will remain stationary, tile installed vertically will be pulled downward. The stone tile is adhered to the subsurface or backup wall with a cementitious mortar-type adhesive, utilizing differing cement mixtures, if the tile is installed directly to a backup surface or if the installation is to use a mortar bed. This type of system is usually selected when the design does not require large modules and the stone tile is available in uniform thin veneers $\frac{1}{2}$ in. thick or less. Tile installed vertically may be applied directly to a masonry backup wall, concrete, or concrete masonry unit (CMU), or to a concrete backer unit (CBU), metal lather and mortar bed, plywood, or gypsum wallboard, with proper substrate and stone selection. Adhered stone veneer systems are most commonly used for interior installations, although they may be used in an exterior environment with consideration given to climatic conditions.

Stone Modules

The Uniform Building Code (UBC) describes an adhered stone veneer system as a system composed of units that are generally $\frac{1}{2}$ in. thick or less, able to withstand a shear stress of 50 lb per square inch, may not be larger than 36 in. in their greatest dimension, may not be more than 5 sq ft in total area, and must weigh less than 15 lb per sq ft. Stone veneer units may exceed $\frac{1}{2}$ in. in thickness; however, to comply with the UBC, stone units that exceed $\frac{1}{2}$ in. thickness are to be installed as an anchored veneer system over exitways, and up to a height of 20 ft. Exceptions are allowed when the stone veneer is used as a wainscot to a height of 4 ft. Generally, the stone tile should be calibrated or uniform in thickness if it is to be thin set directly to a subsurface. Rustic materials or stone modules of irregular thickness, such as quartzite, sandstone, or slates, may require the use of a mortar bed or, with minimum variation, a medium-bed mortar system.

Wall Preparation

The preparation of wall surfaces prior to installation is similar to that used for floor installation. Common concerns, such as the deflection of the backup wall, flatness and trueness of the setting plane, and cleaning of the wall surface, must be reviewed before beginning the stone installation. If the wall surface is to be in a wet environment, such as in a bathtub surround or on the walls of a shower room, or in an exterior installation, a moisture barrier will be required.

Masonry Backup Walls

If the tile is to be installed directly to a concrete wall or CMU, the surface should be clean and have a rough texture to provide a tooth for the mortar to bond to. If the wall has been trowel finished, the surface will require mechanical texturing such as sandblasting, grinding with an abrasive disc, or a light bush hammering. If the concrete wall has been treated with a curing compound or a form-release agent, a good bond may be difficult to achieve; the surface may require aggressive treatment or backer units may have to be used. The wall plane should be checked for cracks and flatness and the installer should confirm that the walls are plumb; any deviance should be corrected for best results. If a concrete wall is to be built, the installer should review the requirements of the stone tile installation with a representative of the concrete trade.

Concrete Backer Board

Durock (produced by U.S. Gypsum) and Hardibacker (produced by James Hardie Building Products) are proprietary names for concrete backer board, to name a few. These products are available in thicknesses of $1/4$ in. to $3/4$ in. and are installed in a similar manner as gypsum board. These types of backer boards are significantly more rigid than gypsum board, making them more difficult to cut and handle; however, they are advantageous when used in wet environments and offer greater stability than gypsum board or plywood. Cement backer units can be scored and snapped to cut, although a reciprocating saw will yield a cleaner cut. The backer boards can be fastened to wood or metal studs with galvanized nails or noncorrosive screws, and the panels should be installed with an $1/8$ in. space around all sides and $1/4$ in. at the perimeter of the wall to allow for expansion. The joints should be taped with fiberglass mesh and receive a coat of mortar, in a manner similar to the taping of gypsum wallboard joints.

Gypsum Wallboard

Gypsum wallboard can be used as a backer material for tile installation in areas where a heavy-duty installation is not required or where moisture will not be in contact with the wallboard. The panels can be fastened in place with galvanized nails or noncorrosive screws and should be installed with an $1/8$ in. space around all sides and $1/4$ in. at the perimeter of the wall to allow for expansion. The joints should be taped with fiberglass mesh and receive a coat of mortar, in a manner similar to the taping of standard gypsum wallboard joints; standard paper tape should not be used, because it will not support the weight and shear of the tile plus adhesive.

Plywood

Exterior-grade plywood will provide a rigid subsurface for wall and floor tile installations and is lower in cost than concrete backer board. Plywood was widely used prior to the introduction of concrete backer board; however, owing to the possibility of plywood delamination when exposed to prolonged contact with moisture, the Tile Council of America (TCA) issued the following caution in regard to using plywood as a subsurface for floor tile in a wet environment:

CAUTION
Substrate Limitations:
The performance of a properly installed thin-set ceramic tile installation is dependent upon the durability and dimensional stability of the substrate to which it is bonded. The user is cautioned that certain substrate materials used in wet areas are subject to deterioration from moisture penetration. (Reference ANSI A108, AN2.5.3.2.1)

Therefore, while every effort has been made to produce accurate guidelines, they should be used only with the independent approval of technically qualified persons.[*]

Plywood panels can be fastened to wood or metal studs with galvanized nails or noncorrosive screws and the panels should be installed with an $\frac{1}{8}$ in. space around all sides and $\frac{1}{4}$ in. at the perimeter of the wall to allow for expansion. The joints should be taped with fiberglass mesh and receive a coat of mortar, in a manner similar to the taping of gypsum wallboard joints.

MORTAR BED

A mortar bed subsurface can be either a three-coat system or a one-coat system. A *three-coat system* is composed of a scratch coat floated over a metal lathe system, followed by a finer leveling coat, and, finally, the bond coat, which is pure cement paste that is used to bond the tile back to the leveling coat. A *one-coat system* is an all-in-one system that is troweled onto the subsurface. The tile is set directly on the plastic mortar bed after receiving a bond coat of pure cement paste or after the one-coat system has set up, in a manner similar to thin-setting

Prior to installation of the mortar bed, the backup wall should be covered with a sheet-type membrane, referred to as a curing membrane. The purpose of the membrane is to prevent the backup wall from absorbing moisture from the mortar bed; moisture is required for the proper curing of the mortar bed. When used with properly spaced expansion joints, the separation between the backup wall and the mortar bed reduces the potential for cracking of the finished wall. Wire mesh or metal lath, attached to the backup wall and set roughly in the center of the mortar bed, is used to reinforce the mortar bed, which is floated over the mesh.

A metal or wood form is used as float strips in the field area of the mortar bed to establish its final thickness. The form and the float strip also assist in the trueing of the mortar bed by providing a support base for a straightedge that is used to screed off excess mortar while leveling the surface of the mortar bed. The straightedge, which can be wood or metal, is pulled across the top of the mortar with a side-to-side sawing motion. The excess mortar is pulled along to level the mortar bed and expose low areas in the mortar bed. Additional mortar is added to the low areas, and a wood float is used to trowel the surface flat.

---

[*]Reprinted from the *1998 Handbook for Ceramic Tile Installation,* published by the Tile Council of America (TCA).

Mortar Mix

The three basic types of mortar mixes used for the vertical installation of stone tiles are those used in mortar beds, of which there are a three-coat and a one-coat system, and thin-set mortar.

Three-coat mortar systems use the tradition mortar mixes that have been used for hundreds of years. The first coat is a coarse mixture, having a larger proportion of sand than cement and water. The coarse texture of the first coat allows for better attachment with a reinforcing mesh. The second coat is finer than the first, with less sand and more cement and water. Both of these coats are allowed to begin the curing process prior to receiving the final coat — the bond coat — which is pure cement mixed with water, used to bond the tile to the mortar bed. This final coat is an important element of the curing process for the entire mortar system. The thickness required for the three-coat system is between $3/4$ in. and $1\,1/2$ in.

One-coat mortar systems accomplish the same results using a one-coat mixture of sand, cement, and water. The advantage of the one-coat system is the reduced overall thickness of the bed, $3/8$ in. to $3/4$ in., as compared with the greater dimension required for the three-coat system. The one-coat system can be allowed to set up and receive tile with a later thin-set application, or the tile can be fresh set into the plastic mortar bed.

Thin-set mortar systems, which are also referred to as dry-set mortar systems, are designed to require a minimum thicknesses of between $1/8$ in. and $1/2$ in. Thin-set systems use a one-coat application, and the material can be mixed with additives for increased flexibility or for quicker curing time. The thin-set, or dry-set, system is the process most commonly used for direct adherence of stone tile to backup walls that are relatively flat and true or where minimum setting thicknesses are required.

Installation

In an adhered veneer system, stone tiles are installed directly to a masonry backup wall, a backer board material, or a mortar bed, with a mortar-type adhesive. The subsurface should be continuous and firmly attached to the building in a manner that provides a rigid surface for the tile to bond to.

EXPANSION JOINTS

Allowing for building movement resulting from seismic activity, expansion/contraction, and building frame movement is a greater concern in installing an adhered veneer tile system as compared with an anchored veneer system. The wall surfaces of an adhered system will experience movement as a larger composition of multiple units, whereas the modules of an anchored veneer system will tend to move as individual units. In using an adhered veneer tile system, an expansion joint system should be incorporated at the beginning of the design process, which can be achieved by planning the location of expansion joints within the wall pattern to accommodate the anticipated movement. The expansion joint is a typical grout joint width that is filled with a nonstaining silicon-type caulking. The joint is filled to the same depth as the grouted joints; however, because of the elastomeric qualities of the silicon caulking, the joint space has the opportunity to compress during periods of material expansion. The spacing of the expansion joints will vary, depending on installation conditions, but as a starting point, regularly shaped areas of approximately 400 sq ft should be isolated to allow for the expansion and contraction of the adhered veneer system. The TCA recommends the frequency of expansion joints as follows:

Recommendations:

- Interior 24' to 36' in each direction.
- Exterior 12' to 16' in each direction.
- Interior tilework exposed to direct sunlight or moisture—12' to 16' in each direction.
- Where tilework abuts restraining surfaces such as perimeter walls, dissimilar floors, curbs, columns, pipes, ceilings, and where changes occur in backing materials.
- All expansion, control, construction, cold and seismic joints in the structure should continue through the tilework including such joints at vertical surfaces.
- Joints through tilework directly over structural joints must never be narrower than the structural joint.

Reprinted from the *1998 Handbook for Ceramic Tile Installation*, published by the Tile Council of America (TCA).

THIN–SET/DRY–SET INSTALLATION

To allow for easier vertical application, the mortar systems that are commonly used in wall installations are more plastic than the mortar systems used on a floor. To achieve this consistency, more water and less sand are used, which gives the tile better gripping ability; however, the compressive strength will be lower and the mortar will be vulnerable to the downward pull of gravity. The tile should be cleaned of dust or debris prior to installation to provide a better bonding surface. The tile is then set directly into a uniform coat of mortar that is troweled to the backup wall surface. Because the mortar is more plastic, additional care is required by the installer when tapping the module into place while aligning the face of the tile with the face of the adjacent modules. If a module is set too deeply, creating a condition referred to as lippage, it is difficult to reposition the module without creating a void at the back. A thin back butter coat applied to the tile prior to setting it in the thin bed will provide more mortar to work the tile into place.

To hold tile stationary while the mortar cures, the temporary use of a nail below a tile or the use of masking tape will prevent the tile from pulling downward. Plastic spacers are placed between the tile modules to maintain uniformity of joint width. The spacers are removed prior to grouting the joints, and excess mortar between the tiles is removed to allow for grouting. The joints should be raked to a depth of $1/4$ in. to accept the grout. Joints that are to receive a sealant should be raked the full depth (see Figures 4-31 through 4-35).

MORTAR BED INSTALLATION

The method of installation of tile in a mortar bed is similar to the methods used for thin-setting the stone directly to a subsurface, including the use of spacers and

Figure 4-31. Back buttering a stone wall cap.
The stone installer is troweling a back butter coat to a stone wall cap prior to installation.

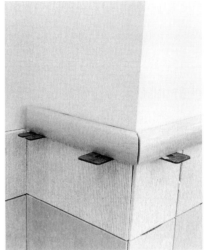

Figures 4-32 and 4-33. Setting the wall cap.
The wall cap has been sawn to create a miter joint at the outside corner. The cap piece is adhered directly to the concrete backer board. A spacer below the cap piece maintains the joint dimension.

Figure 4-34. Stone tile adhered directly to concrete backer board.
Stone tile ½ in. thick adhered directly to a concrete backer board with thin-set mortar. Spacers maintain the joint space between the stone tiles.

Figure 4-35. Stone tile adhered to column, forming a wainscot.

temporary fasteners. The primary difference is the additional time required for the preparation of a mortar bed and the specific method setting the tile in place. There are two methods of setting stone into a mortar bed: fresh set, which means setting the tile into the mortar mix when it is still plastic, and thin set, which allows the mortar bed to partially set prior to setting the tile.

Fresh-set installations allow for the immediate installation of the stone module into a plastic mortar bed. After the mortar bed has been floated to the desired plane, the stone modules can be set into the mortar bed once the stone has been back buttered. The back butter mortar coat is a wet mixture, high in portland cement, and is the consistency of a sticky paste. The back butter coat increases the bond between the stone and the mortar bed and is the final ingredient required for the full cure of the mortar bed system. Back buttering is achieved in two steps: The first is to *flash* a layer of mortar onto the back of the stone. The *flash coat* is a thin layer of mortar that is troweled hard onto the back of the stone, imbedding mortar into the recesses of the stone back. A thicker second coat of the same mortar mix is troweled onto the back of the stone on top of the flash coat. This thicker layer of mortar is the *bond coat*.

The stone is then set in place with a slight twisting motion, when possible, and tamped to its true and level position. Because the fresh-set mortar has not yet set up, the mortar bed is workable and can be manipulated to achieve proper alignment of the stone. As the stone is set in place, the grouting of the joint spaces can be performed. Grouting at this time allows for the grout mixture to cure at the same rate simultaneously with the mortar bed.

Thin-set installations are executed after the mortar bed has partially set; usually after 24 hours, which is when the greatest amount of shrinkage takes place. The mortar bed is firm and ready to receive the stone. The stone modules are back buttered in the same manner used in the fresh-set method, with a thick layer of cement paste. The stone is gently tamped into a true and level plane on the mortar bed and twisted slightly. The bonding of the stone with the setting bed occurs as the wet paste of cement that is buttered onto the back of the stone reacts with the cement in the mortar bed, which allows for the curing of the entire mortar system.

EXTERIOR INSTALLATIONS

A waterproof membrane should be installed between the backup wall and the mortar bed or backer board for all exterior installations and at interior locations where contact with moisture is anticipated. In addition, the design of the wall should incorporate a coping, flashing, and other details to prevent water migration behind the stone veneer, as in any other wall type exposed to the weather.

After the stone veneer modules have been installed, the joint spaces between modules should then be fully grouted. Grout adds further protection from moisture migrating behind the veneer and helps to lock the modules in place. Any voids created between the veneer and the backing will be vulnerable to moisture infiltration, which could result in a failure during a freeze-thaw period. As a void containing water expands during a freeze period, pressure is exerted at the back of the veneer, causing the veneer module to break its bond with the subsurface and resulting in a failure.

Care should be exercised in selecting stone types for adhered veneer installations in exterior locations. The rate of water absorption of the stone tile should be low and considered to be freeze-thaw stable. Generally, stones that have a rate of absorption of 3 % or less are appropriate for use where freeze-thaw stability is a concern. However, for extreme conditions, local practices and comparative data based on previous successful installations should govern the selection of materials for these locations.

The American National Standards Institute (ANSI) measures the permeability of stone tile by comparing the dry weight of a tile with its weight after it has been boiled in water for 5 hours. ANSI has created four categories for ceramic tile based on the water absorption measured. These categories are useful for comparison:

Nonvitreous Tile   Absorbs 7 % or greater

Semivitreous Tile   Absorbs between 3 % and 7 %

Vitreous Tile   Absorbs between 0.5 % and 3 %

Impervious Tile   Absorbs less than 0.5 %

GROUT APPLICATION

The grout mixture is applied to the joint spaces between the tile modules in a slurry. The mixture contains fine sand aggregate for joint widths greater than $\frac{1}{8}$ in.; unsanded grout is used for joints of $\frac{1}{8}$ in. and smaller. The grout mixture is spread over the joint and worked into place with a squeegee or similar tool to force the grout down deep into the joint cavity.

Once the grout has been worked into place, a sponge is used to tool the top of the grouted joint concave. The top of the finished joint should align with the bottom of the bevel, if the tile has a bevel; if the tile has a square edge, the joint should be filled just slightly below the top of the tile.

An area of concern in grouting tiles on a wall surface, as on a floor surface, is the staining of light-colored tiles. If a light-colored stone tile is selected, the color of the grout should not be too dark, which may possibly stain the face of the tile. The longer the grout sits on the surface of the tile, the greater the chance of the fissures, or openings, on the tile to absorb the grout permanently. The challenge is to select a color that will achieve a balance between one that may stain the face of the tile (too dark) and a grout color that is too light, which will eventually darken over time. An installation mock-up executed prior to beginning the tile installation is a valuable tool that can be used to test the absorption of color from the grout.

Advantages of Adhered Stone Veneer (Vertical)

- The primary advantage of using an adhered veneer system is the speed of installation, which translates into overall installation savings. Individual modules can be set in place by a single installer, because of the inherently smaller veneer module, and with far less complication than anchored veneer systems.

- This type of system is also of benefit when the building system cannot accommodate the greater thickness and weight that an anchored veneer system requires.

Disadvantages of Adhered Stone Veneer (Vertical)

- The main disadvantages are the limitation of stone veneer size and the reduced number of allowable locations on a building.

- The number of stones available for this system is reduced because of the greater potential for failure resulting from freeze-thaw instability.

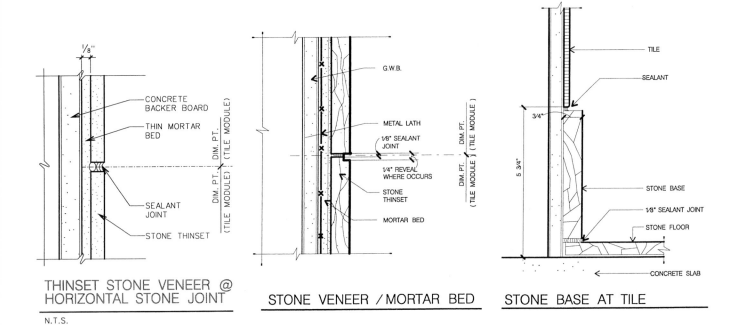

THINSET STONE VENEER @ HORIZONTAL STONE JOINT

N.T.S.

STONE VENEER / MORTAR BED

STONE BASE AT TILE

Figure 4-36. Detail showing stone adhered directly to backer board. A sealant joint is specified at the joint between tile modules, allowing for movement of the modules within the wall system.

Figure 4-37. Detail showing stone set in a mortar bed.

Figure 4-38. Stone adhered directly to a wall to form a base for tile installed above.

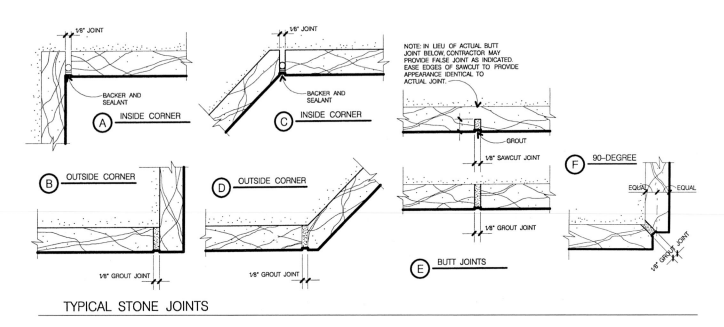

TYPICAL STONE JOINTS

Figure 4-39. Typical stone joints.

ANCHORED VENEER

Anchored veneer systems are also referred to as mechanically fastened stone veneer and handset stone veneer. These are stone veneer systems that utilize anchors in combination with a structural framework for the installation of individual stone units, usually panels, into a wall assembly. Anchors can be mechanical fasteners, continuous metal extrusions, clips, dowels, or wire ties and may be used in combination with stone ledgers and relieving angles. (Stone ledgers are strips of stone that are glued and pinned to the back of a stone panel. The ledger rests horizontally upon a corresponding horizontal structural member on the backup wall. This system is similar to wood cleats used on wall panel systems.) This installation method is usually selected when one or more of the following conditions occur:

- The design requires stone panels that are larger than the sizes available as thin tile modules, typically 24 in. × 24 in.

- The stone installation exceeds the criteria of adhered stone veneer, such as when

  The unit exceeds 36 in. in the greatest dimension.

  Units are larger than 720 sq in.

  Units weigh more than 15 lb per sq ft.

  An exception to these conditions is when the veneer weighs less than 3 lb per sq ft.

- The stone units are greater in thickness than ½ in. and are intended to be installed above exitways or more than 20 ft in height above the adjacent ground elevation.

Anchored veneer systems are suitable for both interior and exterior applications.

Stone panels to be installed utilizing this system will require the thickness of the stone great enough to accept the fabrication necessary for the anchors. Generally, the preferred thickness for interior installations is ¾ in. minimum for exterior installations, 1¼ in. minimum and 2 in. maximum. However, much of the stone used in building construction is imported from countries that are fabricating to metric dimensions, and the standard fabrication dimensions do not convert equally from metric. The standard metric fabrication dimensions are as follows:

1 cm, which is approximately ⅜ in.

2 cm, which is approximately ¾ in.

3 cm, which is approximately 1⅛ in.

4 cm, which is approximately 1½ in.

(UBC (1997) defines the maximum thickness as 2 in. and refers to the stone units as "slab type units" with a maximum panel size of 20 sq ft.)

Any stone fabrication that is greater in thickness than 4 cm is referred to as "cubic" (UBC terms these units "stone units") and is no longer considered a standard fabrication. A thickness of 3 cm or 1⅛ in. is the preferred dimension for exterior veneer systems. Anchors are used to support the weight of the stone panels, to resist live loading, and to position the individual panels within the wall system. The anchors should be located at the bottom edge and top edge of the panel where possible. At areas above windows, doors, and other types of openings it may not be possible to locate anchors at the bottom of the panel, which will require anchors at the side of the panel, or ledgers and liners may be incorporated.

Backup Wall Systems

Typical backup wall systems are structural metal studs, combined with a separate metal frame, and concrete or masonry wall systems.

Structural metal studs that form a building wall system should be sized and spaced by a structural engineer, based on stone veneer load and lateral force resistance (wind load) calculations. The studs are sheathed for dimensional stability and to form a barrier for the building. The sheathing may be composed of gypsum sheathing, plywood, or concrete backer board, although cement wallboard is most common. For moisture protection, the sheathing should be covered by a moisture barrier. A horizontal metal attachment member is integrated with the sheathing and should also be sized by an engineer as part of the overall wall system. The horizontal metal frame, which can be heavy-gauge flat stock or angle sections, is installed continuously and mechanically fastened to the vertical metal studs. The vertical spacing and location of the metal frame is determined by the design of the stone veneer coursing. Both the vertical metal studs and the horizontal metal frame work together as a system to support the stone veneer panels and resist lateral design loads.

Concrete and masonry wall systems are other types of backup walls commonly used for anchoring stone veneer. It is recommended that backup walls composed of CMUs be grouted solid to bear the load of the stone veneer system. A continuous relieving angle, similar to the type used with metal stud backup walls, is used above the first stone course. The relieving angle is fastened to the concrete wall with a wedge anchor, or to a concrete masonry unit wall system with a sleeve anchor fastener. Each stone panel is anchored to the concrete or CMU wall system with the selected anchor system.

Structural metal stud backup walls should be protected from moisture by installing a continuous building paper or Tyvek brand sheeting over the exterior sheathing to create a moisture barrier. The wall surface of a CMU or a concrete backup wall should be treated with an appropriate damp-proofing for water protection. With any of the backup wall systems, the relieving angles and anchors are attached through the moisture barrier to the supporting frame. Weep holes should be located in the joints between panels to allow for the escape of water that has migrated behind the backup wall system.

Stone Veneer Panels

The size of veneer panels is limited to 20 sq ft in area, as stated in the Uniform Building Code. The stone panels that are used in an exterior anchored veneer system are typically 1 1/8 in. (3 cm) in thickness as a minimum and may be as thick as 2 in. The reason for these dimensions is, in part, that the anchors used to support the panels are of a greater dimension than the wire ties and require that the edge of the stone panel be fabricated to receive an anchor. The dimensions of the fabrication or rebate will reduce the stone's effective thickness at the area where the rebate occurs, creating a point of weakness. The rebate, which is a kerf cut-sawn to form a slot, can be continuous throughout the length of the panel or limited to the length required for the specific anchor. The dimensions of the rebate are determined by the type of anchor to be used in the system. The rebate could be a simple hole sized to accept a dowel anchor or a slot sized to coordinate with the width of a split-tail-type anchor. Another type of rebate is a continuous slot that extends the length of the panel and is used with an extruded-type anchor whose shape resembles that of a relieving angle. Regardless of the type of rebate, the UBC states that the anchored veneer and its attachments should be designed to resist a horizontal force equal to twice the weight of the veneer.

Stone panels are fabricated off-site and delivered ready to install. Only a minimum amount of fabrication should occur at the job site, and this should be limited to modification of panels to fit specific field conditions, such as integration of a panel with a fire hose connection, electrical, telephone, or communication outlet boxes, or other building elements. It is recommended that the cut edges of the stone panel be eased slightly to facilitate handling and reduce potential for chipping during installation. This step is accomplished during fabrication, usually consisting of a 45-degree bevel or chamfer of at least $1/16$ in. This treatment is often referred to as an arris; however, by definition, this is incorrect. An *arris* is defined as the sharp edge or ridge formed by two surfaces meeting at an angle, which the easing of the edge is intended to resolve.

Anchors

The type, size, distribution, and design of the anchors and the anchorage system design should be determined by a structural engineer in collaboration with the stone installer. In addition, local building practices, building codes, and possible seismic events should be considered in designing a stone panel system that uses anchors, mechanical fasteners, clips, extrusions, dowels, or wire ties. The UBC provides direction for the distribution of anchors, which states that the tie (anchorage) is to be located in the middle third of the edge of the units, spaced a maximum of 24 in. apart around the periphery of each unit, with not less than four ties per unit.

The most common anchor types are split-tail or two-way anchors, which are L-shaped heavy-gauge stainless steel fabrications, configured with the horizontal leg of the shape split: one half bent up to accept the stone panel above and one half bent down to catch the top of the stone panel below. Other types of anchors include wire tiebacks, wire tiebacks with dowels, strap anchors with attached dowel anchors — all made of steel or stainless steel — and extruded channels made of aluminum, corrosion-resistant steel, or stainless steel similar in section to the L-shaped split tail. Most anchors are engineered and fabricated off-site; however, construction conditions may require that an anchor be modified in the field.

Split-tail anchors, continuous channel anchors, and modified strap anchors are used with 1 1/8 in. (3 cm) thick stone in exterior applications and are load bearing. Wire tieback anchors and tiebacks that incorporate dowels are used with 3/4 in. (2 cm) thick stone in interior applications because of their smaller size. These types of anchors do not support the load of the panels, but are used for securing the position of the panels. Strap anchors that incorporate dowels are also used in interior applications with 3/4 in. (2 cm) thick stone panels. The load is carried by the panel resting on the panel below or by gravity load bearing. This system is referred to as a hand-set installation.

In selecting fasteners, the type of metal and its compatibility with the other metal components of the structural system should be carefully considered so as to avoid the possibility of galvanic corrosion. (See "Galvanic Corrosion" on page 125 and "Stone-Integrated Curtain Wall and Precast Concrete Wall Systems" on page 120.)

Setting Stone Veneer Panels

The first course of stone veneer is usually hand-set, with the use of wire ties but without anchors, independent of the framing system or other backup wall systems. This course is to accommodate the slope and is set below the relieving angle that will carry the load of the stone veneer courses above. Holes are drilled into the concrete slab to accept metal dowels, which are grouted solid, and corresponding holes are drilled into the bottom of the stone panel. High-density vinyl spacers and shims are installed behind and below the panel and are used for the positioning of the individual panels within the wall system. The first course of stone is set, with adhesive, on the dowels projecting up from the concrete. The top of the panel is attached to the backup wall frame with wire ties or strap anchors. In an interior installation, each successive panel is set on the top of the panel below and attached to the backup wall. The load of the panels will be carried by the panels below without the use of load-bearing anchors. Because the panels are attached to the backup wall by hand, the term *hand-set* is used. The height limit of hand-set panels is 12 ft, after which a relieving angle is required.

This first course of stone veneer will be the most vulnerable to impact from pedestrian traffic and susceptible to the maintenance treatments that are commonly applied to the adjacent exterior paving: high-pressure water cleaning and exposure to salts and other deicing agents. The stone that is selected for this location should be extremely durable, and fully grouting the cavity behind the veneer panel is recommended for added resistance to impact. Flashing should be integrated with the design of the fastening system to ensure proper removal of moisture from the cavity behind the first course of veneer panels.

The stone coursing installed above the first course is supported by a metal relieving angle that is mechanically fastened to the framing system. This angle section should be sized to support the load of the courses above. A smaller second anchor is then fastened to the larger relieving angle and oriented with the leg up to accept the kerf in the bottom of the stone veneer panel of the second course. Nonstaining construction adhesive is applied to the slots in the bottom of the panel, and the panel is set in place over the anchor that has been attached to the relieving angle. The load is carried by the relieving angle, and the secondary anchor is used for positioning the panel. The position of the anchors to be installed at the top of the veneer panel can now be determined, and the horizontal frame member or masonry backup wall is drilled to accept the fastener. Each panel is adjusted to be plumb, level, and in alignment with the face of the adjacent panels. Spacers of varying thickness are installed behind the panels to achieve the desired alignment. Once alignment is achieved, the slot in the top of the stone veneer panel is filled with nonstaining construction adhesive and the bolts are tightened through the fastener into the backup wall or frame system. The procedure is repeated with each consecutive course of stone veneer panels as they are installed to the top course, terminating with the head condition.

The final course is often more challenging than the lower courses because of the varying conditions encountered at the top of a wall. Field cutting and customizing of the factory-produced panels are often required by the installer to ensure a proper fit. Special fasteners are often required at the ends or sides of the panels.

The joint sizes between panels must be determined to allow for thermal expansion and contraction, movement of the framing system, and dynamic movement of the building structure. Joint filler materials should be of a type that will create a weather barrier to keep moisture out of the veneer system, permanently adhere to the stone units, accommodate movement, and not cause discoloring of the stone. Backing rods are installed into the stone joints to control the depth of the sealant material and to provide support for the sealant when the joints are installed. The sealant is installed over the backing rods and usually tooled to a concave profile. Although they do accommodate normal movement of the building frame and the stone itself, backing rods should not be used in place of building expansion joints that are required to accommodate movement between adjoining structural frames. Cementitious grout systems are sometimes used to fill the joints between the panels in a wall assembly; however, solid grouts do not allow for the movement that is common in modern construction and are more susceptible, allowing moisture intrusion (see Figures 4-40 through 4-46).

If the top of an exterior stone veneer wall system does not incorporate a canopy or protective overhang, the use of a coping at the top of the wall is necessary. A stone cap often serves as a coping and is further developed as a design feature. The coping must incorporate a flashing and work with other components of the building system to minimize water infiltration and to provide for the removal of any moisture that does get behind the stone system. Water present in the wall system during freezing conditions may initiate a failure in the system; water previously absorbed by the stone will expand when the temperature drops below freezing and can break loose at the point of attachment with the anchor or cause the stone to crack. The main issues here are to provide flashing at the top of the wall to reduce water infiltration, incidental water intrusion, removal of water that does get into the wall system, and to reduce the potential for freeze-thaw damage and allow for a ventilation cavity.

HAND–SET VENEER INSTALLATION—INTERIOR

The difference between the method of installation of an anchored veneer system and a hand-set system lies in the location where they are used; anchored veneer systems are used on exteriors and hand-set veneer systems are used in interior installations. Exterior installations will be exposed to the weather, requiring protective moisture barriers that are not necessary on interiors. In addition, exterior installations will be more vulnerable to impact from pedestrians, which requires 11/4 in. (3 cm) thick stone panels as compared with 3/4 in. (2 cm) thicknesses at interior installations.

Figure 4-40. Relieving angle used to carry the load of the courses above.
The stone veneer panel installed above the lower hand-set course is supported by a metal relieving angle that is mechanically fastened to the framing system. This angle section should be sized to support the load of the courses above. A smaller second anchor is then fastened to the larger relieving angle and oriented with the leg up to accept the kerf in the bottom of the stone veneer panel of the second course, which is used for placement.

Figure 4-41. Preparing the stone veneer panel for placement.
Nonstaining construction adhesive is applied to the slots in the bottom and top of the panel. The panel is set in place over the anchor that has been attached to the relieving angle. The load is carried by the anchor located at the bottom of the panel. The anchor at the top of the panel is used for positioning the panel.

Figure 4-42. Setting the stone veneer panel.

Figure 4-43. Positioning the anchors at the top of the veneer panel.
The position of the anchors at the top of the veneer panel can now be determined, and the masonry backup wall is drilled to accept the fastener. Spacers of varying thickness are installed behind the panels to achieve the desired alignment. Each panel is adjusted for plumb, level, and alignment with the face of the adjacent panels.

Figure 4-44. Fastening the anchor to the backup wall with expansion bolts.
The slot in the top of the stone veneer panel is filled with nonstaining construction adhesive, and the bolts are tightened through the fastener into the backup masonry wall.

Backup Wall Systems

Backup wall systems for interior hand-set installations are composed of structural metal studs sheathed with gypsum wallboard, plywood, or cement board; gypsum wallboard is most common. Metal hat channels are attached horizontally through the sheathing and into the metal studs beyond, spaced in vertical alignment with the coursing of the stone. Spacers are placed behind the metal channel members to create a space of approximately 1/4 in. for the wire ties to sit.

Stone Veneer Panels

The size of veneer panels is limited to 20 sq ft in area, as stated in the UBC. The thickness of the stone panels used in an interior application is generally 3/4 in. (2 cm), because interior veneer systems use wire ties to attach the panel to the back-up wall system. The edge of the stone is drilled to accept the wire ties which are smaller in dimension than load bearing anchors, allowing the use of 3/4 in. thick veneer panels.

Anchors

The purpose of wire ties is to align the panel face and edges from module to module on the backup wall system; they do not carry the load of the veneer panel. The wire ties are to be composed of a noncombustible and noncorrosive material, most often copper wire. The ties are not to be smaller in diameter than No. 9 gauge wire, as stated in the UBC. Copper wire is usually packaged in rolls wrapped around spools. Before the wire is shaped into ties, it can be straightened by attaching one end to a stationary object and the other to a drill. The rotation of the drill unrolls the wire to form a straight and stiffer wire section.

Figure 4-45. Checking the veneer panel for proper alignment.
Each panel is adjusted for plumb, level, and alignment with the face of the adjacent panels.

Figure 4-46. Split-tail anchors supporting the veneer panel.
The anchors used for supporting the stone veneer panel are engineered project-specific and are fabricated off-site. The end of the anchor is split, with one leg oriented up and one down, for positioning the panels. The horizontal section is engineered to carry the load of the panel to which it is anchored, in addition to the courses above.

Figure 4-47. Hand-set veneer panels.
Wire ties are used for securing the panel to the backup wall system laterally, but will not carry the load of the veneer panel. This is referred to as a gravity load-bearing system, in which the load of the panel is carried by the course below. The wire ties are composed of a noncombustible and noncorrosive material, most often copper wire. Copper wire is usually packaged in rolls wrapped around spools. Before the wire is shaped into ties, it can be straightened by attaching one end to a stationary object and the other to a drill. The rotation of the drill unrolls the wire to form a straight and stiffer wire section.

Figure 4-48. Preparing the wire tie and panel edge.
The edge of the stone is drilled to accept the wire tie. One end of the tie is inserted into the predrilled hole in the edge of the panel, and a wood shim is forced into the hole with the wire, securing the tie in place.

The wire is cut to length and bent to form a C shape. One end of the wire tie is inserted into a predrilled hole in the edge of the panel, and a wood shim is forced into the hole with the wire, securing the tie in place. Wire ties are positioned at the middle third of the edge, not more than 18 in. apart, with a minimum of four ties per panel — two top and two bottom.

Setting the Stone Panels
Once the ties are in place along the edges of the veneer panels, the panels are set in place. The first course is set on a metal dowel that is grouted into the finished floor, with neoprene spacers placed between the floor and the panels. Panels set above the first course are set on neoprene spacers directly on the edge of the panels below. This is referred to as a gravity load-bearing system, wherein the load of the panels is being carried by the by the course below. Shims are used to position each panel plumb and in alignment with the wall plane and to wedge the tie between the metal hat channel and the backup wall, securing the panel in place. When the positioning of the panels is complete, casting plaster is

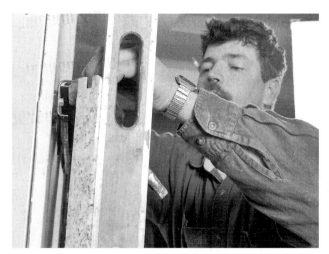

Figures 4-49 and 4-50. Tying the wire to the horizontal metal channel.
Backup wall systems for interior hand set installations are composed of structural metal studs sheathed with gypsum wallboard, plywood, or cement board; gypsum wallboard is most common. Metal hat channels are attached horizontally through the sheathing and into the metal studs beyond, spaced in vertical alignment with the coursing of the stone. Spacers are placed behind the metal hat channel members to create a space of approximately ¼ in. for the wire ties to sit. The wire is cut to length and bent to form a C shape. Wire ties are positioned at the middle third of the edge, not more than 18 in. apart, with a minimum of four ties per panel—two top and two bottom.

Figure 4-52. Immobilizing the wire tie where it is attached to the horizontal channel.
When the positioning of the panel is complete, casting plaster is troweled around the connection of the wire ties, stone panel, and backup wall. The plaster encases the area of attachment, immobilizing the wire tie system.

Figure 4-51. Once it is tied, the panel is checked for accuracy of position.

troweled around the connection of the wire ties, stone panel, and backup wall. The plaster encases the area of attachment, immobilizing the wire tie system (see Figures 4-47 through 4-52). The setting of panels continues to form the stone veneer wall tying the veneer panel with the hat channel mounted to the backup wall to a height of 12 ft - 0 in. The UBC states that a structural relieving angle is required every 12 ft - 0 in. carry the load of the stone veneer panels. If the top course of the stone veneer wall is to be set below a soffit, ceiling, or other horizontal projection, a blind attachment is required, because otherwise the wire tie and hat channel connection will not be accessible. To overcome this obstacle, a basket anchor is created for fastening the top of each panel with the backup wall. A basket anchor is created by cutting a hole in the gypsum wallboard to align with the wire tie at the top of the panel. Wire mesh is bent to line the hole, creating a basket. Plaster is troweled into the basket and onto the wire tie, then the panel is tilted into place. Temporary clamps attached to the backup wall hold the panel in place until the plaster sets, securing the veneer panel permanently in place (see Figures 4-53 and 4-54).

Once the veneer panel wall is installed and the plaster surrounding the attachment ties has cured, the joints between the panels are filled. Interior installations will not be exposed to the weather and are not vulnerable to thermal expansion and contraction; however, movement of the framing system and dynamic movement of the building structure may have an impact on the wall system, depending on the building design. Expansion joints should be planned at regular intervals to accommodate potential building movement. The expansion material should be a flexible caulk-type joint sealant, installed in the joint space between veneer panels. The remaining joint filler material may be a cementitious grout, but more often a flexible caulk sealant is used to create a barrier, permanently adhered to the stone units, and of a variety that will not cause discoloring of the stone. Backing rods are installed into the stone joint to control the depth of the sealant material and to provide support for the sealant when the joint is installed. The sealant is installed over the backing rod and usually tooled to a concave profile. In installing cementitious grout, care should be taken to avoid smearing the face of the veneer panel with excess grout, which may leave a residue or haze. An application of a grout release or stone sealer to the face of the stone is recommended prior to the filling of the joints so as to avoid grout haze and staining.

Advantages of Anchored Veneer Installation

- The primary advantage of using an anchored veneer system is the increased number of design opportunities. Stone modules larger than tile sizes may be considered in designing the overall composition. The limits are largely determined by the stone slab size available and code requirements.

- Another advantage is the increased flexibility of the veneer system and resultant ability to accommodate building movement, expansion, and contraction.

- This method of installation also gives the stone installer the opportunity to achieve alignment of edges and surfaces through adjustment of the anchoring fasteners.

Disadvantages of Anchored Veneer Installation

- The primary disadvantage is the increased cost of materials and labor in this method, as compared with thin-set or adhered installation methods.

Figures 4-53 and 4-54. Setting the panel at the top course.

If the top course of a stone veneer wall is to be set below a soffit or ceiling, a blind attachment is required, because otherwise the wire tie and hat channel connection will not be accessible. To overcome this obstacle, a basket anchor is created for fastening the top of each panel with the backup wall. A basket anchor is created by cutting a hole in the gypsum wallboard to align with the wire tie at the top of the panel. Wire mesh is bent to line the hole, creating a basket. Plaster is troweled into the basket and onto the wire tie, then the panel is tilted into place. Temporary clamps attached to the backup wall secure the panel until the plaster sets, holding the veneer panel permanently in place.

Figures 4-55 and 4-56. Shop tickets.
Shop tickets are used by the stone fabricator as a reference for producing the stone to the required dimensions. The semicircles indicated by the dashed lines show the position of the slots cut into the edge of the stone to accept the anchor.

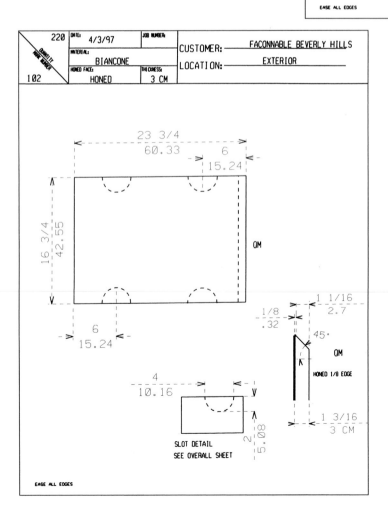

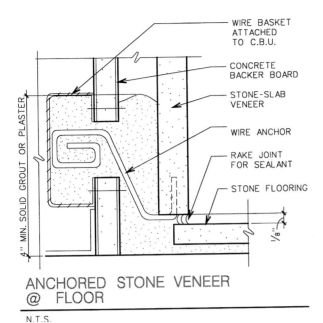

ANCHORED STONE VENEER @ FLOOR

N.T.S.

Figure 4-57. Detail showing the fastening at the base of the wall.
A wire basket is used to form a blind fastener for positioning of the panel at the base of the wall where the back of the panel is not accessible.

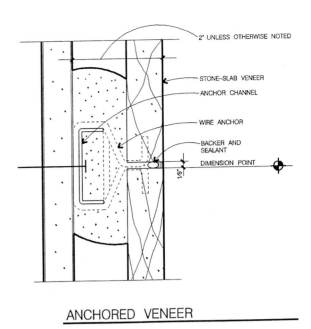

ANCHORED VENEER

Figure 4-58. Detail of a typical wire tie.
A wire tie is used to tie the stone panel back to the horizontal channel used for positioning the stone panel. The load of the panel is transferred to the course below.

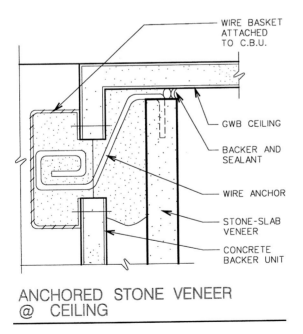

ANCHORED STONE VENEER @ CEILING

Figure 4-59. Detail showing the fastening at the top of the wall
A wire basket is used to form a blind fastener for positioning the panel at the top of the wall where the back of the panel is not accessible.

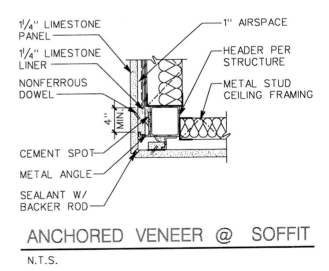

ANCHORED VENEER @ SOFFIT

N.T.S.

Figure 4-60. Detail showing anchored veneer at a soffit condition.

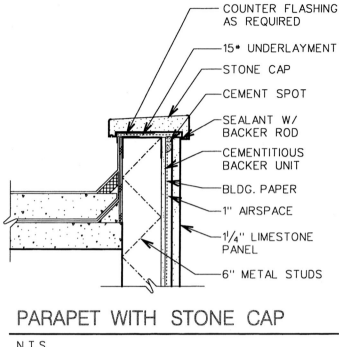

Figure 4-61. Stone cap detail at top of parapet.
If the top of an exterior stone veneer wall system does not incorporate a canopy or protective overhang, the use of a coping at the top of the wall is necessary. A stone cap often serves as a coping and is further developed as a design feature. The coping must incorporate a flashing and work with other components of the building system to minimize water infiltration and to provide for the removal of any moisture that does get behind the stone system.

Labels in figure:
- COUNTER FLASHING AS REQUIRED
- 15# UNDERLAYMENT
- STONE CAP
- CEMENT SPOT
- SEALANT W/ BACKER ROD
- CEMENTITIOUS BACKER UNIT
- BLDG. PAPER
- 1" AIRSPACE
- 1¼" LIMESTONE PANEL
- 6" METAL STUDS

PARAPET WITH STONE CAP

N.T.S.

STONE–INTEGRATED CURTAIN WALL AND PRECAST CONCRETE WALL SYSTEMS

Historically, stone was used primarily as load-bearing units to form exterior walls. As the need for taller buildings increased, load-bearing stone walls became massive in size to support the weight of the floors above. When the iron building frame was introduced and the exterior wall was treated as the skin of the building, stone was adapted to fit within the new building envelope. The lighter-weight, stone-integrated curtain wall was developed for use in multistory buildings, and heavier stone-faced precast concrete wall systems were created for buildings with lower height. The stone industry met the challenges of these refined building concepts by improving processing machinery to saw thinner and thinner stone veneer panels capable of interfacing with the lighter-weight exterior building systems.

Curtain wall systems were developed as modular, prefabricated wall assemblies, originally intended for metal and glass, to form an exterior wall. The exterior wall assembly integrates stone veneer panels within the modular frame, replacing a metal or spandrel panel. The stone-integrated wall assembly is built on an independent structural system that is attached to the overall building structural system. Curtain wall assemblies are not intended to be load bearing within the building system; they form the skin or facade of the building. The weight of the curtain wall creates additional load at the perimeter of the building that the building structure must accommodate. Various anchors are used for attaching stone to the modular frame, including mechanical fasteners, continuous metal extrusions, stone liners, metal clips, and dowels, often imbedded with epoxy adhesives.

There are many benefits to stone curtain wall assemblies, such as the ability to factory fabricate in a controlled shop environment with the opportunity for precision. The installation of a prefabricated wall assembly is faster than traditional anchored veneer and hand-set installations because it is installed as a completed module from within the building, rather than erected as individual pieces on-site.

120

This method requires less labor to attach the assembly to the building exterior, resulting in additional savings in time and cost.

Precast concrete wall systems are based on the same concept as curtain walls; they both rely on the building frame or structural skeleton for support while they create the facade. Stone-faced precast concrete wall systems also enjoy the reduced cost of off-site fabrication and precision production within a controlled shop environment. Because of their increased weight, precast concrete systems are generally used in low-rise buildings and are sometimes used as load-bearing walls in lower-height buildings. The stone veneers are integrated with the panel at the time the concrete wall unit is cast at the plant. The stone veneer can also be attached to anchors integral to the cast panel at the job site. Larger cranes hoist the heavier precast concrete wall systems to the building for attachment with the structure. The installation of the glazing and the required frame is typically performed once the concrete panels have been attached to the building frame. The attachment of the concrete walls is executed in the same manner used in curtain wall systems.

Stone panels that are utilized with these systems require the thickness of the stone to be great enough to accept the fabrication necessary for the anchors; generally, the stone thickness is approximately 1⅛ in. (3 cm) or 1½ in. (4 cm) for panels of smaller areas and up to 2 in. (5 cm) for larger panel sizes. These slab dimensions are based on the standard dimensions of slabs fabricated using the metric system of measurement and the equipment (generally, gang saws) that can be set to saw slabs in increments of 1 cm.

To achieve design features of greater relief and proportion, it is common to use multiple stone panels that are layered, with structural steel configured at the back of the curtain wall assembly to accommodate the changes in plane and profile. Design features such as cornices requiring stone fabrications that are greater in thickness than 4 cm are referred to as "cubic" stone fabrications, and stone panels of this dimension are not considered a standard fabrication and should be accommodated in a modified nonmodular method. In areas where the building design does not facilitate the use of modular panels, more typical anchored veneer systems may be incorporated. The structural metal studs that compose the back-up wall for anchored veneer walls utilize heavy structural steel and are often referred to as "strong-back systems." Structural strong-back should be sheathed for dimensional stability and to form a barrier for the building. Typically, these conditions occur at lower podium levels of the building.

Design and Life Safety Issues

Like other building components, a curtain wall and precast concrete wall assembly are engineered by the fabricator of the assembly. The fabricator of the wall assembly is most often the installer, who is uniquely qualified for this role. However, close coordination between the design team and the construction team is required to ensure success through the construction process.

- The role of the architect is one that is broad, establishing the building design in overall form. This includes determining the visual composition of the panels of the building elevation: the stone, metal, and glass forming the curtain wall. The architect is also responsible for selection of the stone.

- The structural engineer is responsible for engineering the overall building structure, incorporating the load from all of the building components, including the curtain wall system. Within the engineer's scope is the coordination of attachments necessary for the installation of the curtain wall to the perimeter of the building structure.

- The curtain wall fabricator designs and engineers a structural frame to integrate the stone, metal, and glass and build the exterior wall as an independent component. The curtain wall structure is integral with the modular unit, a substructure supportive of the individual members of the panel composition. The engineered wall assembly load and stress resistance is designed into the total building structure by the building structural engineer.

- The general contractor has broad coordination responsibility for all building activity. Paramount is the coordination of all design and construction team members to ensure all are collaborating throughout the process.

In designing and building with natural stone, the financial liability linked to a partial or complete failure of material or its installation is enormous. However, in designing, fabricating, supplying, or installing curtain wall systems, the risk is amplified tenfold. With curtain wall systems the risk is not only financial; issues of life safety are of paramount concern. Stone does not have the same bending characteristics as common curtain wall materials and because of its brittle nature should be used in a manner that does not expose it to stresses that will place it at risk to conditions such as flexure. In addition, the anchors and fasteners used with a curtain wall frame should not impose additional stress at attachment points that can cause the stone to fracture. The design of stone-integrated curtain wall and precast concrete assemblies requires that the structural characteristics of stone be recognized and respected. With the increased financial and safety risks of stone curtain wall installations, the primary concerns for designers and installers of such assemblies are as follows:

1. Proper selection of the stone type to be integrated with the curtain wall assembly
2. Proper design of the systems of anchoring and attaching the stone to the assembly
3. Proper installation of the curtain wall to the building structure

PRIMARY CAUSES OF FAILURE

Chemical corrosion is created by airborne pollutants present in the atmosphere when combined with water from rain. Corrosive agents are produced that attack the stone through its natural microfissures. The stones that are selected for use in industrial regions where the level of air pollutants is high should be carefully reviewed for their resistance to the corrosive agents present in the atmosphere.

The volumetric expansion of water after freezing temperatures causes damage to stone, particularly at areas near the points of attachment, resulting in failure. Water migrates into the stone through the cracks and microfissures within the stone.

The elasticity of the stone is weakened after repeated heating and cooling periods create internal stress which, when transferred to the points of attachment, may cause failure.

Each of these problems is increased when the surface of the stone has been finished with the use of a destructive process such as bush hammering, chiseling, or flaming. These aggressive treatments tend to open the natural microcracks and fissures, allowing for increased moisture migration through capillary action. The climatic conditions should be carefully considered in the selection process, and a review of successful and unsuccessful stone installations is critical to avoid potential failure.

Pressure from the wind is another type of atmospheric stress applied to the face of a stone panel, creating a direct lateral load on the outside of the curtain wall and suction at the interior side of the assembly. The negative impact of wind load is gradual, with flexural stress increasing over time as the resistance of the stone diminishes as a result of freeze-thaw cycles and weakening at the points of attachments owing to corrosion of the stone face, all of which is amplified by the reduced thickness of the stone panel. Because of the destructive nature of the forces created by wind load, the wind intensity and atmospheric patterns of the area where a building is proposed should be carefully reviewed, and the effects of these forces on other buildings in the area of the same construction should be considered.

EXPANSION AND MOVEMENT

Because of the varying rates of thermal expansion of materials used in wall assemblies, a wall system should be examined from two perspectives:

- The rate of expansion for each material and the anticipated movement within the completed assembly.
- The curtain wall and concrete wall as a complete system working within the dynamic movement of the building structure.

The proper design and sizing of joints is as critical as the selection of compatible sealant materials to ensure successful performance of the wall system. Determining the elements that will have an effect on material and system joints should be included in the evaluation.

The stone panels should be allowed to move within the frame and should not be bound or restrained. If the stone panels are rigidly affixed or surrounded by another material without relief for expansion, they will experience stress at the point of contact and at the area of anchorage. Continued stress of the stone will cause failure of the stone within the panel system. The stone panels should be surrounded by joints filled with soft material that accommodate the movement of the stone infill panel. Joint sealant materials must be capable of accommodating the range of expansion and movement of the different wall materials. Joints between panels should be planned and designed to be large enough to allow the movement of the panel assembly on the building frame. The joints should be kept clear of anchors, objects, or debris to provide opportunity for movement within the joint without binding or creating tension by restraint.

The movements of building elements that affect the performance of the panel joints are the compressing of the building, changes in lateral length (vertically and horizontally) from twisting and racking, beam movement caused by floor loading, and changes of building component dimensions owing to fabrication creep and shrinkage. The movement caused by seismic activity must also be accommodated in planning joint sizes. In curtain wall systems the joints between wall system modules should be planned to accept the building dynamics. In a precast concrete wall, an isolation membrane should be located between the concrete and the stone, and grommets made from elastomeric material placed on the pins between the stone and the concrete will allow for building movement.

MOISTURE PROTECTION AND AIR INFILTRATION

Water present in a wall system and absorbed by the stone will expand during freezing conditions, and with repeat cycles will cause the stone to weaken over time. The weakening of the stone may cause an anchor to break loose at the point of attachment or cause the stone to crack, initiating a failure in the panel. To provide a protective barrier, joints must be filled, and a means for the removal of water from within the wall system should be designed.

The joint filler materials should be of a type that will create a weather barrier to keep moisture out of the wall system, permanently adhere to the stone units, accommodate movement, and not cause discoloring of the stone. Two types of materials are used for moisture protection and barriers to air infiltration: sealants and gaskets. Sealants are applied wet, caulked into the joint space, and gaskets are installed dry, surrounding the stone fitting within the joint space. The ability of a sealant to perform as a barrier depends on its adhesion to the stone. Backing rods are installed into the stone joint to control the depth of the sealant material and to provide support for the sealant when the joint is installed. The sealant is installed over the backing rod and tooled to an hourglass profile. Their compression and contact with the stone within the joint space allow gaskets to create a barrier. Although the materials used as joint filler for weather protection can accommodate the normal movement of the building and the stone panels, they should not be used in place of building expansion joints. The effects of movement and weather, and how they work together, should be evaluated within the overall system.

Curtain wall and precast wall systems should incorporate weep holes located in the joints between panels to allow for the escape of water. Combined with weep holes, flashing and gutter systems integrated within the design of the panel system can ensure proper removal of moisture from the cavity behind the veneer panels.

In areas of the building where it is not possible to incorporate curtain wall or precast walls, structural metal stud backup walls with stone veneer panels should be protected from moisture installing a continuous moisture barrier. Flashing and weep holes should be provided for the removal of water that does get into the wall. To reduce water infiltration at the top of the wall, coping that incorporates flashing should be integrated with the wall system.

Air infiltration is also minimized by the use of sealant filled joints and gaskets, as well as by the pressure produced by the building's heating, ventilation, and air-conditioning (HVAC) system. In addition, producing positive pressure within the building will help to reduce the stress on the stone panels caused by suction, which can be greater than wind load.

ATTACHMENT SYSTEM

The design of the attachment system should be a collaborative effort between the panel fabricator and the building structural engineer. Building codes, seismic events, and local building practices should also be considered in designing stone-integrated curtain walls and precast wall assemblies that use anchors such as mechanical fasteners, clips, extrusions, or dowels.

The attachment relationships between the stone and the panel, and the panel and the building, should not be considered independently, because unequal load distribution caused by either attachment may cause stress on the stone. The anchors used to attach the stone to the frame should be located to distribute the load equally around the stone panel. Similarly, the attachments of a curtain wall panel or precast panel to the building should be located to distribute the load throughout the panel and evenly around the building perimeter. The basic concept of curtain wall and concrete wall anchorage and attachment relies on the stone panel's use as an infill panel. The anchors used within the substructure are designed to carry the load of the stone panel within the frame. Moreover, the anchors that compose the system of attachment to the building are designed to carry the load of the panel at the building's perimeter.

The panel frames should be designed to allow for the handling and transporting of the panels to the building, possibly incorporating specific attachments and structure for lifting and loading the panels. The structural system of the panel should be designed to resist the loads and deformation of the panel face in the event that the panel is rotated to a horizontal position during handling.

GALVANIC CORROSION

The performance of each component within the system must be depended on for the full expected life of the building. Care should be exercised in selecting the anchor metal type and its compatibility with the metal types that form adjacent components of the structural system. The primary concern is the galvanic corrosion that may occur when dissimilar metals are in contact. If dissimilar metals are incompatible, they must be isolated from each other and moisture must not be allowed to migrate from one component to another. Moreover, the metal type that is selected must be appropriate for the specific application. If the metal will be exposed to weather, it must be a noncorroding type; if it is steel, it must be coated or galvanized to protect it from exposure to moisture. The second concern is contact between the metal and the stone panel. If moisture is present, the minerals within the stone may react with the metal, causing it to stain the stone.

The interaction of dissimilar metals in contact with moisture will cause disintegration of the less protected, or anodic, metal. When two dissimilar metals are placed in an electrolytic solution, they develop characteristic negative potentials that cause a flow of current, with the resultant galvanic corrosion of one of the metals. The following scale lists the common metals and alloys in an order indicating which is more likely to corrode under conditions favoring bimetallic corrosion. Metals in higher positions, nearer the anodic end, are more subject to corrosion than those nearer the lower, cathodic, end. For example, in seawater, zinc (4), when coupled with copper (15), will corrode in preference to the copper, which is nearer the protected cathodic end. The relative positions of metals on this scale are approximations based on the negative potentials developed in seawater and can vary under other conditions. Metals that are placed near each other on the scale have little tendency to create conditions favoring galvanic corrosion.

Galvanic Corrosion

Anodic End — Corroded

1. Magnesium
2. Magnesium alloys
3. Aluminum
4. Zinc
5. Cadmium
6. Cast iron
7. Carbon steel
8. Stainless steel, Type 304 (active)
9. Soft solder
10. Tin
11. Lead
12. Nickel (active)
13. Brasses
14. Bronze
15. Copper
16. Nickel/copper alloys
17. Nickel (passive)
18. Stainless steel, Type 316 (active)
19. Titanium silver solder
20. Silver
21. Stainless steel, Type 304 (passive)
22. Stainless ateel, Type 316 (passive)
23. Graphite
24. Gold
25. Platinum

Protected — Cathodic End

The following table describes the recommended metal-to-metal contact as it corresponds to the concept of galvanic corrosion.

Recommended Metal-to-Metal Contacts

Metal	Aluminum	Cast Iron	Copper	Galvanized Steel	Phosphor Bronze	Stainless Steel
Aluminum	YES	NO	NO	NO	NO	NO
Cast Iron	NO	YES	NO	YES	NO	NO
Copper	NO	NO	YES	NO	YES	CC
Galvanized Steel	NO	YES	NO	YES	NO	NO
Phosphor Bronze	NO	NO	YES	NO	YES	CC
Stainless Steel	NO	NO	CC	NO	CC	YES

YES=compatible/recommended
NO=noncompatible/not allowed
CC=controlled condition/If presence of moisture is prevented, then use is permitted.

Selection of Stone for Curtain Wall Systems

The feasibility of stone-integrated curtain wall and precast concrete wall systems is based on the use of lighter-weight thin stone panels. Thin stone panels do not offer the same resistance as thicker stone and, consequently, are more vulnerable to the forces of nature. In considering stone types for use in these demanding systems, it is imperative that previous installations of the stone be reviewed and compared with the new conditions to which the stone will be exposed. It is difficult to conceive that stone can warp or bend; however, many stone types have been found to behave in unpredictable ways when sawn to thin dimensions and then experiencing exposure to water. For example, the edges of the white Carrara marble used to clad the exterior of Finlandia Hall in Helsinki are 33 mm thick, which is approximately 1 1/4 in., began to cup at opposite corners, causing the panel to warp within a few years of installation (see "Wintry Discontent," *Architecture,* October 1998). An anchored veneer system was used for the installation of the marble panels that cupped on Finlandia Hall, and experts state that many factors are considered to be responsible, including the reduced number of anchors and a high level of atmospheric pollution. In any case, the fact remains that the thickness of the marble used in this failure is the same thickness that is used in many curtain wall and precast wall systems, and the exposure to nature is the same as many buildings in northern urban centers will experience. The expected high performance of stone in its intended use dictates that selection criteria be higher than those for stone used in any other manner. Practical considerations that should be part of a stone's performance evaluation in designing curtain wall and precast concrete walls include the following:

- The resistance of a stone to atmospheric pollution requires that the mineral composition of the stone be a preponderance of quartz over calcium. The mineral pyrite has been known to cause rust staining of certain granites when exposed to water and should be avoided.

- In the selection of finishes, consider that a polished finish will repel moisture more than open, textural finishes.

- Finishes that are achieved through destructive processes, such as a flamed finish, will weaken the stone.

- Stones with lower rates of absorption will be less vulnerable to the destructive results of freeze-thaw cycles.

Based on the higher level of expected performance that is imposed on curtain wall and precast concrete wall systems, selection criteria should be strictly performance-driven.

Performance-Based Criteria for Stone Selection

1. Physical characteristics of the stone and its ability to resist stress: chemical resistance to atmospheric conditions, strength, and a low rate of absorption
2. Aesthetic appearance of the stone: predictable range of variation, availability of required sizes
3. Cost of the stone

APPLICABLE TESTING

In testing stones for use in a curtain wall system, it is advisable that the stone that is tested be of the same thickness and the same finish as that proposed. This will give the reviewer an opportunity to evaluate the proposed stone in equally comparable conditions and will provide data that represents more realistically the anticipated reaction of the stone in its intended application. The following tests are specifically applicable to the selection of stone for use in curtain wall and precast concrete wall systems.

ASTM C97-96   Standard Test Methods for Absorption and Bulk Specific Gravity of Dimension Stone
Purpose: This test is used to determine the water absorption and the density of stone. Water absorption is expressed in percentages and the values for density are expressed as bulk specific gravity. Stones that have a higher rate of absorption are more vulnerable to the penetration of water carrying corrosive agents, which weaken the stone and the areas where the stone is thinner as a result of slot, hole, and continuous kerf fabrications. In addition, the negative effects of freeze-thaw exposure are increased in stones with higher rates of absorption.

ASTM C99-87   Standard Test Method for Modulus of Rupture of Dimension Stone
Purpose: This test method measures the combined shear strength and diagonal strength. The test determines the load a stone can resist before breaking. Measuring the modulus of rupture of a stone is valuable in determining the flexural strength as it applies to the strength of the stone at its point of attachment with anchoring devices after exposure to the forces of wind load and suction created by wind load. To increase the value of the data produced by this test, it could be modified to use samples of the stone that are of the same thickness and finish as that which is to be used in the panel assembly and to test the stone after it has been tested for its resistance to rapid freeze-thaw cycles, as outlined in ASTM C666, *Resistance of Concrete to Rapid Freezing and Thawing.* This concept is an attempt to create the actual conditions to which the stone will be subjected once it has been installed in the panel assembly and attached to the building.

ASTM C170-90 Standard Test Method for Compressive Strength of Dimension Stone
Purpose: The test to measure compressive strength determines the load that a stone can resist before it will crush. The results of this test are directly applicable only to load-bearing installations, such as where large cubic-sized stones are used as a masonry-type wall or a lintel over an opening. The results of compressive strength tests have reduced relevance for curtain wall and precast panel systems because these systems do not put compressive loads on the stone. However, the values derived from this test are useful for comparing the strength of different stones and in reviewing comparable installations.

ASTM C880-96 Standard Test Method for Flexural Strength of Dimension Stone
Purpose: The test method for flexural strength determines the strength of the stone when in tension, or its bending strength. This test is helpful in determining the maximum load a stone panel can withstand when configured in a curtain wall assembly with anchors located at the edges of the panel, and the data assists in the evaluation of the stone's resistance to wind loads. This test could be made

more applicable by modifying the test procedures to include samples of the pro-posed thickness and finish, as described previously for ASTM C99, *Modulus of Rupture.*

ASTM C217-94 Weather Resistance
Purpose: Although the procedures for this test are not intended for direct evalua-tion of curtain wall systems, the data it provides on the ability of a stone type to resist the corrosive action of local atmospheric agents is useful and relevant.

ASTM C666-97 Standard Test Method for Resistance of Concrete to Rapid
Freezing and Thawing
Purpose: This test is designed to determine the resistance of concrete to rapidly repeated cycles freezing and thawing in water and air. The test is geared to evalu-ate the resistence of concrete for comparison with various concrete samples but can be applied to the evaluation of the resistance of stone panels to rapid freeze-thaw cycles.

ASTM E488-96 Standard Test Method for Strength of Anchors in Concrete and
Masonry Elements
Purpose: This test is designed to determine the strength of an anchor as it is installed in concrete and masonry structures; however, the application as applied to a stone panel can be realized. The test is used to determine the static, seismic, fatigue and shock, tensile, and shear strengths of post-installed and cast-in-place anchorage systems.

Other tests that should be considered beyond the standardized tests mentioned are full panel mock-ups subjected to a wind tunnel test, and direct loading of the panel mock-up in a horizontal orientation. Wind tunnel tests are performed within enclosed chambers, where oversized fans are used to produce lateral load and suc-tion on the curtain wall assembly. Water is also forced onto the curtain wall system to test the assembly for its resistance to water infiltration. The forces generated for these tests are usually increased until the panel assembly fails. For curtain wall assemblies, a horizontal load test is suggested in *Modern Stone Cladding,* authored by Michael Lewis, in which the stone face completed panel mock-up is loaded with sand or bricks until the stone panel fails. In both cases, the points of anchorage, the anchorage devices, and areas where the stone cracks are evaluated for their structural integrity.

For additional information regarding the selection of stone, see Chapter 6 "Guidelines for the Selection of Stone."

Advantages of Stone-Integrated Curtain Wall and Precast Concrete Wall Systems

- Assemblies are fabricated off-site in a controlled shop environment and delivered complete, ready for installation. Shop fabrication can produce to precise tolerances, which is not possible in field fabrication.

- Assemblies can be produced economically by designing modular and repeatable panels.

- Curtain wall panel assemblies are lightweight as compared with traditional masonry systems. Panels are mounted to the building from the inside, eliminating the need for external scaffolding and saving time and cost.

- Precast concrete wall systems can be produced in large completed sections, thus reducing erection time.

Disadvantages of Stone-Integrated Curtain Wall and Precast Concrete Wall Systems

- There is increased risk and liability, coupled with the high cost of correcting failures.

- Moisture intrusion is difficult to control over the extended life of the building.

- The increased weight of precast concrete wall systems limits their use to low-rise building types.

- The short history of curtain wall and precast concrete wall systems does not provide many comparable examples of a large number of stone types in varying climatic conditions.

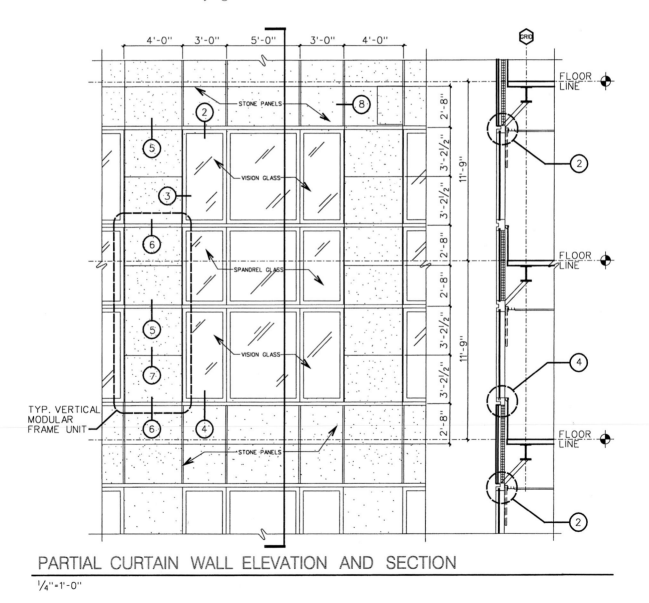

PARTIAL CURTAIN WALL ELEVATION AND SECTION

1/4"=1'-0"

Figure 4-62. Partial curtain wall elevation and section.

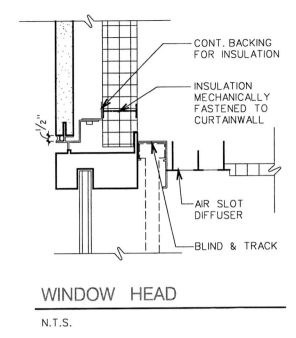

WINDOW HEAD

N.T.S.

CONT. BACKING FOR INSULATION

INSULATION MECHANICALLY FASTENED TO CURTAINWALL

1/2"

AIR SLOT DIFFUSER

BLIND & TRACK

Figure 4-63. Detail at window head.

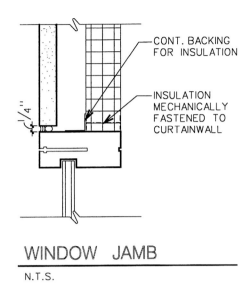

WINDOW JAMB

N.T.S.

CONT. BACKING FOR INSULATION

INSULATION MECHANICALLY FASTENED TO CURTAINWALL

1/4"

Figure 4-64. Detail at window jamb.

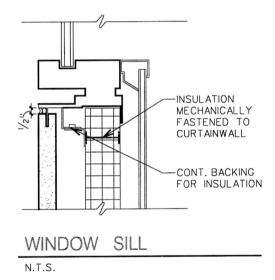

WINDOW SILL

N.T.S.

INSULATION MECHANICALLY FASTENED TO CURTAINWALL

CONT. BACKING FOR INSULATION

1/2"

Figure 4-65. Detail at windowsill.

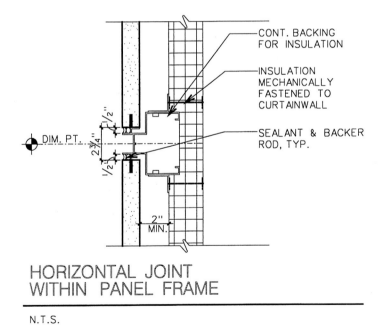

HORIZONTAL JOINT WITHIN PANEL FRAME

N.T.S.

CONT. BACKING FOR INSULATION

INSULATION MECHANICALLY FASTENED TO CURTAINWALL

SEALANT & BACKER ROD, TYP.

DIM. PT.

1/2"

2 3/4"

1/2"

2" MIN.

Figure 4-66. Horizontal joint within panel frame.

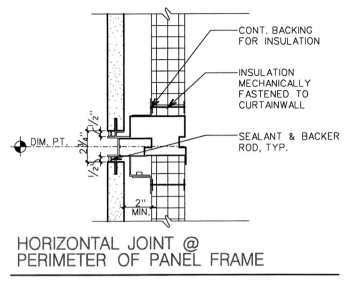

HORIZONTAL JOINT @
PERIMETER OF PANEL FRAME

N.T.S.

Figure 4-67. Horizontal joint at perimeter of panel frame.

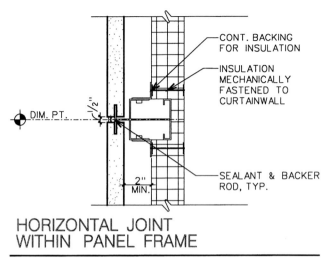

HORIZONTAL JOINT
WITHIN PANEL FRAME

N.T.S.

Figure 4-68. Horizontal joint within panel frame.

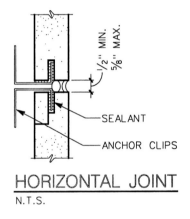

HORIZONTAL JOINT

N.T.S.

Figure 4-69. Detail at horizontal joint.

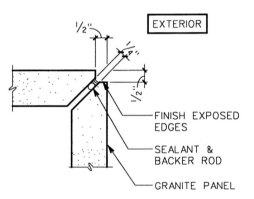

NOTE: DETAIL ASSUMES GRANITE PANELS
ON BOTH SIDES OF JOINT ARE UNITIZED
WITHIN ATTACHMENT SYSTEM

TYPICAL OUTSIDE CORNER

N.T.S.

Figure 4-71. Detail at typical outside corner.

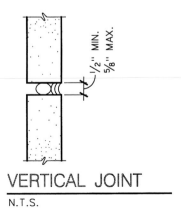

VERTICAL JOINT

N.T.S.

Figure 4-70. Detail at vertical joint.

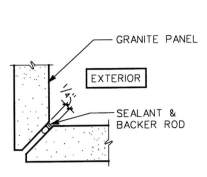

GRANITE PANEL

EXTERIOR

SEALANT &
BACKER ROD

NOTE: DETAIL ASSUMES GRANITE PANELS
ON BOTH SIDES OF JOINT ARE UNITIZED
WITHIN ATTACHMENT SYSTEM

TYPICAL INSIDE CORNER

N.T.S.

Figure 4-72. Detail at typical inside corner.

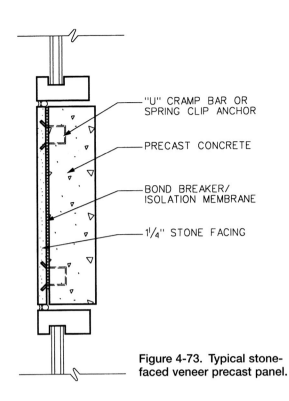

"U" CRAMP BAR OR
SPRING CLIP ANCHOR

PRECAST CONCRETE

BOND BREAKER/
ISOLATION MEMBRANE

1¼" STONE FACING

Figure 4-73. Typical stone-faced veneer precast panel.

MORTARS, SETTING MATERIALS, AND GROUT SYSTEMS

Mortars and Setting Material Systems

The historical origins of mortars and setting materials can be traced to ancient times where early examples of cement have been found in the ruins of cities inhabited by Romans and other Mediterranean cultures thousands of years old. The first types of mortar were produced from indigenous ground limestones composed of the same naturally occurring minerals used in modern-day portland cement. The early builders discovered that the powder produced from certain ground limestones, when mixed with water, produced a sticky paste that hardened when dried. They discovered that the limestone paste could bond stones together to form rigid masonry walls capable of carrying loads and could produce concrete by mixing the cement with sand, aggregates, and water. Because of the durability of the early cement and the resulting masonry construction, many examples of the early builders' work have survived throughout history.

In the early 1800s, Joseph Aspdin, an English mason, created a mixture of cement that produced a concrete that, when finished, resembled a local limestone, Portland stone, which was then used in the construction of stone buildings on the island of Portland, England. Because of this similarity to Portland stone, the type of cement he produced was named "portland cement" and is considered to be the first modern cement. This early portland cement was produced by mixing lime with clay or shale and was heated until a bricklike material formed. This brick or "klinker" could be ground after it hardened, producing a cement powder. The term *cement* can be defined as any adhesive material that can be used to bond two materials together to form a single unit. This is a broad definition that can include an infinite number of adhesives used in everyday life, such as glue and epoxy, a definition appropriate to describe the infinite combinations of materials that are used in mortar systems of today. The basic ingredients of the portland cement used in the construction industry are lime produced from limestone, clay or shale, alumina, and silica. Portland cement mixed with aggregates and other types of additives is used to produce various types of concrete and mortars with fast-curing characteristics, greater water resistance, and increased flexibility to suit modern construction requirements.

Portland cement mortars provide a mechanical bond between the stone and substrate, as opposed to a chemical or adhesive bond. In any concrete, mortar, or grout mixture the only reacting or binding agent is the portland cement contained in the mix, and water is the only catalyst capable of generating the chemical or hydraulic reaction known as *hydration*. When water is introduced to the mix and "wets out" the cement crystals, a gel-like substance called *tobermite* is formed around each of the cement particles, wrapping them completely on all faces. Tubular fibrils, which look like sprouts, begin growing in all directions away from the center of each crystal. At first these sprouts are short, thin, and fragile, but as the curing process continues and as long as water is retained in the mix, the sprouts grow longer, thicker, and stronger over time. The sprouts interlock with each other and penetrate the voids between the aggregate and sand particles, grasping them like millions of tentacles. Once the hydration or curing process is complete, a tight-knit web of crystallized hooks mechanically fasten all particles together into a cohesively strong mass.

The surface of a properly prepared and cleaned substrate is full of holes and cavities; when viewed under magnification, the surface has the appearance of Swiss cheese. When the mortar is wet and pressure is applied with the flat edge of a trowel, it penetrates into the substrate, filling the cavities, and, once cured, allows the crystalline sprouts to permanently grasp beyond the surface. Although natural stone looks smooth and even to the unaided eye, a magnified view reveals a crater-like surface full of voids. When the stone is set in fresh mortar and "beat in," the mortar penetrates the surface of the stone, interlocking within the cavities and voids. As the mortar cures, the crystallized sprouts grow and mechanically fasten themselves to the structure of the stone.

PORTLAND CEMENT MORTAR / THICK–BED MORTAR

The thick-bed mortar system is considered to be the traditional sand and cement mortar system and most closely resembles the mortar used during ancient times. A thick bed mortar system is also referred to as a *mortar bed* or a *mud bed* mortar system. The TCA recommends a ratio of roughly one part portland cement to five parts sand for floor installations, and proportions of one part portland cement to five parts sand and one-half part lime for installation of stone tile to walls.

Thick-bed mortar systems can be used as thick as 2 in., which allows it to accept larger variations in stone thickness, such as flagstone, ungauged slates, ungauged sandstones, and thicker stone modules. A thick mortar bed can be prepared to accept stone in two ways:

1. Fresh set while the mortar is still workable; the stone is set directly into the mortar bed with a wet slurry of pure portland cement and water.

2. After the mortar bed has been set and is cured, the stone is thin set onto the mortar bed. The use of metal lathe on walls, and wire reinforcing mesh integrated into the mortar bed for floors, is recommended for greater strength and stability. Thick mortar beds can be modified with latex polymers to increase the performance of the mortar mix.

When to Use a Thick-Bed Mortar System

- Thick beds are used to facilitate slopes to drains or for creating true planes and plane changes on floors and on walls. In addition, mortar beds can be applied over rough subsurfaces or dissimilar materials and can be floated to level irregular surfaces.

- This mortar system can be used when a deflection of the substrate greater than L / 360 is anticipated.

- A thick bed is also used to compensate for the variations of thickness in the stone.

Recommended Subsurfaces

Floor: Brickwork; concrete; rough, irregular surfaces that are stable; existing stone and other stable finished floors; wood floors.

Wall: Masonry surfaces, concrete, foam insulation board, gypsum board, and gypsum plaster.

THIN–SET MORTAR

Thin-set mortar is a term applied to general mortar systems that are used with thin, flat stone units for both floor and wall installation. Additives may be mixed with thin-set mortar to enhance its bonding characteristics and for special conditions. The term *thin-set* is defined by the Tile Council of America (TCA) in its *Handbook for Ceramic Tile Installation* to describe the method of installing tile with a bonding material, usually $3/32$ in. to $1/8$ in. in thickness. In certain geographic areas, the term *thin-set* is used interchangeably with *dry-set portland cement mortar.* A dry-set mortar is defined by the TCA as a mixture of portland cement and sand, with additives imparting water retentivity, that is used as a bond coat for setting tile. Dry-set mortar is suitable for thin-set installations over a limited variety of surfaces and is used in one layer as thin as $3/32$ in. after the tile is set in place. Dry-set mortar is available as a factory-sanded mortar to which only water need be added.

When to Use a Thin-Set Mortar System

- Thin-set mortars are suitable when using calibrated, uniformly thin stone and when the face of the stone is relatively flat.

- Stone with a natural cleft face, such as slate, quartzite, and sandstone, can be installed in thin-set mortar. When the variation in thickness is moderate, a medium bed or mortar bed may be necessary.

- Thin-set mortar can be used in renovation installations where the overall available thickness is limited.

- According to ANSI A108.5 installation standards, thin-set mortar installations are restricted to surface conditions with a variation in the subsurface of $1/4$ in. in 10 ft.-0 in. maximum from the desired plane.

Recommended Subsurfaces

Floor: Concrete, cured portland cement mortar beds, existing stone and other stable finished floors, and dry countertop areas.

Wall: Masonry surfaces, concrete, and cured portland cement mortar beds.

LATEX–MODIFIED PORTLAND CEMENT MORTAR

Latex mortar systems are portland cement mortar systems that contain latex additives to improve the elasticity of the setting bed, allowing the final stone installation more flexibility in the occasional lateral movement of the subsurface. The TCA *Handbook* states, "Latex additives also provide improved adhesion, higher bond strength, reduced water absorption, and a greater resistance to shock and impact." Latex additives are mixed with the mortar system either in a powder form at the factory at the time of manufacture, or on-site as a liquid additive in lieu of water. Latex additives can be mixed with thin-set, medium-set, and mortar bed systems.

The term *polymer-modified mortar* is becoming more widely accepted to identify factory-blended mixes that incorporate dry polymers, powdered forms of latex that are water dispersed, as compared with liquid-latex-added formulations, which the ceramic tile industry has referred to as *latex portland cement mortar.* A polymer is a natural or synthetic substance, usually a synthetic rubber substance, whose molecules are usually formed in linked sequence of identical chemical units; or combinations of various polymers termed *co-polymers.*

The term *acrylic thin-set mortar* is often used to describe a mortar system that uses a liquid latex additive that utilizes an acrylic co-polymer emulsion.

When to Use a Latex-Modified Mortar System

- When increased flexibility (after the setting bed has cured) is desired to accommodate occasional lateral movement, a latex-modified mortar system may be used.

- This type of system can be used in exterior installations where freeze-thaw resistance is desired.

- A latex-modified mortar system is also used for increased bond strength.

- Latex-modified mortars should be used almost exclusively for stone setting.

Recommended Subsurfaces

Floor: Concrete, cementitious backer units, cured portland cement mortar beds, existing stone and other stable finished floors, and dry countertop areas. Some special latex formulations are suitable for setting over exterior grade plywood, when recommended by the manufacturer. However, exterior grade plywood is restricted to interior residential floors and dry countertop applications.

Wall: Masonry surfaces, concrete, cementitious backer units, cured portland cement mortar beds, gypsum plaster, and gypsum board.

RAPID–SET THIN–BED MORTAR

Rapid-set thin- or medium-bed mortar systems are fast-setting cementicious mortar systems, some of which are latex or polymer modified, that are used to expedite the setting and curing process of the mortar bed. Rapid-set thin-bed mortar systems are advantageous when a stone tile must be walked on within a short period of time, such as required in occupied renovation projects. Systems of this type have chemical additives that retard the initial curing process, keeping it from occurring too soon and allowing the mortar to remain workable for a sufficient time to properly set the tile in place.

Fast-setting mortar systems can also be modified with high concentrations of latex to increase flexibility.

When to Use a Rapid-Set Thin-Bed Mortar System

- This type of system can be used when conditions require the stone installation to be walked on within a short period of time, such as in renovations of occupied areas that have high volumes of traffic.

- Several types of fast-setting modified mortars are formulated for setting moisture-sensitive marble and stone.

Recommended Subsurfaces

Floor: Concrete, cementitious backer units, cured portland cement mortar beds, existing stone and other stable finished subsurfaces. Some special latex formulations are suitable for setting over exterior grade plywood, when recommended by the manufacturer. However, exterior grade plywood is restricted to interior residential floors and dry countertop applications.

MEDIUM–BED MORTAR

The components of a medium-bed mortar system are the same as those in a dry-set mortar system, adapted to achieve greater thickness. To accomplish the increased setting bed thickness, a coarser grade of sand is used with the mix of cement. The thickness of the setting bed can be increased to $9/16$ in. in depth to incorporate the use of thicker stone modules or stone that is not calibrated, with slight variation in module thickness. This type of mortar system can be modified to accept polymer modified additives to achieve similar goals as latex-modified mortar systems: flexibility of the cured setting bed and increased adhesion and bond strength.

When to Use a Medium-Bed Mortar System

- This type of system is appropriate when thicker stone modules are used, when stones of different thickness are used, and when the stone has not been calibrated and the variation in thickness is not too great.

- When the subsurface requires a small degree of leveling this type of system can be used, but not as a substitute for slab leveling.

Recommended Subsurfaces

Floor: Concrete, cementitious backer units, and existing stone and other stable finished floors Some special latex formulations are suitable for setting over exterior grade plywood, when recommended by the manufacturer. However, exterior grade plywood is restricted to interior residential floors and dry countertop applications.

Wall: Masonry surfaces, concrete, cementitious backer units, gypsum plaster.

RAPID–SET MEDIUM–BED MORTAR

A rapid-set medium-bed mortar mix has the same mortar mix components as the standard medium-bed system, combined with latex or polymer-modified additives to achieve rapid setting characteristics.

Recommended Subsurfaces

Floor: Concrete, cementitious backer units, cured portland cement mortar beds, and existing stone and other stable finished floors.

POLYURETHANE REACTIVE RESIN THIN-SET MORTAR

Polyurethane resin mortars, also referred to as polyurethane adhesives, were designed specifically for use with nonconventional substrates that are smooth, such as steel and glass. The system includes either a two-part resin (polyurethane or epoxy) and a hardener that does not require water, or a single-component moisture-cured compound. Because the two-component mortar mix does not require the use of water, it is often recommended for use with water-sensitive marbles.

When to Use a Polyurethane Reactive Resin-Modified Mortar System

- This system can be employed when using water-sensitive stone.
- It is appropriate when using nonconventional substrates such as steel, glass, and plywood.
- The system can also be used in exterior installations.

Recommended Subsurfaces

Floor: Nonconventional substrates such as steel, glass, and plywood. Traditional substrates such as concrete, cementitious backer units, cured portland cement mortar beds, and existing stone and other stable finished floors.

100% SOLIDS EPOXY MORTAR

One hundred percent solids epoxy mortars are thermosetting, contain no water, and are capable of generating extremely high bond strength and providing exceptional performance. The mortar system consists of two components: hydrocarbon resins and a reactive hardener or curing agent. When the hardener is mixed with the resin, the system undergoes a chemical interreaction. During this reaction the hardener is consumed and becomes an integral part of the reacted mortar. The two components remain integrated in the final product without molecular weight loss; the absence of weight loss is what defines a 100% solids epoxy. Epoxy mortars are resistant to chemicals and high impact.

When to Use an Epoxy Resin Mortar System

- Epoxy mortar systems are designed for application where chemical resistance is required; however, stones are not intended for use where there is a presence of chemicals.
- This type of system can be used for grouting when increased stain resistance is desired.
- The system is also appropriate when using water-sensitive stone, such as green marble, or large units of agglomerate stone.
- An epoxy resin mortar system can be employed when using nonconventional substrates, such as steel, glass, and plywood.

Recommended Subsurfaces

Floor: Interior use only. Nonconventional substrates such as steel, glass, and plywood. Traditional substrates such as concrete, cementitious backer units, cured portland cement mortar beds, and existing stone and other stable finished floors.

ORGANIC ADHESIVES

Organic adhesives, also referred to as *mastics,* are noncementitious adhesives premixed at the factory and ready to use without mixing or the addition of water. Mastics are composed of latex and mineral fillers and are suitable for use on light foot traffic / light-duty residential floors and walls; they are intended for interior use only. Organic adhesives are generally intended for the installation of ceramic tile and are generally not suitable for use with most natural stones and agglomerates.

When to Use Organic Adhesives

- Organic adhesives were designed for use with ceramic tile and are not recommended for use with natural stone and agglomerates.

Recommended Subsurfaces

Floor: Not recommended for commercial floor application or for use with natural stone and agglomerates.

Wall: Not recommended for use with natural stone and agglomerates.

Grout Systems

The purpose of a grout is to permanently close all of the spaces, voids, and cavities between stone tiles. A filled joint should always be used in floor and wall installations, with a minimum joint width of $1/16$ in.; butt joints should not be used. Unfilled joints will allow for the migration of water between and beneath the stone modules, which may compromise the bond of the stone, particularly in areas where freezethaw exposure exists. In addition, unfilled joints will allow for the accumulation of dirt and debris within the joint, creating unsanitary conditions.

Grout systems are formulated in the same manner as mortar systems. The available grout systems are as follows:

1. Portland cement grouts and dry-set latex portland cement; these contain portland cement, graded aggregates, water dispersing agents, and colorfast pigments. Based on the intended use, aggregates can vary, ranging from fine for use with narrow joints to coarse for wider joints.

2. Epoxy solids grouts, which are recommended for stain resistance and for food and beverage service installations.

3. Silicone and urethane sealants for use as expansion joints.

SELECTION

The selection of a grout system should be based on criteria similar to those used in selecting mortar systems: desired performance, stain resistance, extra strength, rapid curing, and flexibility to accommodate expansion and contraction. In addition, a grout system should be compatible with the mortar system to ensure proper bonding of the two systems.

Most grout systems are available in several colors, which can be selected to complement or contrast with the color of the stone. Light-colored grouts can be used on walls without concern, but light-colored grout used for high-traffic floor installations will darken and stain within a short period. Often, the grout in areas of lower traffic will not stain as rapidly as in the higher-traffic areas, making it appear that the grout product was not uniform in color. The opposite concern is that dark-colored grout may stain the edges of light-colored or highly absorptive stones, creating an undesirable effect referred to as "picture framing." Grout joints can be sealed after installation, and epoxy grout systems can be used when stain resistance is of concern; however, the best defense in considering grout color for floors is to establish a strategy to balance the benefit of soil hiding versus staining of the stone:

- To avoid staining the stone, the grout colors selected should be as light as possible.
- To conceal the eventual darkening of the grout caused by traffic and staining, the grout color should be as dark as possible.

A grout mock-up prior to installation is recommended to evaluate the impact of the grout color on the stone, balancing the two opposing concepts.

For narrow joints, $1/16$ in. to $1/8$ in., unsanded grout is recommended, to allow for better filling of the joint space. Coarse-graded sand and aggregates are added to the grout when wider joints are used. The exception may be when polished marbles or limestones are used, which are vulnerable to surface scratching by coarse grades of sand.

JOINT WIDTH

Joints should always be filled to protect a stone installation, as previously described; butt joints or filled joints smaller than $1/16$ in. should not be used. Joint widths that are less than $1/16$ in. are difficult to fill and pack properly, allowing for water migration. Narrow joints will also negate the performance benefits of latex grout systems, such as flexibility for expansion and contraction, improved water resistance, and increased strength.

The Materials & Methods Standards Association (MMSA) in Bulletin No. 9, *Materials for Grouting Ceramic Tile, Dimension Stone, and Agglomerates*, recommends joint widths for each type of grout system, as follows:

Material Type	Joint Filler	Joint Width
Grouts Containing Portland Cement	Commercial, sanded	$1/8$ in.–$5/8$ in.
	Dry set, portland cement, unsanded	$1/16$ in.–$1/8$ in.
	Commercial or dry set, portland cement with latex	$1/16$ in.–$5/8$ in.
Non-Portland Cement Grout	100% solids epoxy	$1/16$ in.–$5/8$ in.
Expansion Material	Silicone or Urethane	$1/16$ in.–$1/4$ in.

SECTION 04851
STONE VENEER SYSTEM

Master specifications for the installation of stone veneer.

MASTER

**SECTION 04851
STONE VENEER SYSTEM**

PART 1 GENERAL

1.1 SUMMARY

A. Section Includes:
1. Interior and exterior stone veneer systems, mechanically attached.
2. Contractor design of stone anchorage systems.

B. Related Sections
1. 05120—Structural Steel: Supports and inserts.
2. 07810—Applied Fireproofing: Protection of structual steel supports.
3. 07842—Fibrous Fire Safing
4. 07920—Joint Sealants.
5. 08920—Glazed Curtain Wall: Adjacent construction.

1.2 REFERENCES

A. American Society for Testing and Materials (ASTM):
1. A653—Steel Sheet, Zinc Coated (Galvanized) or Zinc-from Alloy-Coated (Galvannealed) by the Hot-Dip Process.
2. C99—Modulus of Rupture of Dimension Stone.

B. Marble Institute of America (MIA).

C. National Building Granite Quarries Association, Inc. (NBGQA)

1.3 SYSTEM DESCRIPTION

A. The System consists of stone veneer, veneer supports and anchors to the construction indicated, fire safing barriers, and sealing systems for joints. [The system may be either field assembled or factory fabricated into light gauge metal-framed stone veneer panels.] The stone anchorage system shall consist of a mechanical connection to supports and shall not consist of an adhesion bond.

B. The design of the stone veneer system shall be the responsibility of the Contractor, subject to the specified requirements.]

C. Appearance: Design stone veneer system to conform to the general appearance as indicated on the drawings, including locations of joints, shapes, and dimension points.

D. Interface: The stone veneer system shall be designed for secure anchorage without modifications to the indicated building structure, except as approved. All modifications to the indicated building structure shall be paid for by the Contractor without additional cost to the Owner.

E. Exterior System Structural Design:
1. Seismic: Design the system to conform to the seismic requirements of [UBC zone [ ]] [ ].
2. Wind loads shall be calculated in accordance with requirements indicated on the Structural Drawings [the wind load diagram in Section [ ]] [ ].
[3. Design prefabricated panels for live load deflection of the panels not to exceed 1/600 the span.]

[F. Interior System Structural Design:
1. Seismic: Design the system to conform to the seismic requirements of [UBC zone [ ]] [ ].
2. Veneer: Design the veneer attachment system to resist 15 psf or 1 g. normal to the surface, whichever is greater.]

G. Building Dynamics: Design the system to accommodate building dynamics without damage to the stone veneer, sealing systems, backup wall systems, or surrounding construction. Building dynamics is defined as the singular and combined effect of thermal movement, floor or roof deck deflection, and singular effect of wind or seismic movement.
1. Maximum wind and seismic movement shall calculated as a maximum story drift of .015 [ ] times the story height.
2. Maximum floor or roof deflection shall be calculated as 1/2 [ ] in.
3. Calculate thermal movement for a temperature range of -20°F to 140°F [ ].

H. Water Penetration: Design exterior system to remain watertight under full wind load conditions, or provide secondary means of preventing water infiltration.

1.3 SUBMITTALS

A. Make submittals in accordance with Section 01330, prior to fabrication of the mock-up.

B. Samples:
1. Stone: 12 in. × 12 in. samples of each color and finish combination of stone proposed for the Work. Provide samples as necessary to represent the possible range of color, marking, and texture variations from the Architect's sample. The Architect will select the samples which indicate the maximum range of variation which will be accepted. [Duplicates of the approved samples shall be kept at the supplier's quarry and fabrication plant.]
[2. Each type of anchorage device proposed for the work.]

C. Shop Drawings:
1. Indicate pertinent dimensioning, layout, anchorages, construction details, method of installation, and adjacent construction.
2. Submit installation instructions and field erection drawings.

D. Product Literature: Submit complete literature for the following:
[1. Metal framing components.]
2. Recommended stone cleaners and cleaning methods.

E. Design: Submit complete design drawings and calculations which verify that the proposed stone veneer system meets the specified structural requirements. These submittals shall be stamped by the designing structural engineer.

[F. Test Reports: Submit test reports in accordance with ASTM C99.]

[G. Certification: Upon delivery of stone materials, submit a written certification that all stone was visually selected to match the physical characteristics of the stone tested and accepted.]

1.4 QUALITY ASSURANCE

A. All welds shall be performed by welders approved by the local jurisdictional code authorities.

B. Qualifications:

1. Supplier: Associated Imports [ ]

Prefabricated panelized systems:

2. Fabricator:

    a. Minimum of 3 years experience in the production of factory fabricated metal framed stone veneer panels.

    b. Minimum of 3 projects completed.

    c. Sufficient plant and personnel to perform the work.

3. Installer: A minimum of 3 years experience in the field installation of stone veneer systems, comparable in size and scope to the work of this project [under the direct supervision of the stone fabricator].

C. The system shall be designed by a structural engineer licensed to practice in the State of [ ].

D. Mock-up: In accordance with Section 01450.

    1. Prior to commencing full fabrication and installation of the work, fabricate and install a mock-up, as detailed on the Drawings. Use all equipment, materials, and techniques proposed for the work.

    2. Mock-up section shall be a complete full-size assembly, including framing, fastening, anchorages, finished stone, setting beds, and sealant.

    3. Modify or provide additional mock-up as required by the Architect, until a mock-up is approved.

E. Pre-Installation Conference: In accordance with Section 01312.

    1. Administer a pre-installation meeting prior to starting the work of this Section.

    2. Attendance:

        a. Owner.

        b. Architect.

        c. General Contractor.

        d. Stone installer.

        e. All other parties affected by work of this Section.

    3. Agenda: Include the following:

        a. Mock-up review.

        b. Acceptance criteria.

        c. Review installation details.

        d. Coordination and installation requirements for related work.

        e. Delivery, storage, and protection procedures.

        f. Sealants.

F. Testing: Representative samples of the proposed stone shall have been tested by an independent testing laboratory, in accordance with ASTM C99.

1.5 PRODUCT HANDLING

A. In accordance with Section 01600.

B. Stone: Use no packing materials which would cause staining, or discoloration. Store on platforms at least 4 in. off the ground. Cover with polyethylene and protect stone from contact with materials which would cause staining or discoloration.

[C. Panels: Handle panels in a manner to ensure against cracking, staining, distortion, or other damage. Replace all damaged panels, unless approved otherwise.]

1.6 PRECONSTRUCTION CONFERENCE

A. Contractor shall schedule and administer a meeting prior to the installation of the stone veneer. Include in attendance the Architect, Contractor, Installer, and all other parties affected by this work. The minimum agenda shall be as follows:

    1. Review installation details.

    2. Review installation requirements for related work.

    3. Review delivery, storage, and protection procedures.

1.7 GUARANTEE

A. In accordance with Section 01770.

[B.   .]

PART 2 PRODUCTS

2.1 [GRANITE] [ ]

A. General: Standard grade free from cracks, seams, and starts which may impair its structural integrity or function. Provide stone within the color, texture, and finish range approved by Architect. Replace non-conforming stone to meet the project schedule.

B. Types: As quarried by [ ].

    Type A:

    Type B:

    Type C:

    Type D:

    Type E:

C. Thickness: [ ][1¼] in.[, unless otherwise indicated or approved].

2.2 OTHER MATERIALS

A. Veneer Accessories

    1. Exterior Stone Anchoring Devices: Type 304 stainless steel or suitable nonferrous metal.

    2. Setting Buttons: Plastic.

[B. Light Guage Framing: C shaped stud sections; minimum 18 gage; G90 galvanized finish in accordance with ASTM A653.]

C. Primer: Red iron-oxide alkyd type.

[C. Cold Galvanizing Compound: Zinc-rich organic type; minimum 80 percent zinc in the cured film.]

C. Structural Steel Supports: [ ]

D. Safing: In accordance with Section 07842.

2.3 STONE FABRICATION

A. General: Fabricate stone as indicated, and in compliance with recommendations of NBGQA [MIA]. Cut accurately for proper fit and clearance.

1. Maximum variation in face dimensions of any piece: $\frac{1}{16}$ in.
2. Maximum variation in thickness indicated: $\frac{1}{16}$ in.
3. Edge Straightness: Maximum variation of $\frac{1}{16}$ in.
4. Maximum variation from true plane on flat finished surfaces: $\frac{3}{64}$ in.

B. Edges: Dress edges straight and at 90° angle to face, unless indicated otherwise; cut to provide uniform joint width. Finish exposed edges to match face finish.

C. Slope exposed top surfaces of panels and horizontal sill surfaces for natural wash.

D. Finishes:
   1. As indicated, and to match the Architect's sample.
   2. Backs: Saw or roughly dress back of pieces to approximate true planes.

E. Select stone for physical characteristics similar to the stone tested and approved.

[2.4 PANEL FABRICATION

A. Fabricate panels in configurations approved on the shop drawings, with provisions for attachment to adjacent construction.

B. Shop Welding:
   1. Chip and wire brush all welds.
   2. Protect welds with primer; protect welds between galvanized surfaces with cold galvanizing compound.

C. Fabrication Tolerances:

Characteristic	Tolerance
Surface flatness:	Maximum deviation of $\frac{1}{8}$ inch when tested with a 10 foot long straight edge; no abrupt variations.
Overall height and width:	
Dimensions to 10 ft:	Plus or minus $\frac{1}{8}$ in.
Dimensions to 20 ft:	Plus $\frac{1}{8}$ in., minus $\frac{3}{16}$ in.
Dimensions to 30 ft:	Plus $\frac{1}{8}$ in., minus $\frac{1}{4}$ in.
Dimensions over 30 ft:	Plus or minus $\frac{1}{16}$ in. for each additional 10 ft
Difference in diagonal dimensions	$\frac{1}{8}$ in. per 6 ft but not to exceed $\frac{1}{4}$ in.
Edge straightness	Maximum variation of $\frac{1}{8}$ in.
Location of inserts	Maximum $\frac{3}{8}$ in. variation from indicated location
Location of stone joints	Maximum $\frac{1}{8}$ in. from indicated locations and openings

D. Apply stone to panels as specified herein.

PART 3 EXECUTION

3.1 EXAMINATION

A. Prior to starting work, carefully inspect installed work of other trades and verify that such work is complete to the point where work of this Section may properly commence. Notify the Architect of conditions detrimental to the proper and timely completion of the work.

B. Do not begin installation until all unsatisfactory conditions are resolved. Beginning work constitutes acceptance of site conditions and responsibility for defective installation caused by prior observable conditions.

3.2 SUPPORTS AND OTHER MATERIALS

A. Provide field supports and attachments as approved on the shop drawings.

B. Field Welding:
   1. Wire brush all welds.

Interior:
   2. Protect welds with primer.

Exterior:
   3. Protect welds with cold galvanizing compound.

[C. Coordinate with Section 07842 for installation of fire safing.]

3.3 STONE APPLICATION

A. Do not use stone with chips, cracks, voids, stains, or other defects which might be exposed to view in the finished work.

B. Clean stone prior to installation, leaving edges and surfaces free of dirt or foreign material. Do not use wire brushes or implements which mark or damage exposed surfaces.

C. Establish accurate lines, levels, and coursing.

D. Install stone in accordance with the approved shop drawings and the stone supplier's recommendations. Obtain Architect approval prior to making field modifications.

E. Allowable Installation Tolerances:
   1. Joint Width: Maximum of plus or minus $\frac{1}{16}$ in. from the joint width indicated.
   2. Joint Taper: $\frac{1}{8}$ in. in 10 ft maximum taper, with the joint face width not exceeding the tolerance specified.
   3. Step in face alignment between stone faces: $\frac{1}{16}$ in. maximum.
   4. Jog in joint alignment between stone sections: $\frac{1}{8}$ in.
   5. Surface Flatness: Maximum deviation of $\frac{1}{8}$ in. when tested with a 10 ft long straightedge; no abrupt variations.

F. Sealant: Specified in Section 07920.

3.4 PANEL INSTALLATION

A. Erect veneer panel assemblies plumb, true, in accurate position, and in accordance with the tolerances specified.

MASTER

SECTION 04851
STONE VENEER SYSTEM

B. Adjust and secure prefabricated panels within the following tolerances:

1. Joint Width: Plus or minus ⅛ in. from the joint width indicated.
2. Joint Taper: ⅛ in. in 10 ft maximum taper, with the joint face width not exceeding the tolerance specified.
3. Step in face alignment: ⅛ in. maximum.
4. Jog in joint alignment between panels: ⅛ in. maximum.
5. Maximum deviation from plumb and level: ⅛ in. in 10 ft, and ¼ in. overall.

C. Field Welding:

1. Chip and wire brush all welds.
2. Protect welds with cold galvanizing compound.

D. Sealant at Panel Joints: As specified in Section 07920. Remove all panel erection shims and joint spacers prior to sealing.

[E. Coordinate with Section 07842 for installation of fire safing.]

3.5 CLEANING

A. Clean soiled surfaces using solution which will not harm stone, joint materials, or adjacent surfaces. Consult stone supplier for recommended type.

B. Use nonmetallic tools in cleaning operations.

3.6 PROTECTION

A. In accordance with Section 01500.

END OF SECTION
—————

SECTION 09380
CUT NATURAL STONE TILE

Master specifications for the installation of stone tile.

PART 1 GENERAL

1.1 SUMMARY

A. Section Includes:
1. Interior stone wall tile.
2. Interior stone floor tile.
3. Reinforced waterproof membranes.
4. Crack isolation membranes.
5. Tile backer board.
6. Screeds.
7. Sealer.

B. Related Sections:
1. 02225—Selective Demolition: Preparation of existing substrates.
2. 03300—Cast-in-Place Concrete: Substrate.
3. 07920—Joint Sealants: Expansion joint fillers.
4. 09250—Gypsum Board: Substrate.

1.2 REFERENCES

A. American National Standards Institute (ANSI):
1. A108.1—Ceramic Tile Installed with Portland Cement Mortar.
2. A108.4—Ceramic Tile Installed with Water-Resistant Organic Adhesive.
3. A108.5—Ceramic Tile Installed with Dry-Set and Latex Portland Cement Mortar.
4. A108.6—Ceramic Tile Installed with Chemical-Resistant, Water Cleanable Tile-Setting and Grouting Epoxy.
5. A108.10—Installation of Grout in Tilework.
6. A118.3—Chemical-Resistant, Water Cleanable Tile-Setting and Grouting Epoxy.
7. A118.4—Latex-Portland Cement Mortar.
8. A136.1—Organic Adhesive for Installation of Ceramic Tile.
9. A137.1—Ceramic Tile.

B. American Society for Testing and Materials (ASTM):
1. C144—Aggregate for Masonry Mortar.
2. C150—Portland Cement.
3. C206—Finishing Hydrated Lime.
4. C207—Hydrated Lime for Masonry Purposes.
5. C1028—Determining the Static Coefficient of Friction of Ceramic Tile and Other Like Surfaces by the Horizontal Dynamometer Pull-Meter Method.

C. Tile Council of America (TCA): *Handbook of for Ceramic Tile Installation,* current edition.

D. Marble Institute of America (MIA).

E. National Building Granite Quarries Association, Inc. (NBGQA).

1.3 DEFINITIONS

A. Expansion Joints: Unless otherwise detailed, expansion joints in tile fields are sealant-filled joints to accommodate expansion and contraction of tile and possible substrate movement at slab control and construction joints.

B. Reinforced Waterproofing Membrane: Proprietary waterproofing membrane system installed in combination with tile application, as part of the ceramic tile work.

1.4 SUBMITTALS

A. Make submittals in accordance with Section 01330.

Custom fabricated stone tile, only:

[B. Submittals Required Prior to Fabrication
   1. Product Data:
      a. Epoxy adhesive proposed for attachment of cleats [and joining
          of prefabricated units].
      b. Backing material and proposed system.
      c. Filler material, including test data and application instructions.]
   2. Shop Drawings: Include the following:
      a. Layout of stone.
      b. Shapes and dimensions of all typical and special shapes.
      c. Thicknesses, materials, and finishes.
      d. Surrounding construction, as relevant.
      e. Specific cuts and the quantity of each piece to be furnished for
          extra stock.
      f. Fabricator's mark for identification of each type and shape.
      g. Grain direction, as applicable for stones with directional pattern.
      h. All metric dimensions shall have conversions to the English system.
   [3. Shop Cutting Tickets: For information only, submit shop tickets simultaneous with commencement
       of stone fabrication. Include one ticket for each shape or group being fabricated; indicate material,
       marks, count, face dimensions, thickness, curvature, and finish.]
   [4. Test Data: Submit available test data for properties of each type of stone. Include the following test
       data:
      a. Maximum absorption.
      b. Minimum abrasion resistance.
      c. Minimum coefficient of friction for each proposed finish.
      d. Range of density.
      e. Minimum compressive strength.

f.   Range of modulus of elasticity.

g.   Minimum modulus of rupture.

h.   Testing agency and test standard for each category.]

B   Product Data: Submit for each type of grout, adhesive, additive, accessory, and membrane specified.

[C. Shop Drawings: Indicate general layout, surrounding construction, location of expansion joints in substrates and tile fields, edge details, and special conditions.]

D. Samples:

1.   Stone: Submit a minimum of 3 samples of each type and finish of stone as proposed for the work. Make additional samples as necessary to determine the full range of variation for each stone. Submit additional samples as may reasonably be requested by the Architect.

a.   Submit samples unsealed.

b.   Samples shall exhibit proposed finishes and approximate range of color, grain, and veining variations.

c.   Tile samples shall be similar in size to that proposed for the work.

d.   Each sample shall be labeled on the back with the name of the supplier, the name of the stone, and the name of the quarry.

2.   Grout: Submit cured samples of each grout color. [Furnish 2 cured samples of approved grout colors to the expansion joint sealer installer for color matching.]

[3. Screeds: Submit samples of each type and finish of screed; minimum 3 in. length.]

F.   Schedule: Submit a schedule of each tile type, grout, and joint width combination proposed.

1.5 QUALITY ASSURANCE

A. Supplier Qualifications:

1.   Stone suppliers shall have a consistent record of on-time stone delivery on previous projects similar in type and scope to the work of this project, be able to supply the specified stones, be able to produce accurate shop drawings for the fabrication of stone in the absence of a subcontracted installer, and be able to demonstrate additional qualifications as may be required by the Architect or by the Owner.

2.   Suppliers shall be prequalified by the Architect and Owner prior to bidding. To request prequalification, contact [ ] at the office of the Architect.

B. Mock-Up: [In accordance with Section 01450.]

1.   Commence installation of one approximately 10 × 10 ft section of interior stone tile [Mark ST 1] in a location as directed by the Architect.

2.   Mock-up will be reviewed for conformance to tolerance requirements, and installer workmanship.

3.   [Approved mock-ups may be incorporated into the work; rejected mock-up(s) shall be removed.] Repeat mock-up installation as required to obtain approval.

C. Pre-Installation Conference:

1.   In accordance with Section 01312, schedule and administer a meeting to review and discuss the stone tile installation a minimum of one week (7 calendar days) prior to start of setting tile.

2.   Require in attendance the Architect, the tile installer, and all other parties affected by work of this Section.

3. Agenda: Address installation scheduling and procedures, coordination, preparation and protection requirements, grout and expansion joint locations, tile quantities required, material and installation tolerances, overage required for waste, overage for maintenance stock, sealant joint locations.

1.6 DELIVERY, STORAGE, AND HANDLING

A. In accordance with Section 01600.

B. Shipping:
1. Pack fabrications to correspond with reasonable installation sequencing; clearly label each container to identify contents.
2. Stone shall be cleaned of grit prior to packing, as necessary to prevent scratching during shipment.
3. Ship stone in a manner to protect from damage.
4. Require the stone fabricator to accept full responsibility for the shipment of the stone to the [site] [Contractor's storage facility].

C. Damage and Replacement:
1. Upon receipt of the packaged stone, the Contractor shall inspect the crates and furnish to the supplier a signed statement that shipment was received in apparent good order or itemization of damage to crates.
2. Promptly inspect contents of damaged crates and replace all materials damaged as a result of shipping procedures.

D. Storage:
1. Maintain all stone tile materials in dry, protected areas.
2. Prevent stone tile from coming into contact with materials which could cause staining or discoloration.
3. Unload and store the stone fabrications in the warehouse in locations as directed.
4. Catalog stored materials.
5. Comply with industry standards for stacking and storing of materials.
6. Promptly replace all stone damaged as a result of damage due to storage or handling procedures.

1.7 GUARANTEE

A. In accordance with Section 01770, furnish from the tile installer, a two year written guarantee, executed to the Owner, against defects in workmanship and materials.

1.8 MAINTENANCE

A. Overage:
1. General:
   a. Furnish overage stone in typical face sizes and thicknesses furnished for the work; furnish panels in sizes typical to that of the largest size required, in order to permit onshore fabrication.
   b. In addition to that quantity required for overage to be furnished to the Owner, furnish additional pieces as necessary to allow for breakage, and on-site fabrication error.
2. Furnish as a minimum the following overages for each typical floor and wall tile and base shape for each type of stone, except that for each type of stone to be used as floor tile, furnish not less than 10 pieces, cut to typical tile size:

Usually a larger percentage for accents than for field stone:

      ST-1: 2.5 percent

      ST-2: 5 percent

      ST-3: 5 percent

      . . .

3. After inspection and verification of acceptability, overage stone shall be properly packaged and labeled for delivery to the Owner's warehouse. Overage stone shall be undamaged and in full compliance with specification requirements.

4. With the exception of damaged and unusable pieces, all stone purchased for potential use in the Work, including Contractor's allowance for breakage, shall be furnished to the Owner, whether or not in excess of the specified overage quantity, unless otherwise approved by the Owner.

5. Special Shapes: For each type of stone panel indicated for wall and casework installation, furnish quantity of panels equal to 10 percent of the total area furnished, in sizes as required to permit onshore fabrication of panels damaged prior to project acceptance.

B. Leave extra stock at site where directed, in clearly marked sealed cartons.

C. Tile which is used to satisfy extra stock requirements shall be free of damaged tiles, seconds, or tile which is not in conformance with these specifications.

PART 2 PRODUCTS

2.1 STONE

A. Stone Types:
    1. ST-1: [Marble] [Granite]; [NAME], as supplied by [ ].
    2. ST-2: [Marble] [Granite]; [NAME], as supplied by [ ].
    3. ST-3: [Marble] [Granite]; [NAME], as supplied by [ ].

B. Stone shall be first quality, free of irregularities, and within the range of characteristics of the approved control sample sets, including the following:
    1. Free of localized structural defects.
    2. Free of crystal deposits.
    3. Free of inclusions uncharacteristic of the stone.
    4. Uniform in color and free of dark or light spots, and concentrated features which would affect the appearance of uniform color [except as otherwise specified and as follows.

       . . .

       . . .]
    5. Free of fillers, except as specified.
    6. Free of fissures and cracks visible at the face of the tile [in excess of those permitted for filler].
    7. Free of open veins and holes in excess of those allowed for filler.
    8. Backs of each stone tile for installation to floors shall be structurally sound, with defects not to exceed the following:
       a. Open holes of depth greater than one third the stone thickness.

MASTER

SECTION 09380
CUT NATURAL STONE TILE

---

    b. Cracks and fissures (or similar defects which are linear in form) which are either open to a depth greater than one third the stone thickness, greater than two in. in length, or closer than two in. to the stone tile edge.

    c. Relief, regardless of depth, with surface area greater than one square in. for each continuous defect, or greater than five percent, aggregate, over the back surface of the tile.

2.2 FABRICATION

A. Fabricate stone as specified, in accordance with the approved quantity statements and shop drawings, and matching the approved samples.

[B. Fabricate stone only from blocks matching those inspected and approved by the Architect. Do not use portions of the rough cut blocks which do not match the approved samples.]

    C. Directionality: Cut stone which exhibits a distinct grain direction shall be fabricated as follows:

    1. For Installation on Floors: Fabricate with the grain roughly parallel to the cut edges of the stone.

    2. For Installation on Walls: Fabricate with grain direction as indicated on the approved shop Drawings.

D. Except as otherwise specified, shop fabricate all shapes to minimize requirements for field cutting. Unless otherwise approved by the Architect, field cutting requirements shall be limited to cutting of [field tile edges adjacent to special tile patterns, and] tile or panel edges at intersections with walls, columns, or other building components to be installed prior to tile installation.

E. Curved Cuts: Where radius patterns are indicated for floor tile, factory cut and prefit radii; mark stone to identify special shapes as specified.

F. Transition Strips: Fabricate to detail, from same stone as indicated for adjacent stone floor, unless otherwise indicated.

Indicate special conditions:

G. Stone Sizes:

    1. Fabricate stone tile to nominal [12 in. × 12 in. × ⅜ in.] [　] size, unless indicated or specified otherwise.

    2. Fabricate stone base to nominal [12 in. × 6 in. × ¾ in.] size, unless indicated or specified otherwise.

    3. Fabricate stone border tile to nominal [12 in. × 6 in. × ⅜ in.], unless indicated or specified otherwise.

    4. Diagonal cut tile shall be typical rectangular size tile with diagonal cut to match grout joint width.

    5. Cut stone to the sizes as necessary to fit the special conditions indicated on the Drawings.

H. Actual Dimensions: Fabricate tile for uniform grout joint widths of [　] unless otherwise indicated.

I. Finishes:

    1. Provide finishes in accordance with the following suffixes included with the stone types designations on the Drawings:

        a. Suffix "H": Honed; minimum grit honed finish as required to meet a minimum coefficient of friction of .6 when tested with the approved sealer in accordance with ASTM C1028.

        b. Suffix "P": Polished.

        c. Suffix "S": Sandblasted.

        d. Suffix "T": Thermal.

    2. Finishes shall match the approved samples, unless specified otherwise.

3. Edges: Fabricate all tile and base edges with a 0.75–1.0 mm 45° bevel at exposed face. Finish all edges to remain exposed in the finished work to match scheduled surface finish.

J. Fillers: Proprietary mix of epoxy or other approved binder, blended with stone dust or chips, fillers, and pigments, as necessary to approximate stone color. Do not use silica or other fillers with hardness rating greater than that of the stone for which the filler is intended

1. Filler is not permitted in Stones [ ], [ ], and [ ].

2. Fillers will be permitted under the following conditions:

    a. Fillers shall match color of stone in which they are used.

    b. Fillers shall match stone in durability, and shall be resistant to staining and yellowing.

    c. Distribution:

        1) Filled areas in stone surfaces shall be limited to 0.1 percent (one one-thousandth) of the total surface area of the stone piece, with no filled areas greater than 2 in. in any dimension for filled areas in Stones [   ], and ¾ in. in any dimension for other stone types.

    2) Quantity and distribution of fillers shall not be substantially different than that of the control samples.

        d. Filled areas shall be of sufficient depth to prevent flaking or dislodgment due to wear or maintenance operations.

        e. Filler shall be capable of taking and holding a finish similar to that of the stone.

        f. Cracks and other structural defects in stone shall not be filled; such stone shall be rejected.

K. Fabrication Tolerances:

    1. Shop cut stone tiles and shapes shall be fabricated square and true, with exposed flat surfaces true; free of imperfect edges, cracks, seams, and dimensional defects.

    [2. Curved cuts and cylindrical surfaces shall be uniform and true to radius within ⅛ in. or 0.5 percent of radius—whichever is less.]

    3. Stone shall be fabricated to the dimensions indicated within the following tolerances:

        a. Variation in face dimension: Plus 1⁄16 in. or minus 0.

        b. Square: 1⁄16 in. difference in diagonal measure.

        c. Edge straightness: Linear to within 1⁄32 in.

    4. Finished Thickness:

        a. Overall Thickness Tolerance: Specified thickness plus 1⁄16 in. minus 0 for floor tile; plus or minus 1⁄16 in. for casework tops and panels, wall panels, and other components to be mechanically attached.

        b. Uniformity (Maximum Variation in Thickness Across Face of Each Single Floor Tile): Uniform to within 1⁄32 in.

    5. Fabricate marble in compliance with the requirements of the MIA, [and granite in accordance with the requirements of the NBGQA,] with additional tolerance requirements as specified.

L. Identification: For purposes of properly locating special floor tile shapes, in particular in areas where special shapes and patterns are indicated, individual tiles shall be marked on the back with designations corresponding to marks on the shop drawings, using marble crayons.

2.3 ACCESSORY MATERIALS

A. Setting Materials:

1. Thin-set Mortar, Resin Modified: [   ].
   [1. Thin-set Mortar: Portland cement with acrylic latex additive; in accordance with ANSI A118.4.]
2. Rapid-Set Thin Bed Mortar: [   ].
3. Medium Bed Mortar: [   ].
4. Rapid-Set Medium Bed Mortar: [   ].
5. Thick Bed Mortar:
   a. Cement: ASTM C150, Type I.
   b. Hydrated Lime: ASTM C206, Type S, or ASTM C207, Type S.
   c. Sand: ASTM C144.
   d. Water: Clean and free from amounts of matter deleterious to setting bed materials.
   e. Proportioning: In accordance with TCA Handbook.
6. Epoxy Mortar: [   ]; ANSI A118.3.
7. Organic Adhesives: ANSI A136.1, type I; furnish primer/sealer as recommended by the adhesive manufacturer.

B. Reinforcing Mesh: 2 in. × 2 in. × 16/16 guage welded wire mesh or approved.

C. Cementitious Grout:
   1. Standard Grout: [   ]; sanded, except unsanded at joints scheduled at ⅟₁₆ in. wide.
   2. Fast-Setting Grout: [   ]; (proportions as recommended by the manufacturer for the setting time required); sanded, except unsanded for joints scheduled at ⅟₁₆ in. wide.
   3. Colors: As selected by the Architect from the manufacturer's standard line.

D. Epoxy Grout: [   ], or approved. Colors as selected from manufacturer's standard.

E. Tile Waterproofing Membrane: [   ].

[E. Crack Isolation Membrane: [   ].].

F. Tile Backer Board and Accessories:
   1. Board: [   ]; ½ in. nominal thickness aggregated portland cement panel, reinforced with glass fiber mesh.
   2. Tape for Glass Mesh Board: Open weave glass mesh joint tape, self-adhesive; 2½ in. wide.
   3. Fasteners: Self tapping; bugle head screws; zinc plated.

[G. Metal Screed: [   ].

H. Sealers: Siloxane type, one of the following:
   1. [   ].
   2. [   ].

PART 3 EXECUTION

3.1 EXAMINATION

A. Prior to starting work, carefully inspect installed work of other trades and verify that such work is complete to the point where work of this Section may properly commence. Notify the Architect in writing of conditions detrimental to the proper and timely completion of the work.

B. Do not begin installation until all unsatisfactory conditions are resolved. Beginning work constitutes acceptance of site conditions and responsibility for defective installation caused by prior observable conditions.

C. Verify that locations of expansion joints [, control joints, and construction joints] in substrate correspond to tile expansion joint locations.

[D. Substrate Examination:

1. Substrates are subject to examination by the Architect prior to installation of tile or slab leveling materials.

2. The examination will determine the need for additional crack isolation membrane at shrinkage cracks and other special conditions.

[3. Provide additional crack isolation membrane in locations as directed, in accordance with provisions of Sections 01025 and 01026.]

3.2 PREPARATION

A. Clean substrate surfaces free of grease, dirt, dust, organic impurities, curing agents, and other materials which would impair bond. Clean floors with "Blast-track" unit if necessary.

[3.3 TILE BACKER BOARD INSTALLATION

A. Install in accordance with the manufacturer's installation instructions.

B. Install units with edges firmly supported.

C. Screw attach units with 1 in. long drywall screws spaced 6 in. on center along framing.

D. Install fiberglass reinforcing tape at joints between panels. Completely embed in a thin-set mortar bed. Trowel mortar smooth with adjacent surfaces.]

[3.4 CRACK ISOLATION MEMBRANE

A. Install crack isolation membrane in accordance with the manufacturer's instructions, unless indicated or specified otherwise.

B. Provide crack isolation membrane at following locations:

1. At control and construction joints in concrete floors.

2. At changes in substrate materials.

[3. Surfaces of suspended slabs minimum 15 in. each side of building column grid lines (total of 30 in., minimum).]

[4. Surfaces within 5 ft-0 in. of escalator landing plates at suspended slabs.]

[5. On each side of building floor joint cover assemblies installed in grouted pockets; extend a minimum of 12 in. beyond grouted pocket.]

6. Shrinkage cracks [$\frac{1}{16}$ in. or larger] in slabs [on a unit price basis][as directed by the Architect]. [Include a minimum of [1000] sq. ft of crack isolation membrane in the Contract amount.]

C. Extend a minimum of 12 [ ] in. each side of crack or joint.

D. Do not apply crack isolation membrane at joints which will be reflected as expansion joints in the tile.

[E. Omit crack isolation at floors indicated for waterproof membrane.]

MASTER

SECTION 09380
CUT NATURAL STONE TILE

3.5 SLAB LEVELING

A. General:
1. Prior to installation of thin-set floor tile, where local irregularities in the substrate surface would prevent level installation of the tile, the substrate shall be brought to plane surface with variations not to exceed ⅛ in. in 4 ft (cumulative) and ¼ in. in 10 ft (non-cumulative).
2. Smooth all abrupt changes in plane.
3. Maintain slope to drain where indicated.

B. Use thin-set mortar or other filler for slab leveling. Other fillers are subject to endorsement by the setting mortar manufacturer. Submit manufacturer's letter of approval to the Architect, and the Owner's Representative.

C Screed or float to appropriate thickness and specified surface tolerance. Allow to set prior to proceeding with installation. Do not exceed the maximum thicknesses for thin bed mortar as recommended by the manufacturer.

3.6 WATERPROOF MEMBRANE INSTALLATION

A. Install waterproof membranes in strict accordance with manufacturer's installation instructions.

B. Install waterproof membranes at [   ].

C. At slab on grade locations, install waterproof membranes only along the perimeter of tile areas. Extend the membrane up the wall and a minimum of 6 in. out onto the floor surface.

D. At above grade locations, install waterproof membrane completely over floor surfaces indicated, and up the wall.

E. Where the waterproof membrane is extended up the wall, extend to one tile height. Do not expose the waterproof membrane to view.

F. Use embedded reinforcing mesh at changes in plane and material.

G. Protect waterproof membrane from damage until after tile installation is complete.

[H. Install waterproof membrane into clamping ring of floor drain.]

3.7 INSTALLATION OF TILE

A. Interior Floor Application—Thin-set over Concrete Substrate or Waterproof Membrane.
1. TCA System: Similar to F113.
2. Installation Standard: ANSI A108.5.
3. Setting Materials: Thin-set mortar; $\frac{3}{32}$ in. minimum thickness.

B. Interior Floor Application—Thick-set Over Concrete Substrate:
1. TCA System: F112.
2. Installation Standard: ANSI A108.1.
3. Bond Coat: Thin-set mortar over thickset mortar bed; $\frac{3}{32}$ in. minimum thickness.
4. Slope the mortar bed evenly to the floor drains.

C. Interior Floor Application—Thin-set Epoxy System:

1. TCA System: F131.
2. Installation Standard: ANSI A108.6.
3. Bond Coat: Epoxy mortar.
4. Slope the mortar bed evenly to the floor drains.
5. Use this system where tile type F is indicated, except at depressed floor slabs.
6. Use epoxy grout.

D. Interior Floor Application—Thick-set Epoxy System:
   1. TCA System: F132.
   2. Installation Standard: ANSI A108.6.
   3. Bond Coat: Epoxy mortar over thick-set mortar bed.
   4. Slope the mortar bed evenly to the floor drains.
   5. Use this system where depressed floor slabs are indicated.
   6. Use epoxy grout.

E. Interior Floor Application: Thin-set Epoxy System over Metal Substrate:
   1. TCA System: F131.
   2. Installation Standard: ANSI A108.6.
   3. Bond Coat: Epoxy mortar; minimum 1/8 in. thickness.
   4. Use this system to install tile base at walk-in coolers and freezers.
   5. Prior to installation clean metal substrate with a mild solution of TSP, and rinse.
   6. Use epoxy grout.

F. Wall Application—Gypsum Board Substrate:
   1. TCA System: Similar to W243.
   2. Installation Standard: ANSI A108.5.
   3. Setting Materials: Thin-set mortar.

G. Wall Application—Gypsum Board Substrate:
   1. TCA System: W223.
   2. Installation Standard: ANSI A108.4.
   3. Setting Materials: Organic adhesive.

H. Wall Application—Concrete Backer Board:
   1. TCA System: Similar to W244.
   2. Installation Standard: ANSI A108.5.
   3. Setting Materials: Thin-set mortar.
   4. Use vapor barrier behind tile backer board; overlap at joints a minimum of 2 in.; overlap waterproof membrane at base 3/4 in.

I. Countertop Application—Plywood Substrate:
   1. TCA System: Similar to C512.
   2. Installation Standard: ANSI A108.6.
   3. Setting Materials: Epoxy mortar.

[J. Special Requirements for Thick Mortar Bed:
1. Apply setting and mortar beds to thicknesses required for ultimate proper alignment of tile surfaces with adjacent floor materials. At carpet, tile shall align with carpet crush line elevation. Compensate for indicated pitches, tile thicknesses, and bond coat thickness.
2. Install reinforcing mesh at mid depth of all thick mortar beds at floors and decks. At ramps formed by tapered setting beds, terminate mesh near low end of ramp; maintain ¼ in. mortar cover.]

J. Joint Pattern:
1. Lay out tile pattern prior to commencing tile installation.
2. Accurately locate grout joints on lines indicated; where not indicated, adjust grout joints within specified tolerances to minimize use of cut tiles at field edges.
3. Where cut tiles are necessary, position tile such that cut tile at each edge of each rectilinear field is not less than half of a full size unit, unless indicated otherwise.
[4. Align tile joints across changes in plane, including wall to floor intersections.]

K. Tiles shall be blended as required to avoid pattern repeats and "patches" of adjoining tiles of distinctive color or character within each field area. [Coordinate distribution of tiles with the Architect.]

[L. Tiles which exhibit directional patterns shall be set with grain direction as indicated on the shop drawings, or, if not indicated, as directed by the Architect.]

[M. Install tiles aligned with adjacent finishes, where indicated. Provide mortar fill as necessary for proper alignment.]

N. Clean joints of mortar to minimum depth of ¼ in. to allow subsequent grout installation.

[O. Provide temporary setting buttons and shims as necessary to maintain wall tiles in position until setting mortar has set.]

P. Tolerances:
1. Joint Width Variation: Plus or minus 25 percent of the proposed joint width.
2. Taper: Plus or minus 25 percent from one end to the other.
3. No portion of a tile surface shall vary more than $\frac{1}{16}$ in. above or below an adjacent tile surface.
4. Install tile fields level to within tolerance specified for finished substrate.
[5. Tile set on thick mortar beds shall be installed level within ⅛ in. in 10 ft when tested with a straightedge in any direction across the tile field.]

Q. Special [Stone] Floor Tile Installation Requirements:
1. Wash backs of each tile to remove all dust and soil which would compromise adhesion.
2. Dampen substrate as necessary to prevent excessive suction. Trowel mortar onto surfaces to receive tile.
3. Apply mortar bond coat with notched trowel as required for proper level.
4. Set tile within time span recommended by mortar manufacturer.
5. Back butter tiles prior to setting to achieve maximum mortar coverage over back of tile and substrate.
6. Set tiles in accurate alignment. Beat in with a wood block, rubber hammer, or twist as necessary to level tiles.

[R. Ungauged Stone Tile:

1. Apply mortar to back of each tile by using the box screed method.

2. A box screed is a jig used to apply mortar to the backside of ungauged stone tile of varying thickness in order to achieve a uniform unit of thickness of the tile and mortar combined.

3. Press and push the tile into the mortar ridges using a slight movement perpendicular to the notched mortar ridges.]

S. Screed Installation:

1. Install screeds at tile field edges at the locations indicated.

2. Accurately cut to length for flush tightly butted joints. Provide miter-cut angle joints. Remove burrs at field cuts.

3. Install in longest possible lengths, except that no screed section shall be longer than 12 ft or shorter than 4 ft in length for continuous runs greater than 16 ft.

4. Install screeds free from waves and variations in height, flush with top of adjacent tile surfaces.

5. Set screeds directly in setting bed as the tile installation proceeds. Comply with screed manufacturer's instructions to achieve mortar tightly compacted between screed and tile edge.

6. Grind screed joints as necessary to correct minor misalignment and to ease sharp outside corners.

3.8 EXPANSION JOINTS

TCA recommends 24 to 36 ft for interior, assuming ¼ in. joints; change to 16 ft spacing (interior) for ⅛ in. grout/expansion joints (10 ft for special conditions, such as floor tile under skylights). Avoid ⅛ in. joints in exterior locations.

A. Place expansion joints at maximum 30 ft intervals for interior installations[, and at maximum 15 ft intervals for exterior installations].

B. Place expansion joints at control and expansion joints in concrete slabs, and at intersections with walls and columns.

C. Joint Sizes: Set to match width of typical grouted joint [; but in no case less than ¼ in.].

D. Leave expansion joints free of mortar.

E. Sealant materials and installation are specified in Section 07920.

3.9 GROUTING

A. Comply with provisions of ANSI A108.10.

B. Mix grouts in accordance with manufacturer's instructions.

C. Grout all joints, except expansion joints, in accordance with the manufacturer's recommendations. Float joints to a slightly concave profile.

D. Remove excess grout from tile surfaces in accordance with the grout and tile manufacturer's recommendations. Do not use excess amounts of water.

E. Protect adjacent surfaces from damage caused by cleaning agents. Do not use cleaners which would damage tile or grout surfaces.

MASTER

SECTION 09380
CUT NATURAL STONE TILE

F. Do not grout joints indicated to receive sealants, including inside right angle corner joints between floors and walls of column bases. Grout joints perpendicular to expansion joints shall be finished flush with tile edges.

G. Cured grout joints shall be made free of efflorescence, prior to sealing.

3.10 CURING

[A. Cure installation in accordance with the grout manufacturer's recommendations. Protect tile and grout during curing operations.]

B. Protect tile surfaces during curing. Keep traffic off tile surfaces for a minimum of 4 days, unless recommended otherwise by the grout or mortar manufacturer.]

[C. Test cured grout, in the presence of the Architect, to confirm complete and proper hydration. Remove and replace with new, all grout which fails to cure properly.]

3.11 PROTECTION

A. Protect stone tile installations from damage, in accordance with Section 01500.

B. Replace all damaged tiles.

3.12 CLEANING

A. In accordance with Section 01500 and Section 01770.

B. Coordinate final cleaning with work of Section 07920. Do not begin cleaning operations until tile expansion joints sealants are fully cured.

C. [Prior to substantial completion,] wash and thoroughly rinse all tile. Leave all tile surfaces clean.

3.13 TILE SEALING

A. Apply stain repellent sealer to all floor tile, including those with previous treatments, in accordance with the manufacturer's recommendations to achieve maximum penetration into tile

B Apply sealer at earliest possible date allowed by grout and sealer manufacturer.

C. Wipe tile surfaces after application as necessary to remove all visible sealer residue.

END OF SECTION

———

5

Protection and Maintenance of Stone Installations

THE IMPORTANCE OF PROPER SELECTIONS

The protection of stone installations includes preventative measures such as the sealing of the stone, application of antigraffiti coatings, and the use of walk-off mats to remove dirt and grit from shoes. Maintenance refers to regularly scheduled activities intended to keep the stone clean and free from contaminants, maintaining the factory finish, and to replace damaged stone. The success of these activities is dependent on the proper stone selection and the selection of the finish. If an improperly selected stone is installed in a high-traffic location, the demands on both the protection and maintenance systems will require additional time, effort, and money. Even with extra attention it may not be possible to maintain an improperly selected stone in its original condition. In considering the protection and maintenance of stone installations, the selection of the stone should be given equal, if not more, attention.

Figure 5.0. Sealed and unsealed stone tile.
Proper protection of a stone intended for floor installation requires that a sealer be applied to the surface. Sealers, whether they are topical or penetrating, are intended to protect the stone from stains and soiling carried by water—or other liquids—and soiled matter that is tracked to the surface from pedestrian traffic. The stone tile at top has been treated with a penetrating sealer which is repelling the water that has been spilled on the surface, while the untreated stone (underneath) has absorbed the moisture. The use of a sealer is a critical part of an overall maintenance and protection program.

163

STONE SELECTION

The selection criteria used in evaluating stone protection and maintenance are similar to those described in Chapters 4 and 6, on the installation and selection of stone, and the guidelines outlined there will have direct application. The performance issues of concern are the mineral composition of the stone, rate of absorption, hardness, and, finally, the intended application of the stone. For comparison purposes, the following descriptions are based on examples of stone installed in flooring applications. Furthermore, this comparison uses material extremes—limestone and granite—to emphasize the importance of addressing the selection criteria.

The mineral composition of stone can be divided into two general categories: calcareous and siliceous stones. Calcareous stones are stones composed of calcium, such as limestone and marble. Siliceous stones are composed of quartz and silica, such as granite, sandstone, slate, and quartzite. Quartz-based stones will have greater resistance to acids and high alkaline detergents than calcium-based stones. There are many types of acid found in everyday materials, such as Orange Julius and Coca-Cola drinks, that have negative effects on the finish of limestone and marble. If an orange juice drink is left on the surface of limestone or marble, the finish will be etched in the area of the spill; however, if the same drink is left on a granite surface, there will be no change to the finish.

Stones with a high *rate of absorption* will stain more easily than stones with a lower rate of absorption. Most of the staining that occurs on stone installations results from contaminants carried in water and other liquids that are absorbed into the stone. As the liquid evaporates, the contaminants carried into the stone remain attached to its cell structure below the surface. The longer the material is attached to the stone, the more difficult it is to remove the stain. If the stone is granite, which is composed primarily of quartz, aggressive cleansers can be used without damaging the stone; if the stone is a calcium based limestone, it will not tolerate cleaning agents of the same strength.

A stone's *hardness* will determine its ability to resist wear caused by scratching produced by foot traffic. The harder the stone, the more difficult it is to achieve a polish and, consequently, the more difficult to walk the polish off. The hardness of a stone is determined in part by the mineral composition and by the density of the stone. Granites, as a group, have good hardness characteristics; however, there are many limestones and marbles that are extremely hard owing to the geologic deposition and metamorphism experienced at the time of their formation.

In addition to the performance-based criteria described, the color and textural character of the stone should be considered. (The term *texture* in this context refers to the natural mottling, veining, or contrast of colors that constitute the character of the stone, and is not related to roughness of the surface.) Stones that are lighter in color or do not express any textural character show staining more easily than stones that have variation, which assists in hiding soil and stains.

FINISH SELECTION

The first line of defense in the protection of a stone is the finish. The greater the degree of polish gloss a stone receives from factory finishing, the greater the repelling action of the stone surface. Polished finishes repel moisture more than a honed finish, and both polished and honed finishes repel moisture better than a flamed or split-face finish. This is because the pore structure of the face of the stone is closed when a stone is polished, as compared with flamed or split-face textures. In addition, the greater the roughness of the stone face, the greater the attraction of soil and debris by mechanical adhesion.

The porosity of a stone is also important in considering the finish of the stone. The term *porosity* is used to indicate openness or holes within a stone, which will ultimately appear on its surface. If a stone is highly porous, the structure may be open, and regardless of the finish the face may remain open, allowing the infiltration of contaminants into the stone. In evaluating limestones, the unfinished back of the stone should be reviewed for the frequency and sizes of holes that have a spongelike appearance. With marbles, the unfished back of the stone will expose dry seams, fissures, and cracks, which, like the holes on limestone, will be express lanes for moisture to travel into the stone. This is also true of some coarse-grain granites that have a more open pore structure.

STONE PROTECTION

Stone protection is commonly thought to consist of coatings applied to a stone as protective sealers, but building features can also have a positive impact on the life of a stone installation and should be considered as protective measures. Protective features include canopies and overhangs, vestibules, and walk-off mats, which help to prevent weathering elements from making contact with a stone installation. If possible, a stone installation should be separated from streets and parking lots by coarse-textured concrete or other materials to allow for water, soil, asphalt, and debris to be loosened from shoes. Protective coatings include grout release treatments, sealers, and anti-graffiti coatings. All of these tools should be considered for the protection of a stone installation.

Grout Release/Grout Presealer

Grout release treatments are often of the same or similar formulation as sealers. Their purpose is to aid in the removal of grout residue and haze produced during the grouting process. A grout release creates a barrier on the stone that makes cleanup easier. Most medium- to dark-colored stones that have a low rate of absorption and a closed face do not usually need application of a grout release. For lighter-colored stones, stone types that have dry seams, large open fissures, or rougher-textured finishes, the use of a grout release should be considered. If the grout color is too dark and the stone light colored with a high rate of absorption, the edges of the stone may absorb the dark pigment and stain the perimeter of the stone. (As mentioned earlier, this is referred to as "picture framing.") When considering the use of a grout release, particularly for protection of a stone edge, consult with the manufacturer for proper product selection to avoid impairing the necessary bond of the grout to the stone. Whenever possible, mock-ups using all of the specified products should be produced for review prior to beginning installation.

Sealers

A sealer is intended to protect the stone from staining, allowing for easier day-to-day cleaning. The two sealer systems are topical sealers and penetrating sealers, which are completely different in regard to mechanics, chemistry, and philosophy of use. Penetrating sealers are sometimes referred to as impregnating sealers. In selecting sealers, several issues should be considered:

- What are the stone type and characteristics that necessitate protection?
- Where is the stone installation, and what type of contaminants will the stone be exposed to?
- What is the desired appearance of the stone after sealing: low gloss, high gloss, color enhanced, etc.?

TOPICAL SEALERS

As the name implies, topical sealers are coatings designed to create a barrier on the surface of the stone. The goal is to produce a sacrificial barrier on the surface that protects the stone from contact with foot traffic and contaminants. This barrier does not breathe, but encases the surface with its protective film and does not allow the passage of vapor through the stone. In earlier days, wax products were used to provide this protection. Technology has improved in recent years, however, introducing more durable materials than the earlier waxes. Most topical sealers contain either urethane resins or acrylic emulsions as the primary material in their formulation. These materials work well to prohibit the passage of water, water-carried contaminants, and oil-based contaminants. They are produced in liquid form and applied directly to the surface of the stone. Most topical sealers produce a gloss sheen that can be buffed between applications to increase the surface luster in heavily trafficked areas. Some topical sealers are available in lower-gloss sheens, although most are high gloss, and matte finishes are somewhat limited. Older formulations had a tendency to change color and yellow; this is no longer a concern with the new formulations. However, topical sealers usually darken the stone color, requiring sample testing of the product on the stone prior to application.

The frequency of application depends on the level of traffic and the occurrence of soiling. For example, the foot traffic of an office building lobby, although focused, will most likely be lighter than the traffic in an airport concourse or in a shopping center. Food courts and other food service installations are exposed to a higher frequency of spills than a retail store. The heavier the traffic, the more frequent the reapplication of topical sealers.

The frequency of reapplication is the major disadvantage of topical sealers. In areas where traffic is focused, paths will be worn, with pedestrians walking off the protection more rapidly than in perimeter areas of lighter traffic. Prior to reapplication, removal of the built-up sealer areas will be required. The materials used to remove or strip the old sealer should not be so aggressive as to cause harm to the stone. Because topical sealers create a film on the surface of the stone, they tend to show scuffs and markings, which are removed during the reapplication process.

Topical sealer

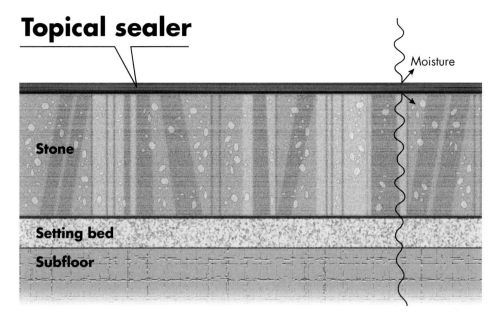

Figure 5-1. Topical sealers.
Topical sealers are coatings that create a sacrificial barrier on the surface of the stone which protects the stone from making contact with foot traffic and contaminants. These types of sealers work well to prohibit the passage of water, water-carried contaminants, and oil-based contaminants. However, because they produce a non-breathable barrier that encases the surface with a protective film, they do not allow the passage of vapor through the stone.

Advantages of a Topical Sealer

- Some formulations contain additives that produce non-slip characteristics.

- Creates a protective sacrificial barrier between contaminants, foot traffic, and the stone. This barrier protects the stone from surface scratching and etching caused by acidic materials: Coke, orange juice, etc.

- If a gloss finish is desired, topical sealers can produce a gloss that can be buffed, allowing for the maintenance of a high-gloss sheen.

Disadvantages of a Topical Sealer

- Changes the appearance of the stone by adding a gloss sheen and may deepen the color of the stone.

- Traps moisture within the stone by not allowing for the transmission of vapor through the protective barrier.

- The sacrificial barrier tends to show scuffs, can be walked off, and shows paths at heavy traffic areas. Requires continual reapplication as it wears in traffic areas, resulting in additional cost.

- The process of stripping the old topical sealers can be detrimental to the surface of some stones.

PENETRATING SEALERS

The purpose of penetrating sealers is to penetrate the stone with a material that will carry the protection into the structure of the stone. Once the sealer has penetrated the stone, the protection adheres to the cell walls without closing the pore

Penetrating sealer

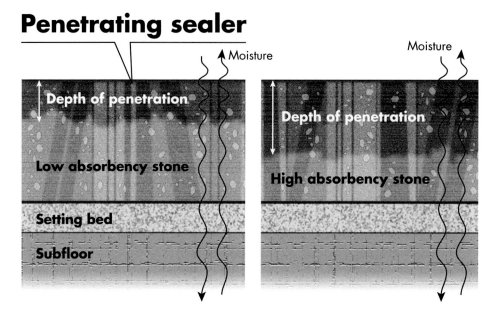

Figure 5-2. Penetrating sealers.
Penetrating sealers penetrate the stone with a material that carries the protection into the very structure of the stone. Once the sealer has penetrated the stone, the protection adheres to the cell walls without closing the pore structure, allowing the stone to breathe. Although these types of sealers do not provide protection on the face of the stone, they do protect the stone below the surface.

structure, thus allowing the stone to breathe. Sealers of this type are designed to be low in viscosity, which permits greater "wetting" of particles within the structure of the stone. When the vehicle has evaporated, the protective material remains to create a long-lasting, invisible barrier of protection from water, dirt, oil, and acid. Solvent-based sealers are formulated to penetrate below the surface of the stone without leaving a coating on the surface. The stone below the surface will be protected by the penetrating sealer, however, sealers of this type do not provide protection on the surface, which is considered a disadvantage. If Coca-Cola or Orange Julius is spilled and left on the surface of a stone treated with penetrating sealer, the surface finish will etch, dulling the affected area.

To provide surface protection, natural vegetable soap cleansers should be used with penetrating sealers, which build up a thin film layer, between periodic deeper cleaning. Natural vegetable soaps emulsify dirt and debris left on the stone surface in the same manner as detergent soaps, only milder. The thin oily layer repels liquids, yet complements penetrating sealers because of their low density, allowing the properties of penetrating sealers to work

There are two types of carriers or vehicles in penetrating sealers: solvents and water. A solvent vehicle also provides better durability because solvents are lower in viscosity, allowing for deeper penetration of the surface. When water is used as the vehicle, the protection cannot penetrate any deeper than the stone will absorb it. In many dense stones, water will not penetrate as deeply, leaving the protection just below the surface and on top of the surface of the stone, providing less protection over a long period of time. Stones with high rates of absorption will take the protective sealers deeper into the stone.

Penetrating sealers are durable, requiring periodic reapplication based on the frequency of deeper and more aggressive cleaning. Reapplication may also be required after pressure washing.

The most common protection materials used in penetrating sealers are silicone, siloxane, and fluoropolymers. These materials are a group of semiorganic polymers used in adhesives, lubricants, protective coatings, and synthetic rubber. Unaffected by outside elements, they can be damaged only by temperatures that range from 900°F to 1200°F or exposure to strong caustic solutions. Silicone, in many cases, may last longer than the surfaces to which they have been applied. Silicone, silane, and siloxane, form solvent-base sealers and work well to repel water-borne stains. Fluoropolymers, which are relatively new, contain fluorine and carbon. Flourine does not commonly occur in nature and is found combined with other elements. When flourine is extracted and combined with carbon, new compounds are created that have oil-repellent characteristics. Generally, fluorocarbon sealers are water based.

All of these penetrating sealers will work well to protect stone, some better at repelling oil and others at repelling water. Because there are many formulations, the manufacturers should be contacted for specific recommendations.

Advantages of a Penetrating Sealer

- Penetrates into the stone and attaches its protection to the cell walls within the pore structure. This allows for total vapor transmission through the stone.
- Does not change the color or sheen of the stone.
- Does not need to be reapplied after each cleaning.
- Because the sealer does not remain on the surface, the sealer coating will not scratch or scuff. Without a surface coating to wear off, this type of sealer does not require reapplication as frequently as topical sealers.

Disadvantages of a Penetrating Sealer

- By itself, penetrating sealers do not protect the surface of the stone from scratching or etching.

Graffiti Protection

Coatings protecting against graffiti are available in topical and penetrating formulas and perform in a similar manner as sealers. The manufacturers of topical systems generally produce their own cleaners for graffiti removal that are compatible with the base sealer. The topical sealer creates a sacrificial barrier to protect the stone. The sacrificial barrier will be removed during the cleaning process, requiring reapplication after each cleaning. Some topical cleaners may darken the color and increase the sheen of the stone being protected.

Penetrating systems provide protection from within the stone, preventing graffiti from penetrating the stone. Penetrating sealers do not change the color or sheen of the stone. Sealers of this type rely on other cleaning products and pressure washing to remove the graffiti, based on the durability of the graffiti; the more resistant the graffiti, the more aggressive the cleaning treatment. Because the sealer protection is located within the stone, aggressive cleaners will not harm the sealer and will not require reapplication after each cleaning.

Penetrating sealers do not provide the sacrificial barrier that topical sealers provide. If a treated stone can be characterized as being soft and requires an aggressive cleanser to remove durable graffiti damage, the surface may not tolerate the cleaning treatment. This demonstrates the importance of stone selection and finish. If the stone is to be used in an area where the probability of damage caused by graffiti is high, only stone types that can withstand aggressive cleaning treatments should be considered.

MAINTENANCE OF STONE

It is not uncommon to hear the statement that stone, marble, granite, and limestone do not require maintenance, that left alone a stone will develop its own patina, creating its own protective barrier. Examples of Old World installations will be cited as successes that have endured the test of time. For instance, there is a salesman who uses the steps of St. Peter's Basilica in Rome to illustrate the durability of Roman travertine, and that it is suitable for high-traffic applications. "The treads of St. Peter's are walked upon by thousands of people daily, get rained on, and have been in place for 1,000 years. If a stone can withstand that kind of traffic, it can be used anywhere." What the salesman fails to point out to the unknowing listener is that the treads of St. Peter's are more than 6 in. thick (that is, except for the areas that are worn to 5 or $5\frac{1}{2}$ in. and that the most common thickness of stone that is installed in the U.S. is $\frac{3}{8}$ in.! Ancient installation examples should not be used to evaluate materials intended for modern construction. Stone floor installations should not be left alone; they must be maintained.

The selection of the proper stone for the specific application is the most important issue to consider. After selection, the maintenance of stone is the second most important issue; stone installations should be treated with protective sealers and cleaned as often as the budget will permit. Many protective treatments have been developed in recent years, and the technology continues to improve. Cleaning products and procedures are also improving. The discussion that follows focuses on the most critical issues of a maintenance program.

Cleaning Methods (Sweep/Dust Mop/Wet Mop/Wet Vacuum)

Two important activities in a maintenance regime are the removal of dust, grit, and sand and the cleaning of accidental spills.

- Frequent dust mopping or vacuuming of stone surfaces will slow the rate of surface deterioration caused by foot traffic grinding sand and grit into the face of the stone, ultimately scratching the finish. Daily sweeping will also prevent the accumulation of grit and grime on the stone surface.

- Spills should be wiped up as soon as possible. Left unattended, the spills will etch the polish, dulling the finish of a stone. Many of the beverages consumed by humans contain acidic materials that, when in contact with

pH Scale

pH	Household Solutions	Acid
0.0	Hydrochloric acid	
1.0	Gastric juices	
2.3	Lemon juice	
2.9	Vinegar	
3.5	Wine	Increase in acidity
4.1	Tomato juice	
5.0	Black coffee	
5.6	Acid rain	
6.0	Urine	
6.5	Rainwater	
6.6	Milk	
7.0	Pure water	**Neutral**
7.4	Blood	
8.4	Baking soda solution	
9.2	Borax solution	
9.9	Toothpaste	Increase in alkalinity
10.5	Milk of magnesia	
11.0	Limewater	
11.9	Household ammonia	
14.0	Sodium hydroxide	**Alkaline**

calcium-based stones, will slowly deteriorate the stone. The beverage will not burn a hole through the stone; however, the stone will loose its factory finish in the area of contact.

In addition to dust mopping and spot-wiping spills, the stone should be wet mopped using soap and water from a mop bucket. There are as many cleansers on the market today as there are sealers, and choosing which products to use will depend on the volume of traffic the installation receives and the budget available.

After dust mopping, the floor is ready to be wet or damp mopped with a soap and water solution. Many qualified technicians in the floor care industry believe that damp mopping with clear water to emulsify any soiled areas should be all that is necessary to keep a stone floor clean. If this procedure can be done diligently every day or the floor area is small enough to take care of easily, this recommendation can be met with greater acceptance. More often, the case is that the floor will be damp mopped less frequently, requiring that the water be assisted with a soap solution.

The most common cleansers in use today are natural soaps, detergents, poultices, and diluted acid solutions. In selecting cleaning products, the chemical composition of the cleansers should be evaluated, using the pH scale to determine their compatibility with the stone. Cleaning products should be only strong enough to do the required task and no more; more is not better.

The term *pH* refers to the measure of a solution acidity, which is determined by the concentration of the hydrogen ion in solution. A small change in the pH value is a large change in the concentration of hydrogen. The pH value of lemon juice is 2.3, which is 63 times greater than that of tomato juice, whose pH value is 4.1, and 50,000 times greater than that of water, with a pH of 7.0. To use clean water for damp mopping a stone floor, as recommended, would be to use a solution that is pH balanced or neutral, which would not be harmful to the surface of the stone no matter what the stone's mineral composition is. In reviewing cleaning products, the focus is usually directed to materials containing acid solutions. Acid in diluted strength will deteriorate the face of calcium-based stone; consider that lemon juice has a pH value of 2.3 and that leaving an Orange Julius on the face of a limestone will etch the polish in a matter of a few hours. The alkalinity of cleansers, at the opposite end of the scale, are often overlooked, and these can be detrimental to some stones. Many household cleaners contain ammonia, some in strong solution. Consider the fact that household ammonia is 11.9 on the pH scale. In choosing a cleanser, it must be remembered that the level of acidity should be as close to neutral as possible.

Natural soaps, which have been used more frequently recently, are made from natural vegetable oils. The solution creates little or no suds and does not require a rinse step. A thin oil film is left on the surface that will build until a stronger cleansing soap is used. Supporters of the use of vegetable soaps recommend their use with penetrating sealers as a type of sacrificial barrier that is thin enough to allow vapor transmission.

Cleansers that use *detergents,* similar to those used for washing clothes, are the most commonly used cleansers and have a pH value of approximately 9.2. Cleaners of this type are generally used in mild solution as daily cleaners and in more concentrated solution as periodic deep cleaners. Strong solutions of detergents should be avoided, because they may have a detrimental impact on calcium-based stones, eroding the surface of softer stones.

Poultices are stronger solutions of detergents. The detergents, usually in powder form, are mixed with water to a paste consistency. They are generally used for concentrated spot-cleaning and will have a destructive effect if left on a surface for extended periods of time or if used too frequently.

Acid solutions have been used historically in the masonry trades for cleaning mortar residue from brickwork. There may be occasions when very mild acid solutions may be necessary for specific cleaning problems. As a rule, acids should be avoided whenever possible, and when used, they should be used with extreme caution. Acid in strong concentration will destroy calcium-based stones.

Cleaning Procedures

A well-executed cleaning program should include a strategy addressing daily, periodic, and spot-cleaning procedures. As previously mentioned, the most effective cleaning program includes the removal of dust, dirt, and grit, accomplished by damp mopping as frequently as the budget can afford. A routine should be established that provides for frequent dust moping and damp mopping—daily for both, if possible. If the stone installation is smaller in size, this routine should be possible; for larger installations such as shopping centers it may be difficult to achieve. For cleaning large areas, automated cleaning equipment such as auto-scrubbers can speed the cleaning process. Many auto-scrubbers can be fitted with vacuum systems that draw up the mop water that is applied while scrubbing with soft rotating bristles.

A daily cleaning schedule should be accompanied by *periodic deep cleaning,* using slightly more concentrated detergent cleansers to remove soiling that may have worked into the pores of the stone. The use of a penetrating sealer can prevent soil particles from staining the stone and permit the detergent cleaner to emulsify the soil and allow for easier extraction.

A *spot-cleaning* strategy should include daily cleaning, which consists of simple wipe-up incidents and the periodic removal of deep staining. The cleaning of more deeply soiled areas should begin with slightly stronger solutions of detergent and progress to a poultice if the detergent cleaner is unsuccessful. The increase in product strength should always be effected cautiously and in small steps.

Finally, the maintenance program that is developed and implemented should be documented. A well-documented program can assist in the training of new personnel and make very clear the products that are part of the cleaning program. New materials should not be used without proper testing and evaluation. Another important benefit of a well-documented program is the opportunity to determine the source of a problem when it occurs. It is easier to undo a problem when the procedures and products that have been used can be identified.

Guidelines for the Selection of Stone

SELECTION CRITERIA AND PRACTICAL CONSIDERATIONS

Stone is a product of nature and therefore cannot be weighed or measured in the same manner as manufactured materials or ceramic tile. Each type of stone — granite, marble, limestone, and slate — was created differently and, as one would expect, will have differing physical characteristics. These differences go beyond the physical appearance of the various types of stone; there can also be greatly differing performance characteristics resulting from the manner in which they were created or their geologic formation. It is the differences in the way stone types were created that makes stone an interesting building material, yet sometimes unpredictable, full of inconsistencies and, consequently, risk for those who select and specify stone.

Tests have been created to measure the physical properties of stone, most of which have been developed for the application of stone in a building system, such as a curtain wall design or vertical application as a veneer on a building exterior. However, not all of these tests are directly applicable to all uses of stone integrated with modern building systems that utilize lightweight construction methods.

For example, when a stone is selected for use in a shopping center as flooring, what should be the criteria the stone must meet? The shopping center industry is big business, whose focus is to maximize the investment of its specific prop-

Figure 6.0. Selecting stone.
With the increasing number of stones available each day, how does the architect, designer, or specifier of stone establish criteria for the selection of an appropriate stone for their specific application? To determine whether or not the stone is suitable for the intended use, several important questions need to be addressed: 1. What are the characteristics of the stone? 2. Has the stone been tested? What do the test results tell us? 3. Where has the stone been used before? And finally, to reduce the risk of a stone failure, the most important criteria is to determine whether the stone under consideration has performed successfully in a like installation.

erty. To achieve this goal, shopping centers are designed and built using technology to push the limits of building materials, squeezing the costs as low as possible to maximize every construction dollar. While standards of life safety and adherence to building codes are maintained, one way construction costs are reduced is by extending the structural system to its maximum design limit, combined with a lightweight concrete and metal deck system for the flooring on upper levels of the shopping center. The result of this construction cost saving is a higher rate of deflection in the subfloor; recall your last visit to a shopping center and the bounce of the floor that you experienced as two families passed on an upper level. This deflection will be a permanent characteristic of the concrete slab that is the subsurface for a ³⁄₈ in. thick stone tile, directly adhered with a thin setting bed of mortar as little as ¹⁄₄ in. in thickness.

What can we learn from the results of tests that are designed to measure compressive strength? How much load can a stone module carry before it crushes? Consider the modulus of rupture: When will the stone break under point loading or its bending strength? The dimensions of the samples used for these tests are 2 × 2 in. cubes for compressive strength and a sample of 4 × 8 × 2¹⁄₄ in. to test the modulus of rupture; the dimensions of the stone tile that will be installed in the shopping center will be 12 × 12 × ³⁄₈ in. thick. What will these test results tell us about a stone that will be installed to a surface designed to bounce the length of its life and be subjected to the wear of hundreds of thousands of shoppers in a year? Probably not very much!

Is the Stone Suitable for the Intended Application?

Determining the suitability and appropriateness of a stone for use in a built environment is a responsibility with enormous consequences, yet a task that is often given to individuals who may not have the necessary tools available to shoulder the responsibility. This is of particular concern when materials under consideration are new or have not been used outside their own region and most likely have not been used in modern building systems. A designer recently spoke of one of the best clients he had ever worked with, Bud Ericksen, the director of store planning for a major national retailer, who was particularly sensitive to the use of new materials.

> As a designer, and also being competitive by nature, I wanted to be the first with new ideas and materials, to give my client the most creative solutions and to express my personal creativity through my projects. I believed that this approach to design would enable me to stand taller than my associates. Bud Ericksen, whose role was that of being the owner, and who also happened to be an architect, also wanted his projects to be creative, yet they had to be sound and able to stand the test of time. The expression Bud used was, "We do not want to be first, and we do not want to be last." We used large quantities of stone on the projects under Bud's direction, at a time when the use of thin stone modules was taking off, and with the personal design philosophy that I described, it is a miracle that we had as few failures as we did. The number of new stones that were brought to us for our consideration, often by individuals who were less experienced than we were, was staggering.

How does one determine the suitability and appropriateness of a stone, and what is the process that should be followed? For a few applications, there are specific guidelines that have been developed, such as for the use of stone in curtain wall systems, their anchors, and attachments, and for the use of stone as veneer. However, for many more types of installations there are no yes-or-no guidelines that can be followed; often the process becomes more art than science. A great deal of information does exist relating to the use of stone; the key is the evaluation of the available information and how to apply the data to the specific use for which the stone is being considered. A way to begin the process is to ask the following questions at various points in the review process and use these questions as guidelines in pursuing the information required to make a responsible decision.

Is the stone suitable for the intended application?

- What are the characteristics of the stone?
- Has the stone been tested? What do the test results tell us?
- Where has the stone been used before?

What Are the Characteristics of the Stone?

In selecting stone an important consideration in the evaluation process is how a stone was formed geologically, which has a great deal to do with how it can be expected to appear and perform. Whether by the layering of material, molten magma, or the product of a metamorphic event, the formation will have an impact on the characteristics and performance of a stone. The geologic formation will also have an effect on its mineral composition. The two basic mineral types present in all stones are silica or calcium, and which mineral base the stone is composed of will have a significant effect on the performance of the stone and its usage.

For ease of comparison, the following descriptions focus on granites, limestones, marbles, and slate as representatives of the three main geologic formation groups: igneous, sedimentary, and metamorphic.

Granite is an igneous stone. Igneous stones began as a material that was molten, or plastic, emerging from the core of the earth, mixing with many types of elements as it flowed. The slower the flow of magma (intrusive formation) during a granite development, the coarser the grain structure; the faster the flow of magma (extrusive formation), the finer the grain structure. As the molten material moved toward the surface it began to cool, consequently hardening and then densifying over the millions of years of the earth's formation. Because of their molten beginning, granites can be characterized as being very uniform in appearance with occasional veining. Many granites are surprisingly porous, some with high rates of absorption. This characteristic is most common in intrusive granites that have a larger grain structure, which will produce larger pores in their structure. Regardless of the grain size or pore structure, granites are extremely hard and resistant to acids and abrasion. This natural resistance is due to the presence of feldspar and quartz particles that were formed during the molten stage of development. It also contributes to the high level of hardness that is consistent with all granites. This hardness makes it difficult to achieve a mirror polish in granites under fabrication, and, conversely, once a granite achieves a polish it is difficult for foot traffic or atmospheric agents to wear off its polish. The hard polish a granite is capable of achieving will also repel the water- and airborne acids contained in acid rain and will maintain a highly reflective surface longer than any other type of stone.

Figure 6-1. Characteristics of granite.
Because of their molten beginning, granites can be characterized as being very uniform in their appearance. They are composed of various sized aggregates within a uniformly colored matrix material, with occasional veining. Generally, the aggregates can be categorized by their similarity of size and color. Because of the homogenous structure of granite, multiple granite samples from a single deposit generally test uniformly from sample to sample.

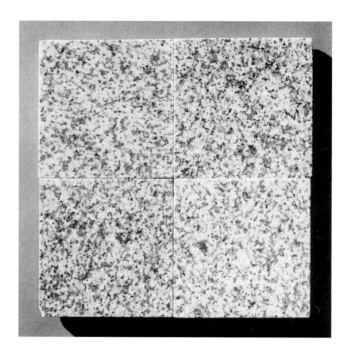

Because of the homogenous structure of granite, multiple granite samples from a single deposit will generally test uniformly from sample to sample, and therefore their test data can be considered very reliable from test to test. Again, this is due to the manner in which granite was created.

Characteristics to Look for When Selecting Granites

- Granite that has a larger pore structure will most likely have a higher rate of water absorption. If the granite is intended for use in an exterior installation, the water absorption should be low; less than 0.5% to withstand the effects of freeze-thaw cycles.

- The presence of the mineral pyrite within a stone that is exposed to moisture may result in rust staining of the stone surface.

- Light colors are generally softer than dark-colored granites, with the exception of the black granites, which are from the gabbro igneous subgroup.

Limestone is a sedimentary stone created by the accumulation of finely eroded particles of rock and other fine materials carried by the wind or water, most often collecting in basins or seabeds. These deposits densified over the millions of years of the earth's development to create uniform layers or formations. The layers of sediment contain organic material that is cemented with other materials that are sometimes inorganic in origin. The infinite types of materials that accumulated to form these deposits throughout the world resulted in a variety of characteristics; many are extremely dense with low rates of absorption, and many are very soft with high rates of absorption. Because limestones were formed by the deposition of different types of materials, their performance as a group is not as predictable as as that of granites, which are more homogenous and therefore easier to predict because of their molten beginnings. For example, many stereotypes have been drawn based on an evaluator's experience with a soft limestone and, hence, a negative categorization of the characteristics of limestone as a group. There are many limestones that have hardness values approaching the hardness of granites and rates of absorption that are often lower than those of some granites. Thus, the categorizing or stereotyping of limestones or any other stone as a group is not appropriate in evaluating an individual limestone.

Characteristics to Look for When Selecting Limestones

- Many limestones are sawn parallel to the bedding plane (fleuri cut) or perpendicular to the bedding plane (vein cut). The faces of limestones that are fleuri cut have a greater compressive strength than the same stone vein cut, because the fleuri-cut layer has been has been subjected to greater forces of compression than the same stone sawn in the opposite orientation—vein cut. However, the stone that is fleuri cut yields wilder variation in color and character than the more predictable color and variation of a vein-cut stone.

- Because of the layering process of sedimentary stones, there is an increased opportunity for fissures to be exposed than in metamorphosed marbles. This is particularly true of fleuri-cut limestone. Few limestone producers fill the open areas and fissures on the face of the stone with any material; if a fill material is used, it is seldom a hard resin-based fill. Over time, aggressive abrasive action will expose fissures that have been filled with soft materials, and if no fill is used, the fissure will open and collect dirt. Rarely is this a detriment to the integrity of a stone's strength or its performance; however, once the fissure is fully compacted with dirt, it appears as a crack. Most often the depth of the fissure is too shallow to accept a fill.

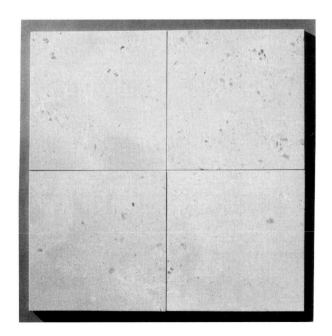

Figure 6-2. Characteristics of limestone. Limestones are formed by the accumulation of eroded particles of rock and other fine materials carried by the wind or water, most often collecting in basins or sea beds. The infinite types of materials that accumulate to form these deposits throughout the world result in a variety of characteristics: many are extremely dense with low rates of absorption, while others are very soft with high rates of absorption. Because limestones were formed by the deposition of different types of materials, the performance of limestones as a group is not as predictable as granites, which are more homogenous and, therefore, easier to predict.

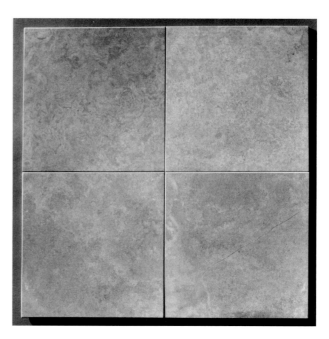

Figure 6-3. Vein-cut limestones.
Vein-cut limestones are produced by sawing the stone perpendicular to the bedding plane; the bedding plane is parallel to the earth. Because limestones are created through the deposition of material, generally in large, low-lying areas, the variation of color and character should be consistent within adjacent areas vertically within the deposit.

Figure 6-4 Fleuri-cut limestones.
Fleuri-cut limestones are produced by sawing the stone parallel to the bedding plane. Stone that is produced in this method will express more variation than vein-cut stones because the yield is produced by sawing through and between the sedimentary layers. Due to the degree of contrast between different layers of sediment, the finished surface of one stone may be inconsistent in color and character from another taken within the same area.

Figures 6-5A and 6-5B. Finished and unfinished faces of low-density limestone.
Many of the less dense limestones will have an open pore structure. Examine the unfinished back side of the stone to observe the character of the pore structure. If the surface of the stone appears open or spongelike, this characteristic is a sign that the stone has a high rate of water absorption. These stones will show staining easier and the stain will be more difficult to remove once the stain has been absorbed.

- Many of the less dense limestones have an open pore structure; the face of the stone looks like the texture of a sponge under magnification. If the face of the stone has been filled or has a higher sheen, it may be difficult to see the degree of openness of the surface. To determine the character of the pore structure, the finished stone face is turned over and the unfinished back side of the stone is examined. If the surface of the stone appears open or spongelike, the application of the stone should be carefully considered because this characteristic is certainly a sign of a stone with a high rate of water absorption. These stone types will show staining more easily, and a stain will be more difficult to remove once it has been absorbed.

Marbles are metamorphic stones. They began as limestone from a sedimentary deposit, then experienced one or more metamorphoses that included dramatic movement and extreme heat. These dynamic forces acting on the deposit cause new minerals, not present in the original deposit, to recrystallize to form marble. This stone type is typically more colorful than the other types and far less predictable in range of color and variation — from individual tile to individual tile, for example. Marbles usually have dramatic veining and deposits of various material types, adding to their beauty. However, it is this accumulation of varying characteristics present in a specific marble that may create a weakness in the marble or unpredictable performance of the same material quarried at different times. The test data on marbles may not be as reliable as the data on limestones or granites, because of their formation. Conversely, the metamorphic process that a marble has experienced can create a material that is stronger as an overall composition than the individual components of the stone deposit.

Characteristics to Look for When Selecting Marble

- Often a metamorphosed stone is harder and more durable than the original limestone from which a marble was produced. The calcium carbonate of limestone becomes calcite when metamorphosed to marble. Pure calcium carbonate yields pure white marble. The impurities of the metamorphosis and the dramatic forces that form marbles are what create the infinite range of color, texture, and veining and vary its structural characteristics. Therefore, with all of the potential variation in the structure of a marble, it is often difficult to evaluate the test data between marbles and stones from the same deposit.

- The calcitic material that composes marble, similar to the calcium carbonate of limestone, makes it vulnerable to the agents of acid, and marbles should be located in areas where they will not be exposed to weather. Conversely, if the goal is to achieve a weathered appearance rapidly, calcite-based stones are desirable.

- The structure of a marble under consideration should be carefully examined, focusing on the structure of the dry veins, quartz veining, fissures, and other noncharacteristic inclusions. The bond between the surrounding material and the vein or inclusion should be without interruption or separation. When a vein shows a separation between two materials, it is referred to as a "dry vein," which will most likely crack and break under pressure. If there is no separation, the bond between the vein and the surrounding material can be extremely strong, similar in strength to two pieces of metal welded together.

- Large white-colored quartz spots should be examined for their soundness and compactness. Often these concentrations of quartz are hollow or can separate easily from the surrounding material. This is of particular concern when there is a significant difference between the hardness of the quartz inclusion and the hardness of the surrounding marble. The greater the difference, the easier it is for the two materials to separate, which is similar to the negative action of a dry vein.

- Large variations in color and character of a marble should be anticipated because of the dynamic forces that combined to create it. Several samples of the specific marble should be viewed to determine its full range of variation prior to making a decision based on its appearance.

Slate is a metamorphic stone. The origins of slate are the sedimentary deposits of finely sorted silt that compressed to form clay and shale. The primary mineral components of slate are quartz and mica. Slate is formed by the metamorphosis of shale and clay. The density of slate types is determined by the degree of metamorphic action that occurred during its formation. Many shales are extremely dense, and many are very loose in compaction. The consolidation of the shale and clay deposit during the metamorphosis created linear planes, referred to as foliation, which is the folding or layering of metamorphic rock that occurs when focused pressure is applied from one direction. The mineral structure of shale is platy and linear, which reorients perpendicular to the force of the metamorphic activity. This alignment creates a texture that is a layered cleavage, which gives slate its characteristic cleft face.

Characteristics to Look for When Selecting Slate

- The density of slate types can vary dramatically as a direct result of the amount of force and the heat exerted on the deposit at the time of their formation. The greater the pressure and heat experienced, the greater the density. The density of the slate determines the looseness of cleaved layers; lower-density slates separate more easily than higher-density slates. The edge of a tile or slab of slate and the cleaving at the surface should be examined. Slates that are composed of loosely compacted cleaved layers should be avoided in high-impact or heavy-traffic areas and in exterior locations that are exposed to freeze-thaw cycles. Water can work its way into the open areas between the cleaved planes and expand as the temperature drops, breaking the loosely cleaved layers away from the body of the stone.

- Many types of slate that are loosely cleaved have a more rustic appearance and greater degrees of irregularity on the surface of the stone, which increases the variation in overall thickness. The variation in thickness can be reduced by grinding or sawing grooves on the back side of the stone, allowing for the slate to be installed in a thinner setting bed. Slates that are not capable of receiving treatment on one side may require medium or thick setting beds. In addition, slates that have dramatic variation in height across the face of the module are difficult to place next to each other in floor applications without incident of lippage. Using larger grout joint widths or chiseling the high spots is required to avoid this misalignment at the edge of the stone tile.

Figure 6-6. Variation in marble surface.
Marbles are typically more colorful than other stone types, and are far less predictable in their range of color and variation. Marbles usually have dramatic veining and deposits of various material types, adding to their beauty. However, it is the accumulation of noncharacteristic minerals and geologic inclusions present in a specific marble that may create a weakness in the marble or unpredictability in its range of variation.

Figure 6-7. Low-density slates.
Low-density slates will generally have more dramatic cleaving; high and low areas will be found across the face of the stone. The cleaved areas of low-density slates will separate more easily than higher density slates. Squareness of fabricated edges and consistency of thickness are difficult to achieve with low-density slates.

Figure 6-8. High-density slates.
High-density slates will be flatter across the face of the stone, allowing for trueness of edge fabrication and thickness, which will produce more precise installations.

Figure 6-9. Quartzites.
Quartzites are often confused with slates because quartzite will produce a cleaved plane when split, similar to slate. The primary difference between slate and quartzite is the fact that quartzite has a higher content of quartz and an increased density. The higher density is a result of the greater force and heat that is required to create a quartzite deposit.

- If the slate is fabricated with a natural cleft face on both sides of the module, it is difficult to achieve square modules or to fabricate large panels owing to the rocking that occurs while the slate is sawn because the face is not flat.

- Many types of slate are extremely soft and not suited for high-traffic floor application. To determine the hardness of a slate, drag a blunt metal object such as a standard screw driver or a blunt blade from a pocket knife across the face of the slate and examine the depth of the scratch that is created.

- In designing with slate and other rustic types of stone, it is important to be aware of the limitations of the material and to avoid application where precision is required. Wider grout joints between modules, thicker setting beds, and the use of smaller stone modules should be considered, so as to avoid disappointment when using rustic stones.

Has the Stone Been Tested?

Why do we test materials, and what do we expect to obtain from the tests we perform? The purpose of testing is to establish a value that measures the strength of a stone, which can be used to determine the suitability of the stone in the application for which it is intended. Many of the test methods that have been developed are specific and attempt to approximate the anticipated behavior of the stone in the manner that it is to be installed, such as flexural strength and compressive strength. Other test methods produce general information about the stone, such as the rate of water absorption and density, which can be utilized in multiple conditions. Unfortunately, in developing a standardized test procedure, it is difficult to create a mock-up of exact conditions that are then applied to a variety of differing construction circumstances. It is also important to note that in many applications of stone, such as flooring, there have been no minimum requirements established to clearly determine that a proposed stone is appropriate for the intended application. For example, the test value for abrasion resistance describes hardness and a stone's ability to resist abrasion, which is useful in comparing the same data on other stones. But there have been no tests developed to adequately evaluate stones for flooring application, such as a test to measure the impact a stone can resist when subjected to heavy foot traffic or the effects of foot traffic on a stone characterized by its inclusion of dry seams. Specific guidelines are needed to reach a yes-or-no conclusion, which are not always available in reviewing the values established through current test methods. The pursuit of test data is valuable for comparisons; however, tests performed on field mock-ups may provide more direct conclusions.

TESTING OF STONE

The purpose of stone testing is clear: to measure the strength of a stone. The next hurdle is to develop tests that can consistently predict the performance of the stone in a specific application through the use of similar conditions or mock-ups. The tests that have been developed that are specific to the selection of stone are the tests for water absorption, density, abrasion resistance, modulus of rupture, compressive strength, and flexural strength. Several tests have been developed to determine the strength of anchoring systems and fasteners, which are described in Chapter 4.

ASTM TEST STANDARDS

In an effort to determine a stone's ability to resist stress, the American Society for Testing and Materials (ASTM) has developed tests to measure the physical properties and strength of stones. The tests provide values for water absorption, density, compressive strength, flexural strength, and abrasion resistance and are useful for determining the appropriateness of a stone for a specific application. Care should be exercised in evaluating the data to ensure that the tests and the procedures used in the tests are comparable to the application for which the stone is intended. The tests that have been developed for the selection of stones and for comparing their values for appropriateness are presented in the following paragraphs.

ASTM C 97   Standard Test Methods for Absorption and Bulk Specific Gravity of Dimension Stone
Purpose: This test is used to determine the water absorption and the density of stone. Water absorption is expressed in percentages, and the values for density are expressed as bulk specific gravity.
 The test procedure: The absorption of a stone is determined by weighing the stone sample in a dry condition and weighing the sample again after the stone has been immersed in water for 48 hours. Bulk specific gravity is measured in a similar manner. The samples that are used may be cubes, prisms, cylinders, or any regular shapes, with the smallest dimension at least 2 in. and the greatest dimension not more than 3 in.

ASTM C 99   Standard Test Method for Modulus of Rupture of Dimension Stone
Purpose: This test measures the combined shear strength and diagonal strength of a stone. The test determines the load the stone can resist before breaking. Measuring the modulus of rupture of a stone is valuable in determining the strength of the stone at its point of attachment with anchoring devices.
 The test procedure: An assembly is used to support a stone sample 8 in. long × 4 in. wide × 2 in. thick at each of its ends. A point load the width of the sample is applied at the center of the span and is increased until the stone fails.

ASTM C 170   Standard Test Method for Compressive Strength of Dimension Stone
Purpose: The test to measure compressive strength determines the load a stone can resist before it will crush. The results of this test are only directly applicable to load-bearing installations, such as when large cubic-sized stones are used for a masonry-type wall or for lintels over openings. The results of compressive strength tests have little direct relevance for precast panel and curtain wall systems unless the stone is tested after freeze-thaw cycle tests. This indicates the effects of the stress produced by repeat freeze-thaw cycles. However, compressive strength tests are useful in evaluating different stones for floor application if density, hardness, and comparable installations are also considered.
 The test procedure: A cube or core sample, 2 in. × 2 in. minimum, is placed in an assembly that applies a load evenly on the sample until it crushes.

ASTM C 241   Standard Test Method for Abrasion Resistance of Stone to Foot Traffic
Purpose: The test for measuring the abrasion resistance of a stone determines the resistance of a stone to the abrasion caused by foot traffic on a floor or stair tread.

The test procedure: A sample 2 in. × 2 in. × 1 in. thick is measured prior to applying a grinding wheel with an abrasive grit of No. 60 alundum onto the surface of the sample. The sample is subjected to 225 revolutions of the grinding wheel. The sample is weighed again and is then tested for its bulk specific gravity (density). The calculation determines the loss of material from the grinding process; the higher the value, the greater the resistance to abrasion.

ASTM C 99   Standard Test Method for Flexural Strength of Dimension Stone
Purpose: The test for flexural strength determines the strength of a stone when in tension, or its bending strength. This test is helpful in determining the maximum load a stone panel can withstand when configured in a curtain wall assembly with anchors located at the edges of the panel.

The test procedure: A sample 12 in. long × 1½ in wide × 1 in. thick is placed on elevated supports located near the ends of the span. A load is placed on the sample spread between two supports that are one-quarter the distance from each of the two supports below. This configuration distributes the load toward the ends of the span and places the sample in tension. The load is increased until the sample fails.

ASTM C 1028-96 Standard Test Method for Determining the Coefficient of Static Friction of Ceramic Tile and Other Like Surfaces
Purpose: This test was developed to measure the slip resistance of a walking surface. The values expressed in the testing represent a scale of resistance; low resistance of the surface to the material dragged across its face yields a low value; high resistance of the surface to the material dragged across its face yields a high value.

The test procedure: A block of wood with a 3 in. × 3 in. section of shoe material (leather and Neolite are the commonly tested shoe materials) adhered to it is placed on the stone surface to be tested. A 50 lb weight is placed on the wood block, and the assembly is dragged across the surface of the stone. The force in pounds required to cause the test assembly to slide parallel across the surface is measured with a dynamometer. The test is repeated four times, and the measurements are averaged to obtain the coefficient of friction.

Underwriters Laboratory (UL) considers a coefficient of friction value of 0.5 to indicate a slip-resistant walking surface, whereas the Americans with Disabilities Act (ADA) considers a value of 0.6 as slip resistant. The ADA recommends a coefficient of friction value of 0.8 for slip resistance on inclined walking surfaces.

The procedures for each of these tests are published in the ASTM *Annual Book of Standards,* which is available at most public libraries, and a reprint of the dimension stone tests are included in the Marble Institute of America (MIA) *Design Manual IV.* There are many national and local engineering companies, laboratories, and test agencies capable of performing the standardized ASTM tests, such as Smith Emery, SGS-U.S. Testing, Case Consulting Laboratories, and many others.

Most of the building stones that are commercially available have been tested to determine their strength and durability. The results of tests performed on specific stones are available from several sources: national and regional trade organizations, such as the Marble Institute of America (MIA), which has compiled the largest database of information on stones that are produced throughout the world, and Marmi Italiani, which maintains data on stones produced in Italy. Many stone-producing regions have assembled data and published books on the materials produced in their specific areas, such as *Marmi di Puglia,* which describes the stones and provides test results for the stones from the Puglia region of Southern Italy, and *La Piedra en Castilla y Leon,* which describes the stones and provides test results for the stones from the Castile and Leon regions of Spain. When general tests results are required for a project, they can be requested by the suppliers of stone products.

The test methods that have been developed by the American Society for Testing and Materials (ASTM) base their values on the U.S. system of measurement (foot and pound); European agencies have similar standardized test methods, which are based on metric values. For informal comparison of different stone types, reference sources such as *The MIA Color Plate* are useful. However, if an application of stone is intended for areas such as curtain wall systems, precast assemblies, or other high-liability installations, it is critical to provide the testing laboratory with representative samples from the same layer or bench from which the project will be fabricated for the test procedure.

MOHS' HARDNESS

Another method used to determine the hardness of a stone is the Mohs' Hardness Scale, which measures the ability of a material to resist abrasion. Friedrich Mohs (1773–1839), a German mineralogist, created the scale to measure hardness in terms of the durability of a gem: soft minerals can be scratched more easily by a hard material, and hard materials cannot be scratched by soft materials. The Mohs' Scale is commonly used to evaluate a stone's anticipated durability, which is determined by the ability of a stone to resist scratches by known materials. If a fingernail can scratch the surface of a stone that is under consideration, the stone is too soft for foot traffic. However, if a stone can resist the scratches of the mineral feldspar, then it would be considered highly resistant to scratching and suitable for high volumes of foot traffic.

Mohs' Hardness Scale

Mineral	Hardness	Common Test
Talc	1	Scratched by a fingernail
Gypsum	2	
Calcite	3	Scratched by a copper coin
Fluorite	4	Scratched by a knife blade or window glass
Apatite	5	
Feldspar	6	Scratches a knife blade or window glass
Quartz	7	
Topaz	8	
Corundum	9	
Diamond	10	Scratches all common materials

Marble Institute of America, Stone Classification System for Soundness

The Marble Institute of America (MIA) has created a system of identifying the soundness of stones for the purpose of determining the degree of difficulty required to process a stone by categorizing stones into an A, B, C, and D classification. A stone classified as an "A" stone is free of inclusions and imperfections, is structurally sound, and will not require corrective action during the fabrication process; thus, the degree of difficulty to process is low. A stone classified as "D" contains many types of inclusions and voids, which will require corrective action at the time of fabrication to compensate for the imperfections that could otherwise allow the stone to break; thus, the degree of difficulty to process is high. The classification is intended only for this purpose; it does not imply that a stone is good or bad, nor does it state the appropriateness of stone types for specific applications. In addition, the MIA categories are completely subjective, because the classification is assigned by the viewer of the stone, which can be done by several different individuals at different times rather than through the use of mechanical measurement or other objective systems of testing. The MIA classification is intended to identify characteristics of stone types that may be encountered in the fabrication process. Unfortunately, the classification is often misunderstood and misused in selecting stone for architectural application and installation. The following excerpt has been reprinted from the *MIA Design Manual IV,* to clarify the intent of the classification system:

Soundness

As a result of knowledge gained in extensive practical experience of its [Members], marbles have been classified into four groups. The basis of this classification is the characteristics encountered in fabricating and has no reference whatsoever to the comparative merit or value. The classifications merely indicate what method of fabrication is considered necessary practice. Classification of marble is done by MIA producer and finisher members. A written warranty should be obtained from them prior to installation.

These four groups are:

GROUP "A"   Sound marbles and stones, with uniform and favorable working qualities.

GROUP "B"   Marbles and stones similar in character to the preceding group, but with working qualities somewhat less favorable; may have natural faults; a limited amount of waxing and sticking necessary.

GROUP "C"   Marbles and stones with some variations in working qualities; geologic flaws, voids, veins, and lines of separation are common; it is standard practice to repair these variations by sticking, waxing, and filling; liners and other forms of reinforcements employed when necessary.

GROUP "D"   Marbles and stones similar to the proceeding group, but containing a larger proportion of natural faults, and a maximum variation in working qualities, requiring more of the same methods of finishing. This group comprises many of the highly colored marbles prized for their decorative qualities.

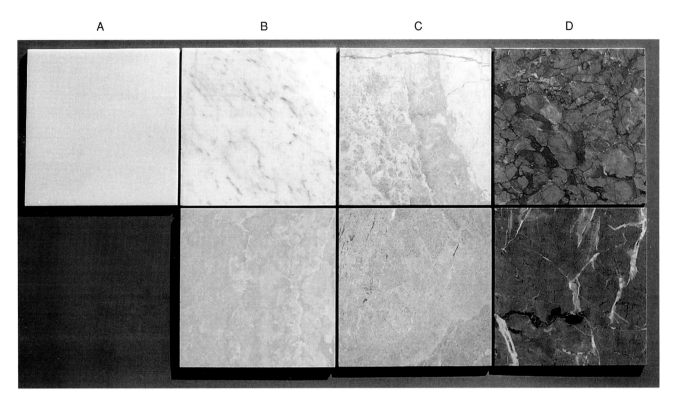

A   B   C   D

Figure 6-10. Classifying stones using the Marble Institute of America classification.
The Marble Institute of America (MIA) has created a system of identifying the soundness of stones based on the effort required to correct any imperfections. There are four classifications: A, B, C, D. A stone classified as an "A" stone is free of inclusions or imperfections and will be structurally sound, requiring no corrective action during the fabrication process. A stone classified as "D" will contain many types of inclusions and voids which will require corrective action at the time of fabrication to compensate for the imperfections that could otherwise allow the stone to break. The classification does not imply that a stone is good or bad; nor does it state the appropriateness of stone types for specific applications.

WHAT DO THE TEST RESULTS TELL US?

Because of the variations in characteristics between stones and their formations, how uniform can testing really be? There can be variation in the physical characteristics of a stone within the same quarry, depending on its location within the quarry, and there can be variation even within the same layer or bench. When materials are evaluated, the manner in which the stone was created should be considered; can the test results of the same stone that were performed 20 years ago from a different quarry location be considered reliable?

The intent of this description is not to paint a picture of the testing process as being less valuable; the importance of testing stones and evaluating stone tests is greatest when the data is used for comparative purposes. If it is known that a specific stone has been used successfully in a similar application, it is of great value to compare the test results of the known material against the results of the proposed material.

In addition, the more uniform or homogeneous the geologic process the stone experienced at its creation, the more likely that the tests results can be considered consistent within the deposit of stone. The tests results for igneous- and sedimentary-type stones should be uniform within a specific deposit. However, the test results from a metamorphic deposit may be less consistent from sample to sample, or from area to area within a deposit, owing to the inconsistencies experienced at the time of formation.

What tests tell us is the strength of a particular stone when subjected to various types of stress. The value of testing will increase or decrease, depending on how the data is interpreted and applied. At the beginning of the design process when several stones are to be considered, the evaluation of each stone's physical characteristics by comparison of tests results is a beneficial strategy. For example, if the abrasion resistance is known for a specific stone that has been used successfully in an application identical to that which is proposed, the abrasion resistance of the stones under consideration can be compared with the known success and conclusions regarding the performance of the proposed stones can be reliably drawn.

Where Has the Stone Been Used Before?

Reviewing the test results of a given stone is only a part of the evaluation process and is certainly only scratching the surface. One of the most important steps in evaluating the performance of a stone is to review installations of the stone — successful installations as well as failures. Reviewing an installation of the stone under consideration is imperative. The owner, architect, and construction team should seek out installations of the stone that are the same in application and project type, and observe the performance of the stone installation by visiting the sites. This will allow the team to make an accurate evaluation of the stone under review in an environment similar to the intended application. Matters of concern are the similarity of project types and building types, manner of installation, amount of traffic or the forces of nature imposed on the installation, such as the climate and seismic activity, the maintenance program, and the length of time the stone has been in place.

If a stone has been used in a residence or in a low-traffic application, or the installation was composed of stone that is ¾ in. thick installed in a thick-set bed, is it realistic to expect that the stone will perform well in a shopping center when cut to ⅜ in. thick and is thin set to a lightweight concrete floor system? A common practice employed by dubious suppliers is to use 100-year-old examples for the basis of a comparison. A comparison that uses the 12 in. thick ancient limestone slabs that form the sidewalks of Jerusalem as the basis of success for a thin-set limestone tile installation is hardly fair. The comparison that should be made would use the same stone, installed in the same manner, and in the same dimension.

The world is getting smaller everyday, and many regions of the world have only recently been explored or have been closed for political reasons. New stones are introduced to the marketplace each day, many of which are sound and many of which are not. Selecting a stone, particularly a stone that is new to the market, is risky business, whether it has been tested or not. If a stone is so new to the market that there are no installations to review, then one must consider whether he or she wants to be the first to try it.

The comparison of installations and the evaluation of a stone's test data is a difficult challenge by itself. The challenge is magnified when the stone has not been tested, is new to the market without a proven history of success, or has a proprietary "fantasy" name linked to it that masks its past usage.

SPECIAL CONSIDERATIONS FOR EXTERIOR INSTALLATIONS AND INTERIOR USE OF STONE

The following discussion of special considerations focuses on issues related to the selection of stone in exterior and interior applications. Issues regarding design safety factors and code requirements are specifically applicable to the installation of building stone and are discussed in previous chapters.

Exterior Considerations

Mineral composition and stone finishes: All stones are composed of one of the two basic mineral groups: silica or calcium. Granite, quartzite, sandstone, and slate contain silica as their primary mineral component, which is highly resistant to acids, making these stones good choices for exterior use. They resist the corrosive atmospheric agents carried in rainwater and air that will etch the finished face of a stone. A granite panel with a polished finish will retain the polish longer than a limestone that is finished to a high sheen, because the silica present in the quartz that composes the granite is more resistive than limestone, which is made of calcium. Limestone and marble are composed of the mineral calcium, which is less resistant to acids as compared with silica. When calcerous stone is used in exterior applications, it should be located in areas where it can be protected by overhangs or recesses within the building. If the stone is not located in protected areas, the surface finish will etch and wear at a faster rate than if it were protected.

This does not imply that calcium-based stones will fail when used in exterior applications, only that the finish will change with exposure to the weather. There are many large-scale government and institutional buildings in United States and throughout the world that are built of limestone that have been in service for hundreds of years. It should, however, be recognized that the stone that was used on these buildings is of greater thicknesses than that used today, and in many cases the stone modules are large in dimension and thickness and were intended for use as load-bearing masonry units. As these larger stone modules age and small cracks develop, causing material to chip or spall from the surface, there is a substantial thickness remaining in the module; this is not the case with the thin stone veneers that are components of modern building systems.

Therefore, the selection of the stone finish is an important design consideration, and the aging of the finish of the stone should be contemplated early in the design process. What will the stone look like five, ten, or many years into the future, as the stone changes color and the surface ages? When a stone is to be considered for exterior use, the design team should review installations of the stone that have been exposed to weather and incorporate the future surface aging into the building design.

The selection of a stone's finish will have an impact on how the finish will retain its appearance over time. The higher the sheen or level of polish, the more resistant to moisture, acidic solutions, and air pollutants the surface will be; coarser surfaces will be more vulnerable to these agents. Rougher surfaces allow for easier migration of solution into the body of the stone. Flamed finishes are particularly vulnerable to weathering agents, because the process that is employed to create a flamed texture uses a destructive high-temperature flame to break the surface, which creates subsurface microcracking. These microcracks and fissures create microscopic channels that draw moisture into the stone through capillary action. In addition, the rougher the texture of a stone surface, the more difficult the surface is to clean, making coarse textures at pedestrian areas particularly vulnerable to graffiti and accelerated soiling.

Freeze-thaw stability: Stones used in exterior installations that are exposed to freezing temperatures must be freeze-thaw stable; that is, they must have low water absorption. A volume of water expands to 8% of its size when it freezes; therefore, stones that have a lower rate of absorption should be used in cold weather exterior conditions. This also applies to all setting materials, caulking, and sealants that are accessories to a stone installation. A stone with a high rate of absorption installed at exterior locations will absorb moisture, and as the water freezes and expands, the surface can break from the stone, cracks may develop, areas near anchors may become vulnerable, and the entire stone module may break free from the setting bed. The ceramic tile industry classifies ceramic products based on the rate of water absorption, as follows, and recommends that materials be vitreous or impervious when installed in exterior locations:

Semivitreous	3% to 7% absorption
Vitreous	0.5% to 3% absorption
Impervious	Less than 0.5% absorption

"Hysteresis" — deformation, shrinkage, and thermal expansion: The thermal expansion of stone types and adjacent materials is an important issue when combining different stones with dissimilar materials in an assembly or in an adjacent installation. Clearances between materials and the incorporation of adequate expansion joints are critical to accommodate the movement of stone as it is exposed to temperature changes and the anticipated expansion and contraction of the stone module when rigidly attached. In addition, the MIA states in its *Dimension Stone Design Manual IV* that laboratory tests of the coefficient of thermal expansion of certain marble have indicated that after several cycles of heating and cooling, a residual expansion of approximately 20% of the original increase can be expected. The rate of thermal expansion varies from stone to stone, and stones should be reviewed on an individual basis.

The phenomenon of curling or the deformation of the stone's flat plane in certain green and red marbles and in agglomerates is not completely understood. To overcome the curling or bending of the corners in stone tile, several mortar and adhesive manufacturers have developed epoxy mortar systems that have successfully inhibited the movement of stone tile once the tile has been set. The difference between the epoxy system and standard cement mortar systems is that the epoxy system does not use water, which suggests that water is responsible for the curious movement of thin stone modules when installed using water as part of the adhering system. The MIA identifies this phenomenon as "hysteresis," as it applies to stone:

> Hysteresis is a phenomenon that affects certain true marbles. Unlike most stones that return to their original shape and volume after exposure to higher or lower temperatures, these marbles show small increases in volume after each rise in temperature above the starting point. This can

result in differential expansion within the stone which is more likely to be accommodated or restrained with thicker stone modules than with thinner stone modules. If the stone is not restrained, bowing of the marble module takes place and produces compressive forces in the backs of the stone. This causes creep which leads to permanent deformation of the stone. Dishing also stretches the face which makes the stone more porous and increases their vulnerability to corrosion from acids in the atmosphere and deterioration from freezing and thawing effects. If marbles of this tendency are considered, it is important to determine the minimum thickness necessary to overcome the effects of hysteresis by testing under conditions which simulate in-place temperature gradients of the back up wall or sub-floor.[*]

Mapei, Inc., a major international producer of setting materials and adhesives, experienced the deformation of thin stone tile when specific types of stone and agglomerate tile had been thin set with standard three-part mortar systems: sand, water, and cement. When the same stone was adhered using a two-part epoxy system, Mapei observed that the occurrence of deformation was diminished, which led its technical department to suspect that water in contact with the stone was responsible for the curling at the edges and corners of the thin tile. This phenomenon caused the technicians at Mapei to conduct tests on a variety of stone types to determine which stones were vulnerable to the effects of water in mortar systems. Tests were performed on a variety of stones, in which the individual samples were placed face down on a measuring device while being supported on three corners. To simulate the moisture contained in a still-wet mortar system, a wet felt cloth was placed on the back of each stone sample. The measuring device used sensors placed at various locations on the stone sample to measure linear movement and detect any possible distortion across the face of the stone. The measuring device was connected to a computer that recorded all directional movement every ten minutes for a period of 24 hours. The technicians reviewed the collected data and determined the dimensional stability of each of the stones, then used the data to make recommendations for the appropriate mortar system. Mapei classified the tested stones in groups according to their dimensional stability based on the presence of moisture:[**]

Group 1
These materials showed a minimum amount of distortion, less than 0.3 mm:

White Carrara

White Thassos

Verona Red

Marquina Black

Granitello Del Carso

Most Granites

---

[*]Marble Institute of America, *Dimension Stone Design Manual IV.* Reprinted with permission.
[**]Adapted from Mapei Technical Bulletin *Installation of Natural Stone Veneers According to Their Dimensional Stability.*

Stones of this group are considered to be stable and free of any particular installation problem related to their deformation. The choice of adhesive can be based on the type of substrate to which they will be installed, the possible mechanical stresses, or the downtime limitations imposed by the project schedule.

Group 2

This group consists of all those materials that are slightly sensitive to water contact and will show evidence of movement between 0.3 mm and 0.6 mm during the first 6 hours:

> Certain slates
>
> White Zandobbio
>
> Various agglomerates

The use of traditional portland cement mortars and dry-set mortars will cause serious distortion problems that are detrimental to the adhesion and evenness of the finished installation. Mapei recommends using a two-part mortar system that utilizes hydraulic binders that chemically link its mixing water, which will securely key the stone tile into the setting bed rapidly (the Mapei system is designed to bond within 3 hours), as compared with the longer time required by traditional mortar systems, which can take up to 24 hours.

Group 3

This group includes highly sensitive materials that show distortion greater than 0.6 mm during the first 6 hours of contact, or otherwise relevant movements within minutes of the initial contact with water.

> Verde Alpi
>
> Rosso Levanto
>
> Rosso D'Italia
>
> Certain slates

This group of stones requires the use of a water-free, two-component reactive polyurethane adhesive; epoxy mortar system.

Staining: Discoloration and staining of stone when exposed to weathering and moisture may occur for several reasons. For example, slates have their beginnings as clay and silts. A few types of slate that did not experience a full metamorphosis, and consequently are not dense but are loosely cleaved, contain materials that, when in contact with acids, may cause the stone color to run or tend to soften the surface. This may be due to the mineral composition of slate and the presence of pyrite, calcite, or carbon, which when exposed to acidic solution may convert the calcite particles to gypsum and ultimately cause softening of the stone to the point of disintegration.

It has been thought that the presence of iron oxides or other iron materials is the cause of rust staining in granites that are exposed to moisture and acidic solution; however, further research suggests that these minerals are usually stable and it is the presence of the mineral pyrite within a stone that may cause rust staining of the stone surface. These examples clearly point out the importance of using existing installations for comparison when selecting stone for exterior use.

Interior Considerations

There are fewer issues of concern in selecting stone for interior, as opposed to exterior installations, mainly because the climate of an interior environment is controlled. Therefore, the selection considerations are focused on matters related to the fabrication and installation of the stone: uniformity of thickness, the finish applied to the stone, and the hardness of the stone.

Uniformity of thickness: The ability of a stone to be fabricated to a uniform and consistent thickness is directly related to the geologic type of stone and its density. This is of concern mainly if the stone is to be installed on a floor. Generally, marbles, granites, and limestones are of a density that is capable of withstanding the pressure applied on their faces by processing equipment which calibrates the thickness of the stone. However, stones such as slate and quartzite that are cleaved will be irregular in thickness when they are split, requiring further processing or hand-selection to allow for a uniform installation. Processing techniques, such as the grinding of one side or sawing parallel cuts across one of the stone faces, can reduce the overall variation in thickness of the stone. If the variation of the cleaved face is too great, it will be a greater challenge to install the stones, aligning the edges to avoid lippage created by adjacent high and low edges. If the slate or quartzite is not capable of receiving additional processing because the stone is not dense enough to withstand the pressure of sawing or grinding of the back, or if processing equipment is not available, the stone will require thick setting, which is costly and not always possible in renovations or where setting bed depths of greater dimension are not allowable.

The impact of finish on staining and slip resistence: The higher the level of sheen or the polish of the stone surface, the more resistant the surface of the stone is to stains and soiling. Conversely, the greater the coarseness of the stone surface, the greater the attraction of soil to the surface. Polished stone has a fully filled face, without a tooth for soil to mechanically attach to, and is relatively closed to stains that can migrate into the stone; a stone with a flamed finish will be a magnet for the mechanical attachment of soil to its surface, and the natural openness of the surface will be increased as a result of the breaking caused by the flaming process. This conceptual description does not incorporate the positive impact of the use of sealers, which can enhance the resistance to staining regardless of the texture of a stone's surface. For a more in-depth description, see Chapter 5, "Protection and Maintenance of Stone Installations."

As mentioned earlier, the higher the gloss, the greater the resistance to soiling; unfortunately, the higher the gloss of the surface, the lower its slip resistance. To establish the value for the slip resistance of a surface, the test procedures of ASTM C1028 are used to determine the coefficient of friction (COF) of a surface. The higher the value, the greater the resistance to slipping across the surface of a material. There are no specific code requirements or laws that state the minimum coefficient of friction; however, the Ocupational Safety and Health Administration (OSHA) Underwriters Laboratories state that "a coefficient of friction of 0.5 and above is the recognized industry standard for a slip-resistant flooring surface, except where local code requirements require higher COF values." There is no predetermined level of sheen by which a surface is considered to be polished, but a continuum. It is the number of abrasives used in the finishing process and the length of time the stone is exposed to the process that determine the level of polish, and there are infinite levels of a polished finish. Many stones with a lower level of polished finish attain a 0.5 COF and can therefore be considered to be slip-resistant walking surfaces. In 1991, the Americans with Disabilities Act Accessibility Guidelines (ADAAG) were developed. According to the Guidelines, the ADA "conducted tests with persons with disabilities and concluded that a higher coefficient of friction was needed by such persons. A static coefficient of friction of 0.6 is recommended for accessible routes and 0.8 for ramps." Although this is a recommendation and not a requirement by definition, if a specifier or owner is involved in slip-and-fall litigation, it is easy to imagine which way the recommendation will be viewed. It is nearly impossible to achieve a 0.6 C.O.F with a polished finish, whether it is a high/high polished finish or a low/high polished finish. If slip resistance is a concern, a balance between the improved stain resistance of a higher polish and the increased slip resistance of a lower sheen should be sought. Stones that can be finished with a lower sheen, such as a honed finish, and can achieve a 0.6 coefficient of friction should be considered for use in areas where the public will be using the stone as a walking surface.

Hardness: Various trade organizations have recommended that when multiple stones are selected for use in a pattern, the hardness value of all of the stones be the same or similar. A further recommendation is made to alert the design team to select stones that will wear at similar rates over the life span of the building. These recommendations must be applied in the appropriate context. Stones with lower hardness values will not wear out; however, those with softer hardness values will show wear more rapidly. This is a valid concern when the building or installation is intended to have a life span of 100 years, such as in planning large-scale government structures, institutions, or civic buildings. For stone installations that are not as permanent, such as tenant improvements, retail stores, and shopping centers, where fashion or turnover will dictate a shorter life span, the concept of similar hardness has a different interpretation. The focus changes to the appearance of the differing stones; the harder stones will retain their factory finish or sheen longer than the stones of lower hardness, which will dull more quickly. Areas of higher traffic will show wear patterns, and areas out of the primary path of traffic will retain the original finish longer.

A minimum hardness value of 10, based on the test procedures for ASTM C241, is recommended by several trade organizations for general paving application, and a hardness value of 12 for stair treads and other high-traffic conditions. Because there are many stones that will achieve a hardness value of 10 (such as many types of travertine), which would be considered too soft or vulnerable for commercial high-wear locations, this recommendation should be considered a starting point for comparison. Reviewing the installation of various stones with known hardness values and comparing the expected level of performance with that of the anticipated installation is a more appropriate use of reviewing the hardness values of stones. A residential stone floor or a light commercial installation in which the stone may be installed a distance from the building entry most likely will not be subjected to the rigorous conditions of a building entry where abrasive exterior grit is tracked over the stone by a large volume of people; softer stones of lower hardness values may be suitable in these areas.

INFORMAL TESTING AND PRACTICAL ANALYSIS

The ASTM standard test methods are tools outlining the procedure for testing to obtain uniform results; however, they do not offer guidelines. The purpose of a test should be to predict the performance of a stone within a specific installation. Yet without a guideline that sets minimum criteria, how can stones be selected? The reality is that the selection process is often more art than science; the scientific approach of reviewing comparative test data should be balanced by visiting installations, practical analysis, and common sense. There are several methods for performing informal tests to give a quick snapshot perspective of what the anticipated characteristics will be and, consequently, how the stone will perform. For example, a good material to use in comparing many of the characteristics of stone is porcelain ceramic tile. Porcelain ceramics are composed of dense clays that are fired at extremely high temperatures to produce a dense vitreous material. The high density and low water absorption of porcelain ceramic make it an excellent material to compare stone with.

Density

The density, or compactness, of a stone can be informally measured by holding the corner of a thin sample of the stone (a $12 \times 12 \times \frac{3}{8}$ in. tile works best) in one hand and knocking the stone sample with the knuckle of the other hand. If the sound produced by the stone sample is a clear ring, similar to that of a porcelain ceramic tile, the stone can be characterized as being dense or compact. The duller the sound that resonates from the tile, the more likely it is that the tile is not dense or compact. However, if the stone has been dropped or has a crack that was incurred through handling, the sound that emits from the stone could sound "cracked" and may not be projecting a true indication of the density of the stone. The sound may also resonate dully if the stone is saturated with water, as occurs during the fabrication process, and some igneous stones may ring dully owing to the open structure that results from intrusive formation, in which case this informal observation may not be conclusive in these examples.

Resistance to Impact

No tests by ASTM or American Stone Industry Organizations have been created to measure resistance to impact on the surface of a stone. The concerns go beyond the premature deterioration of the stone surface, as there will also be a negative impact on stones that are not fully bonded. In a tile installation, if the mortar coverage does not go to the corners of the tile, leaving a void below the tile, focused impact on the unsupported corner will have a high probability of breaking the tile.

An informal test method to simulate focused stress and impact on walking surfaces is to drop a steel ball bearing approximately $\frac{1}{2}$ in. in diameter onto the surface of the stone. The steel bearing should be elevated 6 in. to 7 in. above the stone surface. When a bearing is dropped from this height, the area that comes in contact with the stone is roughly the size of an exposed nail on the heel of a shoe. The steel bearing should be dropped several times and in several locations, including areas where fissures, veins, dry seams, or other inclusions occur. Stones that are crystalline in structure, such as marble, will tend to fracture below the surface of the stone. If the stone is light in color, these markings are usually not noticeable and do not present the potential of future failure. However, the presence of microfractures have been observed below the surface of marbles that are medium to dark gray in color, which may not be desirable to building owners.

Stones that are lower in density will also show damage when subjected to impact, which also has the potential of breaking small areas of stone from the face of the stone. Areas where open veins occur are other sites of vulnerability and should be informally tested to determine the stone's ability to resist impact. Stone tiles that do not receive a bevel at their edges are also vulnerable to impact; a bevel will provide greater resistance to chipping along the edge of the stone module. Stones that are not compact will be vulnerable to chipping along the edges when impacted, particularly in areas where the joints are not fully grouted.

Water Absorption

To review the water absorption of a stone, sprinkle water over its surface and observe the rate at which the water is drawn into the stone. If the water beads on the surface or if it is absorbed slowly into the stone, the stone can be characterized as having a low rate of absorption. Another method for observing water absorption is to submerge a corner or portion of the sample in water. Observe the rate at which the water is absorbed and the rate at which the moisture evaporates. The rate of absorption is influenced by the finish of the stone surface. If the control sample that is being tested has a polished finish, the rate of absorption will be slower because the polished surface will repel the moisture. If the surface has a honed finish, the moisture will be absorbed at a faster rate than a polished finish; conversely, the rougher the finish — sandblasted, flamed, or sawn — the higher the rate of absorption.

Abrasion Resistance and Hardness

To review the abrasion resistance or abrasive wear of a stone, drag a blunt object across the face of the stone. To obtain reliable results, the object or material that is used to abrade the surface of the stone should be harder than the stone. An object such as the flat edge of a screwdriver is an effective tool for abrading the surface of the stone. The flat edge of the tool should contact the surface of the stone and a consistent pressure applied as the tool moves back and forth across the surface. Take care not to dig the corner of the tool into the surface, as this would not be indicative of the actual forces to which a surface would be subjected. The larger the amount of material removed while the stone is scraped, the lower the abrasion resistance, which is characteristic of softer stones. The smaller the amount of material removed, the higher the rate of resistance, characteristic of harder stone.

This test also works well to determine the vulnerability of veins, fissures, and areas of openness on the surface of a stone. As the tool is dragged parallel to the fissure and then perpendicular to the fissure, the effects on the area may give an indication of the soundness of that area or the strength of the fissure or vein.

A common perceived failure in paving applications occurs where a fissure or vein is opened when the factory fill is removed from the fissure by foot traffic. The open vein fills with dirt, and it appears as though the stone is cracked or broken, but, in reality, the stone is most likely sound. However, a stone that has areas of fissures or veins that are softer than the adjacent surface will be to vulnerable to abrasive action caused by foot traffic in high-use areas.

AVAILABILITY OF A STONE

Beyond the performance issues related to the selection of a stone, another area of concern is the availability of a stone: In what size is the stone available? In what country is the stone quarried and fabricated? Is the quarry open year-round, or is it closed because of monsoon rains or freezing temperatures? How efficient is the transportation system of the country where the stone is produced?

To maximize the efficiency of fabrication, the size of the block or slab should be considered. For example, if the panel can be increased or decreased slightly and one additional module can be sawn from the slab, less waste will be produced, which will reduce the overall fabrication cost. Some types of stone are limited in size by the equipment or labor available to extract them from their quarries. Reviewing the available size of the stone will avoid designing to a larger module than is commonly quarried.

Many rustic types of stone, such as slates and quartzite, have recently become available from emerging economies with poor infrastructure, such as inadequate roads, bridges, truck lines, or rail service, which inevitably will require longer delivery times. In some countries the roads from the point of fabrication to the seaport are not built and maintained to accept the weight of trucks loaded with ocean containers and require the use of smaller trucks to ferry the produced goods from the factory to the port. Once the smaller truck arrives at the port, the stone is off-loaded and reloaded into closed ocean containers. This method of transport increases the handling of the stone and exposes it to additional opportunities for damage. In India the transportation of manufactured goods is dramatically slowed during the periods of monsoon rain and for a lengthy time afterward until the roads have been repaired. There are always holdups in production and shipment of stone, even when the infrastructure is good, and delays are commonplace in emerging countries.

With the increased technology available for both communication and stone fabrication, an increasing number of emerging countries are exporting stones that were once used exclusively on a regional scale; these are now being marketed globally. The advantage, of course, is that there are more materials available today than ever before. The disadvantages are that the history of these materials in modern building systems is limited — they have no proven track record — and the infrastructure of a particular region may be inadequate, resulting in long delivery times.

Another concern in selecting stone is the political stability of a stone-producing region. Is the country a regular trading partner, or has the State Department issued a travel advisory recommending against travel to that country? This concern should make the owner of a project rather nervous, wondering whether he or she will receive the selected material and whether it will be available in the future should the owner decide to remodel or expand. The question "Do I want to be first?" should be asked.

IS THE STONE SUITABLE FOR THE INTENDED APPLICATION?

When test results and other information have been gathered from all available sources, what does this data really tell us? The review of a stone's geologic formation gives us insight to the physical characteristics of the stone, and the specific test results give us a point at which we can begin comparison, which will provide valuable clues to how a stone should perform over time. The most important part of the investigation, however, is to examine projects where the stone has been used previously. If the stone under consideration has been installed in the same manner as intended for the proposed application, in a similar project type, similar building type, and similar climatic conditions and is observed to be holding up to the forces and stresses imposed on it, then it can be deduced that the stone should be successful in the intended application. In an age when high technology is readily available, we can become unduly reliant on the collection of scientific data, yet what is critical is the analysis and application of that data. The successful selection of a stone is dependent on the balance of art, science, and common sense.

The anticipated performance of a stone based on test data and the observation of past installations is only part of the puzzle. Even stones with the best test performance characteristics have a potential for failure if the stone is not properly installed and maintained. Because of the complexity of issues relative to a stone's anticipated performance and behavior, the following outline should be used as guide and checklist when considering any stone for use in the built environment.

Stone Selection Criterion Checklist

Is the stone suitable for the intended application?

1. What are the characteristics of the stone?

2. Has the stone been tested? What do the test results tell us?

3. Where has the stone been used before?

Glossary of Common Stoneworking Terms

abrasive finish A flat, nonreflective surface finish for marble.

abrasive hardness Refers to the wearing qualities of stone for floors, stair treads, and other areas subjected to abrasion by foot traffic (see ASTM C241).

absorption Percentage of moisture absorption by weight (see ASTM C97).

adhered Veneer secured and supported through adhesion.

adoquin A volcanic quartz-based stone containing a variety of colored aggregates and pumice in a quartz matrix; quarried in Mexico.

agglomerate stone A man-made product produced from crushed stone combined with resins.

alabaster Fine-grained, translucent variety of gypsum, generally white in color. May be cut and carved easily with a knife or saw. This term is often incorrectly applied to fine-grained marble.

alkaline Pertains to a highly basic, as opposed to acidic, substance; for example, hydroxide or carbonate of sodium or potassium.

anchorage The means by which slabs are attached to a self-supporting structure.

anchors Metal devices for securing dimension stone to a structure. Types for stonework include those made of flat stock (strap, cramp, dovetail, dowel, strap and dowel, and two-way anchor) and round stock (rod cramp, rod anchor, eyebolt and dowel, flat-hood wall tie and dowel, dowel and wire toggle bolt).

apron A trim piece under a projecting stone top, stool, etc.

arkose A sandstone containing 10% or more clastic grains of feldspar. Also called arkosic sandstone, feldspathic sandstone.

arris The edge of an external angle, usually finished to match the surface finish.

ashlar Stone having a square or rectangular shape installed in a pattern of multiple shapes and sizes.

backing rod A flexible and compressible material, ropelike in form, that is used to fill the back of a joint space. The backing rod holds the joint filler material in place. Common materials used for backing rods are closed-cell foam polyethylene, butyl rubber, and open-cell or closed-cell polyurethane.

201

basalt   A dark-colored igneous rock commercially known as granite when fabricated as dimension stone. Volcanic equivalent of gabbro.

base   The bottom course of a stone wall, or the vertical first member above grade of a finished floor.

bearing check   A slot cut into the back of dimension stone to allow entry of a supporting angle or clip.

bed   (1) In granites and marbles, a layer or sheet of rock mass that is horizontal, as developed by fractures. (2) In stratified rocks, the unit layer formed by sedimentation; of variable thickness and commonly tilted or distorted by subsequent deformation; generally develops a rock cleavage, parting, or jointing along the planes of stratification.

bedrock   General term referring to the rock underlying other unconsolidated material, such as soil.

belt course   A continuous horizontal course of flat stones placed in line marking a division in the wall plane.

bevel   An angle between two sides that is greater or less than a right angle.

black granite   Rock species known to petrologists as diabase, diorite, gabbro; intermediate varieties are sometimes quarried as building stone, chiefly for ornamental use, and sold as "black granite." As dimension blocks or slabs, such stones are valued specifically for their dark grey to black color when polished. Scientifically, they are far removed in composition from true granites, although they may be satisfactorily used for some of the purposes to which commercial granites are adapted. They possess an interlocking crystalline texture but, unlike granites, contain little or no quartz of alkalic feldspar and are characterized by an abundance of one or more common black rock-forming minerals (chiefly pyroxenes, hornblende, and biotite).

bleed   Staining caused by corrosive metals, oil-based putties, mastics, caulking or sealing compounds.

blending   Refers to the proper positioning of adjacent veneer panels, or floor slabs or tiles, by their predominant color.

block   (*See* quarry block.)

bluestone   A dense, hard, fine-grained, commonly feldspathic sandstone or siltstone of medium to dark or bluish grey color that splits readily along original bedding planes to form thin slabs. It is considered to be a variety of flagstone, the thin, relatively smooth-surfaced slabs being suitable for use as flagging. The term has been applied particularly to sandstone of Devonian age that is being or has been quarried in eastern New York and Pennsylvania and in western New Jersey, but similar stones that occur elsewhere may be included.

bond   To stick or adhere.

border stone   Usually a flat stone used as an edging material. A border stone is generally used to retain the field of a terrace or platform.

brecciated marble   Any marble composed of angular fragments; term used to describe the textural character of a metamorphic stone.

broach   To drill or cut material left between closely spaced drill holes.

brownstone   A sandstone of characteristic brown or reddish brown color that is due to a prominent amount of iron oxide. The term *brownstone* was applied originally to certain Triassic sandstones of the Connecticut Valley in Massachusetts (Longmeadow sandstone) and Connecticut (Portland sandstone) and to similar-appearing reddish brown sandstone quarried in and near Hummelstown, Pennsylvania.

brushed finish Obtained by brushing a stone with a coarse rotary-type wire brush.

building stone, natural Rock material in its natural state of composition and aggregation as it exists in the quarry, usable in construction as dimension building stone.

bullnose Convex rounding of a stone member, such as a stair tread.

bush-hammering A mechanical process that produces textured surfaces. Textures vary from subtle to rough.

buttering Placing mortar on stone units with a trowel before setting into position.

butt joint An external corner formed by two stone panels with one head.

calcarenite Limestone composed predominantly of clastic sand-size grains of calcite or, rarely, aragonite, usually as fragments of shells or other skeletal structures. Some calcarenites contain oolites (small spherical grains of calcium carbonate that resemble roe) and may be termed oolite limestone. Calcareous sandstones, in which the calcium carbonate is present chiefly as bonding material, are not included in this category.

calcareous Refers to substances containing or composed of calcium carbonate.

calcite limestone A crystalline variety of limestone containing not more than 5% magnesium carbonate.

calcite streaks White or milky-like streak occurring in stone. It is a joint plane, usually wider than a glass seam, that has been recemented by deposition of calcite in the crack and is structurally sound.

cantera A volcanic quartz-based stone with qualities similar to those of adoquin, but not as dense; quarried in Mexico.

carve To shape by cutting a design, as performed by a sculptor.

caulking Making a stone joint tight or leak-proof by sealing with an elastic adhesive compound.

cavity vent An opening in joints of stone veneer to allow the passage of air and moisture from inside the wall cavity to the exterior. "Vents" may be weep holes, plastic tubing, or wicks.

cement butter A thick, creamy mixture made of pure cement and water that is used to strengthen the bond between a stone and a setting bed.

chamfer To bevel the junction of an exterior angle.

chat sawn finish A rough gang sawn finish produced by sawing with coarse abrasives.

chert Hard, dense sedimentary rock composed of interlocking quartz crystals and possibly amorphous silica (opal). The origin of the silica is normally biological, created from diatoms, radiolarian or sponge spicules. Synonymous with *flint*.

cladding Non-load-bearing stone veneer used as the facing material in exterior wall construction.

clast An individual grain or constituent of a rock.

cleavage The ability of a rock mass to break along natural surfaces; a surface of natural parting.

cleavage plane Plane or planes along which a stone may likely break or delaminate.

cleft finish   Stones such as slates that are cleaved or separated along a natural seam, whose surface is rough; referred to as a natural cleft surface. Stones of this description were formed as a result of metamorphic foliation.

coating   A protective or decorative covering applied to the surface or impregnated into stone for such purposes as waterproofing, enhancing resistance to weathering, wear, and chemical action, or improving appearance of the stone.

cobblestone   Historically, a natural rounded stone, large enough for use in paving blocks. Modern use generally dictates that cobblestone be cut to rectangular shapes.

composite   A construction unit in which stone that is to be exposed in the final use is permanently bonded or joined to other material, which may be stone or manufactured material, that will be concealed.

conglomerate   A coarse-grained sedimentary rock with clasts larger than 2 mm.

control joint   A joint providing for dimensional changes of different parts of a structure owing to shrinkage, expansion, variations in temperature, or other causes. Its purpose is to prevent the development of high stresses.

coping   A flat stone used as a cap on freestanding walls.

coquina   Limestone composed predominantly of shells or fragments of shells loosely cemented by calcite. Conquina is coarse textured and has high porosity. The term is applied principally to a very porous rock quarried in Florida.

corbel plates   Plates of nonferrous metal fixed into a structure to support stone cladding at intervals and over openings in such a way as not to be visible.

core   That portion of the interior of the earth that lies beneath the mantle and goes all the way to the center. The earth's core is very dense, rich in iron, and the source of the magnetic field.

cornerstone   A stone forming a part of a corner or angle in a wall.

cornice   A molded, projecting stone at the top of an entablature.

course   A horizontal range of stone units the length of a wall.

coursed veneer   Achieved by using stones of the same or approximately the same heights. Horizontal joints run the entire length of a veneered area. Vertical joints are constantly broken so that no joint will be over another.

cove base   A concave stone molding.

crack   A break, split, fracture, fissure, separation, cleavage, or elongated narrow opening, however caused, visible without magnification to the human eye and extending from the surface into the stone, that extends through the grain or matrix.

cramp   A U-shaped metal anchor used to hold two adjacent units of stone together.

cross-bedding   The arrangement of laminations of strata transverse or oblique to the main planes of stratification.

crowfoot (styolite)   A dark grey to black zigzag marking occurring in stone. Usually structurally sound.

crust   The outermost layer of the earth, typically 3 to 50 miles thick, representing less than 1 % of the earth's volume.

crystalline limestone   A limestone, either calcitic or dolomitic, composed of interlocking crystalline grains of the constituent minerals and of phaneritic texture; commonly used synonymously with marble, thus representing a recrystallized limestone; improperly applied to limestones that display some obviously crystalline grains in a fine-grained mass but do not have an interlocking texture and do not compose the entire mass. (Note: All limestones are microscopically, or in part microscopically, crystalline; the term is thus confusing but should be restricted to stones that are completely crystalline and of megascopic and interlocking texture and that may be classed as marbles.)

cubic stone   Dimension units more than 2 in. thick.

cultured marble   An artificial, man-made product.

curbing   Slabs and blocks of stone bordering streets, walks, etc.

cushion   A resilient pad placed between adjoining stone units and other materials, intended to absorb or counteract severe stresses.

cut stone   Stone fabricated to specific dimensions.

damp-proofing   One or more coatings of a compound or layer of material that is impervious to water applied to a surface about grade.

defect   A feature that affects or may potentially affect the structural soundness of building stone, or may affect the durability of building stone.

deposition   Any accumulation of material by mechanical settling from the water or air, chemical precipitation, evaporation from solution, etc.

diamond sawn   Finish produced by sawing with diamond-toothed saws (either circular or gang).

dimension stone   A natural building stone that has been cut and finished to specifications.

dip   The angle that a bedding plane or fault makes with the horizontal when measured perpendicular to the strike of the bedding plane or fault.

dolomite   A crystalline variety of limestone containing in excess of 40% magnesium carbonate as the dolomite molecule. Generally speaking, its crushing and tensile strengths are greater than those of oolitic limestone and its appearance shows greater variety in texture.

dowel   A cylindrical metal pin used in aligning and strengthening joints of adjacent stone units.

dressed or **hand-dressed**   Rough chunks of stone cut by hand to create a square or rectangular shape. A stone that is sold as dressed stone is generally ready for installation.

drip   A recess cut under a sill or projecting stone to throw off water, preventing it from running down the face of a wall or other surface, such as a window or door.

dripstone   A projecting molding over the heads of doorways, windows, and archways to throw off rain. Also known as a "hoodmould."

dry seam   Unhealed fracture, which may be a plane of weakness.

dry wall   A dry wall is a stone wall that is constructed one stone upon the other without the use of any mortar. Generally used for retaining walls.

durability   The measure of the ability of natural building stone to endure and to maintain its essential and distinctive characteristics of strength, resistance to decay, and appearance, in relation to a specific manner, purpose, and environment of use.

efflorescence   A whitish powder, sometimes found on surfaces, caused by the deposition of soluble salts carried through or onto the surface by moisture.

epoxy resin   A flexible, usually thermal-setting resin made by the polymerization of an epoxide and used as an adhesive.

erosion   Processes (mechanical and chemical) responsible for the wearing away, loosening, and dissolving of materials of the earth's crust.

expansion bolt   A receiving socket that grips the sides of a drilled hole in stone by expanding as the bolt is screwed into it.

expansion-contraction joint   A joint between stone units designed to expand or contract with temperature changes. An expansion joint compresses as panels expand.

exposed aggregate   Larger pieces of stone aggregate purposely exposed for their color and texture in a cast concrete slab.

face   The exposed portion of stone.

fascia   A horizontal belt or vertical face; often used in combination with moldings.

fault   A fracture or zone of fractures in rocks of mappable size, along which there has been displacement of one side relative to the other.

field stone   Loose blocks separated from ledges by natural processes and scattered through or upon the regolith (soil) cover; applied also to similar transported materials, such as glacial boulders and cobbles.

filling   A trade expression used to indicate the filling of natural voids in stone units with cements, synthetic resins, or similar materials.

finish   Final surface applied to the face of dimension stone during fabrication.

finished stone   Building stone with one or more mechanically dressed surfaces.

flagstone   Slabs of stone used for paving walks, driveways, patios, etc. They are generally fine-grained bluestone, other quartz-based stone, or slate. Thin slabs of other stones may also be used.

flamed finish   (See thermal finish.)

fleuri cut   The "mottled" effect obtained when certain stone varieties are cut parallel to their natural bedding planes.

flooring   Stone used as an interior pedestrian walking surface.

fold   Bent rock strata.

foliation   The reorientation of a deposit into linear and directional layers. Caused by a metamorphic event in which the force from one or more sources realigns the platy mineral structure of certain stone deposits; e.g., slate, quartzite, some granite gneiss, and some schist.

fossil   Any evidence of past life, including remains, traces, and imprints, as well as life history artifacts. Examples of artifacts include fossilized bird's nests, beehives, etc.

fracture   A break in a rock produced by mechanical failure. Fractures include faults and joints.

freestone   A stone that may be cut freely in any direction without fracture or splitting.

gabbro   Highly mafic igneous plutonic rock, typically dark in color; rough plutonic equivalent of basalt.

gang saw   A mechanical device, also known as a frame saw, used to reduce stone blocks to slabs of predetermined thickness.

gang sawn   Description of the granular surface of stone resulting from gang sawing alone.

gauging   A grinding process to make all pieces of material to be used together the same thickness.

glass seam   A narrow glasslike streak occurring in stone; a joint plane that has been recemented by deposition of translucent calcite in the crack, which does not necessarily decrease the strength of stone.

grade course   Beginning course at the grade level, generally waterproofed with a damp check or damp course.

grain   The easiest cleavage direction in a stone. "With the grain" same as "natural bed." Also, particles (crystals, sand grains, etc.) of a rock.

granite   A very hard, crystalline, igneous rock, fine to coarse grained, gray to pink in color, primarily composed of feldspar, quartz, and lesser amounts of dark ferromagnesium materials. Gneiss and black "granites" are similar to "true" granites in structure and texture, but are composed of different minerals. (Note: Commercial and scientific definitions of the Granite Group are explained in detail in ASTM C119.)

granite gneiss   A foliated crystalline rock composed essentially of silicate minerals with interlocking and visibly granular texture, in which the foliation is due primarily to alternating layers, regular or irregular, of contrasting mineralogical composition. In general, a gneiss is characterized by relatively thick layers, as compared with a schist. According to their mineralogical compositions, gneisses may correspond to other rocks of crystalline, visibly granular, interlocking texture, such as those included in the definition of commercial granite, and may then be known as granite gneiss if strongly foliated, or gneissic granite if weakly foliated.

granular   Having a texture characterized by particles that are apparent to the unaided eye.

greenstone   Includes stones that have been metamorphosed or otherwise changed so that they have assumed a distinctive greenish color owing to the presence of one or more of the following minerals: chlorite, epidote, and actinolite. Peridotite consists dominantly of olivine and pyroxene. Serpentine consists largely of talc, chlorite, and serpentine; further alteration may result in soapstone.

grout   Mortar used to fill joints.

hand-cut random rectangular ashlar   A pattern achieved by hand cutting a stone into squares and rectangulars. Joints are fairly consistent.

hand- or **machine-pitched faced (rock-faced) ashlar**   A finish given to veneer stone. This is created by chiselling a stone unit, usually with a hammer, from the face of the stone. The intent is to create a rustic finish on the face of the stone.

head   The end of a stone that has been tooled to match the face of the stone. Heads are used at outside corners, windows, and doorjambs, or anyplace where the veneering will be visible from the side.

hearth   That part of the floor of a fireplace of stone on which the fire is laid.

hearthstone   Originally, the single large stone or stones used for a hearth; now most commonly used to describe the stone in front of the fire chamber and often extending on either or both sides of the front of the fire chamber.

honed finish   A satin-smooth surface finish with little or no gloss; the level of gloss is less than a polished finish. This finish is recommended for commercial floors.

igneous   One of the three great classes of rock (igneous, sedimentary, and metamorphic), solidified from the molten state as granite and lavas.

incise   To cut inwardly or engrave, as in an inscription.

joint   The space between stone units, usually filled with mortar or flexible sealant material.

jumper   In ashlar patterns, a piece of stone of higher rise than adjacent stones that is used to end a horizontal mortar joint at the point where it is set.

kerf   Slot cut into the edge of stone with a saw blade for the insertion of anchors.

keystone   The last wedge-shaped stone placed in the crown of an arch, regarded as binding the whole.

laccolith   A batholithic structure that forms as a dome or bubble, lifting weaker, overlying rock.

lava   A general term applied to igneous rocks, such as basalt and rhyolite, that erupted from the earth by volcanic action.

lead buttons   Lead spacers in solid horizontal joints to support the top stones until the mortar has set.

Lewis bolt   Used for lifting; a tapered-head device wedged into a tapered recess in the edge of a dimension stone unit.

limestone   A sedimentary rock composed primarily of calcite or dolomite. The varieties of limestone used as dimension stone are usually well consolidated and exhibit a minimum of graining or bedding direction. (Note: See definitions of Limestone Group in ASTM C119.)

liners   Structurally sound sections of stone cemented and dowelled to the back of thin stone units to give greater strength or additional bearing surface or to increase joint depth.

lintel   A block of stone spanning the top of an opening such as a doorway or window; sometimes called a head.

lippage   A condition in which one edge of a stone is higher than adjacent edges, giving the finished surface a ragged appearance.

lug sill   A stone sill set into the jambs on each side of a masonry opening.

magma   Molten rock generated within the earth.

malpais   Literally, badland; refers to dark-colored rock, commonly lava, in rough terrain. As defined for architectural use, calcium carbonate with other components that give it color, markings, and texture suitable as a desirable building stone.

mantle   That portion of the interior of the earth that lies between the crust and the core.

marble   A metamorphic crystalline rock composed predominately of crystalline grains of calcite, dolomite, or serpentine and capable of taking a polish. Commercial definition: A crystalline rock, capable of taking a polish, and composed of one or more of the minerals calcite, dolomite, and serpentine. (Note: Commercial and scientific definitions of the Marble Group are given in detail in ASTM C119.)

melange   A body of rocks consisting of large blocks (mappable size) of different rocks jumbled together with little continuity of contacts.

metamorphic rock   Rock altered in appearance, density, crystalline structure, and in some cases mineral composition, by high temperature, intense pressure, or both. Includes slate, derived from shale; quartz-based stone, derived from quartzitic sand; and true marble, derived from limestone.

MIA (Marble Institute of America)   An international trade association whose membership is composed of producers, fabricators, contractors, exporters-importers and distributors, sales agents, and those who sell products and services to the dimension stone industry and building owners.

midoceanic ridges   Elongated rises on the ocean floor where molten magma erupts, forming new oceanic crust; similar to continental rift zones.

miter   Generally refers to a joint or cut, sawn on a stone module, where two units are joined. The two units are sawn equally at the midpoint of the joint, usually bisecting the joint at a 45-degree angle.

moldings   Decorative stone deviating from a plane surface by projections, curved profiles, recesses, or any combination thereof.

mortar   A plastic mixture of cement, lime, sand, and water used to bond masonry units.

mosaic   A veneering that is generally irregular, with no definite pattern. Nearly all stone used in a mosaic pattern is irregular in shape.

natural bed   The setting of stone on the same plane as that on which it was formed in the ground. This generally applies to all stratified materials.

obsidian   A glassy phase of lava.

oceanic crust   The earth's crust that is formed at midoceanic ridges, typically 3 to 6 miles thick.

ogee   A stone molding with a reverse curved edge, concave above, convex below.

onyx   A crystalline form of calcium carbonate deposition, usually from cold-water solutions; closely related in form and origin to agate. It is generally translucent and shows a characteristic layering.

oolitic limestone   A calcite-cemented calcareous stone formed of shells and shell fragments, practically noncrystalline in character; found in massive deposits. This limestone is characteristically a freestone, without cleavage planes, having a remarkable uniformity of composition, texture, and structure. It has a high internal elasticity, adapting itself without damage to extreme temperature changes.

opalized   The condition of a rock into which siliceous material, in the form of opal, hydrous silicate, has been introduced.

outcrop   Any place where bedrock is visible on the surface of the earth.

palletizing   A system of stacking stone on wooden pallets. Stone that is delivered palletized is easily moved and transported by modern handling equipment. Palletized stone generally arrives at a job site in better condition than unpalletized material.

panel   A single unit of fabricated stone veneer.

parging   Damp-proofing by applying a coat of mortar to the back of stone units or to the face of the backup material.

parquetry   An inlay of stone floors in geometrical or other patterns.

paver   A single unit of fabricated stone for use as a paving material.

paving   Stone used as a wearing surface, as in patios, walkways, driveways, etc. (*See* flooring.)

perrons   Slabs of stone set on other stones, serving as steps and arches in gardens.

phenocryst   In igneous rocks, the relatively large and conspicuous crystals in a finer-grained matrix or groundmass.

pitched stone   Rough stone face or edge cut with pitching chisel.

plate   Rigid parts of the earth's crust and part of the earth's upper mantle that move and adjoin each other along zones of seismic activity.

plinth   (1) The base block at the junction of a stone base and trim around a door or other opening. (2) The bottom stone block of a column or pedestal.

plutonic   Applies to igneous rocks formed beneath the surface of the earth, typically with large crystals owing to the slowness of cooling.

pointing   The final filling and finishing of mortar joints that have been raked out.

polished finish   The finest and smoothest finish available in stone, characterized by high gloss and strong reflection of incident light; generally possible only on hard, dense materials. A glossy surface that brings out the full color and character of a stone.

porphyry   An igneous rock in which relatively large and conspicuous crystal (phenocrysts) are set in a matrix of finer crystals; characterized by distinct and contrasting sizes of coarse and fine-grained crystals, used as a decorative building stone.

processing   The work involved in transforming building stone from quarry blocks to cut or finished stone. This includes primary sawing into slabs; it may also include both hand and mechanical techniques such as sawing, drilling, grinding, honing, polishing, and carving.

projections   Stones pulled out from a wall to give the effect of ruggedness. The amount each stone is pulled out can vary between 1/2 and 1 1/2 in. Stones can be pulled out to the same degree at both ends, or one end can be pulled out, leaving the other flush with most of the veneer.

pumice   An exceptionally cellular, glassy lava resembling a solid plinth.

quarrier   One who extracts natural stone from a quarry.

quarry   The location of an operation where a deposit of stone is extracted from the earth, through an open pit or underground mine.

quarry block   Generally, a rectangular piece of rough stone as it comes from a quarry, frequently dressed (scabbed) or wire sawed for shipment.

quartz   A silicon dioxide mineral that occurs in colorless and transparent or colored hexagonal crystals or in crystalline masses. One of the hardest minerals that compose stones such as sandstone, granite, and quartzite.

quartz-based stone   This stone may be either sedimentary in formation (as in sandstone) or metamorphic (as in quartzite). (Note: Definitions of the three classes of stone that form the Quartz-Based Stone Group are given in ASTM C119.)

quartzite   A metamorphic quartz-based stone formed in exceedingly hard and stratified layers. In some deposits, intrusion of minerals during the formation process have created unusual coloration.

quartzitic sandstone   A sandstone with a high concentration of quartz grains and siliceous cement.

quirk-miter joint   An external corner formed by two stone panels at an angle, with meeting edges mitered and exposed portions finished.

rabbett   A groove cut into a surface along an edge so as to receive another piece similarly cut.

rake   An angular cut on the face of stone.

rebated kerf   An additional cut that countersinks a kerf from the back edge of the kerf to the back edge of another piece of stone for the purpose of additional anchor clearance. This is not a gauged cut. If used for a bearing surface, it must be shimmed to allow for tolerance in the cut.

recess   A change in plane where an area is set back from another surface.

reglet   A narrow, flat recessed molding, or a kerf cut to receive flashing.

reinforcement   A fabrication technique, often called "rodding"; refers to the strengthening of unsound marble and limestone by cementing rods into grooves or channels cut into the back of a stone unit. Another method of reinforcement is the lamination of fiberglass to the back of tile units.

relief or **relieve**   An ornament or figure slightly, half, or greatly projected from a surface to distinguish it from another surface.

return   The right angle turn of a molding.

return head   Stone facing with the finish appearing on both the face and the edge of the same stone, as on the corner of a building.

rhyolite   Igneous volcanic rock, typically light in color; rough volcanic equivalent of granite.

ribbon   Narrow bands of rock differing to various degrees in chemical composition and color from the main body of the slate or stone bands.

rift   The most pronounced direction of splitting or cleavage of stone. Rift and grain may be obscure, as in some granites, but are important in both quarrying and processing stone.

riprap   Irregularly shaped stones used for facing bridge abutments and fills; stones thrown together without order to form a foundation or sustaining wall.

rise   The height of a stone, generally used in reference to veneer stone.

rock   An integral part of the earth's crust composed of an aggregate of grains of one or more minerals. (*Stone* is the commercial term applied to quarry products.)

rock (pitch) face   Similar to split face, except that the face of the stone is pitched to a given line and plane, producing a bold appearance rather than the comparatively straight face obtained in split face.

rodding   Reinforcement of a structurally unsound marble by cementing reinforcing rods into grooves or channels cut into the back of the slab.

rough sawn   A surface finish resulting from the gang sawing process.

rubbed finish   Mechanically rubbed for smoother finish.

rubble   A product term applied to dimension stone used for building purposes, chiefly walls and foundations, consisting of irregularly shaped pieces, partly trimmed or squared, generally with one split or finished face, and selected and specified with a size range.

rustication   Chamfers or square sinking around the face edges of individual stones to create shadows and give an appearance of weight to a lower part of a building. When only horizontal joints are sunk, the process is known as banded rustication.

saddle   A flat strip of stone projecting above the floor between the jambs of the door; a threshold.

sandblasted   A matte-texture marble surface finish with no gloss, accomplished by exposing the surface to a steady flow of sand under pressure.

sandstone   A sedimentary rock usually consisting of quartz, cemented with silica, iron oxide, or calcium carbonate. Sandstone is durable, has a very high crushing and tensile strength and a wide range of colors and textures. Conglomerate is a sandstone composed in large part of rounded pebbles; also called puddingstone.

sawn edge   A clean-cut edge generally achieved by cutting with a diamond blade, gang saw, or wire saw.

sawn face   A finish obtained from the process used in producing building stone; texture is from smooth to rough and coincident with the type of materials used in sawing; characterized as diamond sawn, sand sawn, chat sawn, and shot sawn.

schist   A loose term applying to foliated metamorphic (recrystallized) rock characterized by thin foliae that are composed predominantly of minerals of thin platy or prismatic habits and whose long dimensions are oriented in approximately parallel positions along the planes of foliation. Because of this foliated structure, schists split readily along these planes and so have a pronounced rock cleavage. The more common schists are composed of micas and other mica-like minerals (such as chlorite) and generally contain subordinate quartz and/or feldspar of comparatively fine-grained texture; all gradations exist between schist and gneiss (coarsely foliated feldspathic rocks).

scoria   Irregular masses of lava resembling clinkers of slag; may be cellular (vesticular), dark colored, and heavy.

sculpture   The work of a sculptor; a three-dimensional form cut from a block of stone.

sealant   An elastic adhesive compound used to fill stone veneer joints.

sealing   (1) Making a veneer joint watertight or leak-proof with an elastic adhesive compound. (2) Application of a surface treatment to retard staining.

sediment   Any solid material that has settled out of suspension in liquid.

sedimentary   Refers to rocks formed of sediments laid down in successive strata or layers. The materials of which they are formed are derived from preexisting rocks or the skeletal remains of sea creatures.

semirubbed   A finish achieved by rubbing (by hand or machine) the rough or high spots from the surface to be used, leaving a certain amount of the natural surface along with the smoothed areas.

serpentine   A hydrous magnesium silicate material; generally dark green in color with markings of white, light green, or black. Considered commercially as a marble because it can be polished. One of the hardest varieties of natural building stone. (Note: The definition of serpentine is given in ASTM C119 under the Marble Group.)

setter   An experienced journeyman who installs dimension stone.

setting   The trade of installing dimension stone.

setting space   The distance from the finished face of a marble to the face of the backup wall.

shaped stone   Cut stone that has been carved, ground, or otherwise processed.

shear   A type of stress; a body is in shear when it is subjected to a pair of equal forces that are opposite in direction and act along parallel planes.

shim   A piece of plastic or other noncorrosive, nonstaining material used to hold joints to size.

shot-sawn   Description of a finish obtained by using steal shot in the gang sawing process to produce random markings for a rough surface texture.

sill   A horizontal flat stone used at the base of an exterior opening in a structure.

siltstone   A fine-grained noncarbonate clastic rock composed of at least 67% detrital grains of quartz and silicate minerals of silt size. Siltstones are rarely marketed as such but are commonly considered as fine-grained sandstones. This class of sediments is texturally transitional between sandstones and shales (mudstones). Many bluestones and siliceous flagstones fall within this category. The term is included in these definitions chiefly to explain the relationship of some siliceous flagstone to the sandstone category.

simulated stone   An artificial man-made product.

slab   A lengthwise cut of a large quarry block of stone, produced by sawing or splitting in the first milling or quarrying operation. A slab has two parallel surfaces.

slate   A very fine-grained, foliated metamorphic rock derived from sedimentary shale rock. Characterized by an excellent parallel cleavage, entirely independent of original bedding, by which the rock may be split easily into relatively thin slabs.

slip sill   A stone sill set between jambs.

smooth finish   The finish produced by planer machines plus the removal of objectionable tool marks. Also known as smooth planer finish and smooth machine finish.

snapped edge, quarry cut, or **broken edge**   A natural breaking of a stone either by hand or by machine. The break should be at right angles to the top and bottom surfaces.

soapstone   A massive variety of talcs with a "soapy" feel, used for hearths, tabletops, chemical-resistant laboratory tops, stove facing and cladding; known for its stain-proof characteristics. (Classified in ASTM C119 as part of the Greenstone Group.)

soil   Unconsolidated materials above bedrock.

soundness   A property of stone used to describe relative freedom from cracks, faults, voids, and similar imperfections found in untreated stone. One of the characteristics encountered in fabrication.

spall   A chip or splinter separated from the main mass of stone.

spandrel wall   That part of a curtain wall above the top of a window in one story and below the sill of the window in the story above.

splay   A beveled or slanted surface.

spline   A thin strip of material, such as wood or metal, inserted into the edges of two stone pieces or stone tiles to make a butt joint between them.

split   Division of a rock by cleavage.

split-face stone   Stone on which the face has been broken to an approximate plane.

spot or **spotting**   The mortar applied to the back of dimension stone veneer to bridge the space between a stone panel and the backup wall. Used to plumb a wall.

stack bond   Stone that is cut to one dimension and installed with unbroken vertical and horizontal joints running the entire length and height of the veneered area.

start   A small fissure.

sticking   A trade term describing the butt edge repair of a broken piece of stone, now generally done with dowels, cements, or epoxies. The pieces are "stuck" together, thus "sticking."

stone   Sometimes synonymous with rock, but more properly applied to individual blocks, masses, or fragments taken from their original formation or considered for commercial use.

stool   A flat unit of stone, often referred to as an interior windowsill.

stratification   A structure produced by deposition of sediments in beds or layers (strata).

strip rubble   Generally speaking, strip rubble comes from a quarry ledge; the beds of the stone, although uniformly straight, are of the natural cleft as the stone is removed from the ledge and then split by machine to approximately 4-in. widths.

strips   Long pieces of stone, usually low height ashlar courses, where the length to height ratio is at maximum for the material used.

styrolite   A longitudinally streaked, columnar structure occurring in some marbles and of the same material as the marble in which it occurs.

subduction   The process of one plate descending beneath another.

template   A pattern for repetitive marking in a fabricating operation.

terrazzo   A flooring surface of marble or granite chips in a cementitious or resinous mix, which is ground and finished after setting.

texture   Surface quality of stone independent of color.

textured finish   A rough surface finish.

thermal finish   A highly textured surface treatment applied by intense heat flaming. Can be achieved with granites and a very few limestones.

thin stone/thin veneer   A cladding less than 2 in. (50 mm) thick.

threshold   A piece of stone under a door.

tile   A thin modular stone unit, generally less than ¾ in. thick.

tolerance   Dimensional allowances in the fabrication process.

tooled finish   A finish that customarily has four, six, or eight parallel, concave grooves to the inch.

translucence   The ability of many lighter-colored marbles to transmit light.

travertine   A variety of limestone that is a precipitant from hot springs. Some varieties of travertine take a polish and are known commercially as marble. (Note: ASTM C119 classifies travertine in both the Limestone and the Marble Groups.)

tread   A flat stone used as the top walking surface on steps.

trim   Stone used as decorative items only, such as sills, coping, enframements, etc., with facing of another material.

tuff   Cemented volcanic ash; includes many varieties.

unconformity   Any interruption of the continuity of a depositional sequence.

undercut   Cut so as to present an overhanging part.

unit   A piece of fabricated cubic or thin dimension stone.

vein   A layer, seam, or narrow irregular body of mineral material different from the surrounding formation.

vein cut   Cutting of quarried stone perpendicular to the natural bedding plane.

veneer   A non-load-bearing facing of stone attached to a backing for the purpose of ornamentation, protection, or insulation. Veneer should support no vertical load other than its own weight and possibly the vertical dead load of veneer above.

venting A method used to allow air and moisture to escape to the outside from a wall cavity.

verde antique A commercial marble composed chiefly of serpentine and capable of taking a high polish. Verde antique is not a true marble in the scientific sense, but is commonly sold as a decorative commercial marble and, as such, requires the adjectival modifier *verde antique*. Verde antique is commonly veined with carbonate minerals, chiefly calcite and dolomite.

volcanic Applies to igneous rock that cools on the surface of the earth, including that part of the surface beneath water; typically with small crystals owing to the rapidity of cooling. Synonym of *extrusive;* antonym of *plutonic.*

wainscot An interior veneer of stone less than full wall height.

wall plate A horizontal member anchored to a masonry wall to which other structural elements may be attached. Also called head plate. Usually steel $3/16$ in. (5 mm) in diameter and formed in a Z shape or a rectangle.

wall tie A bonder or metal piece that connects wythes of masonry to each other or to other materials.

wall tie cavity A rigid corrosion-resistant metal tie that bonds wythes of a cavity wall.

wash The slope on the top of a stone unit intended to shed water.

waxing A trade expression referring to the practice of filling minor surface imperfections such as voids or sand holes with melted shellac, cabinetmakers wax, or certain polyester compounds. It does not refer to the application of paste wax to make surfaces shinier.

weathering Natural alteration by either chemical or mechanical processes caused by the action of constituents of the atmosphere, soil, surface waters, and other groundwaters, or by temperature changes.

wedging The splitting of stone by driving wedges into planes of weakness.

weep holes Openings for drainage in veneer joints or in the structural components supporting the veneer.

wire sawing A method of cutting stone by passing a twisted multistrand wire over the stone. The wire may either be immersed in a slurry of abrasive material or be fitted with spaced industrial diamond blocks.

Bibliography

BOOKS

Amrhein, James E., and Michael W. Merrigan. *Marble and Stone Slab Veneer*. Los Angeles: Masonry Institute of America, 1985, 1989.

Busbey, Arthur B. III, Robeft R. Coenraads, Paul Willis, and David Roots. *Rocks and Fossils*. Alexandria, VA: Nature Company/Time Life Books, 1996.

Byrne, Michael. *Setting Tile*. Newtown, CT: Taunton Press, 1996.

Catella, M., E. Corbella, C. Costa, G. Montani, A. Morandini Frisa, M. Pinzari, A. Ricci, and S. Sachelli. *Marmi Italiani*. Rome: Italian Institute for Foreign Trade, 1982.

Cotecchia, Vicenzo, Bruno Radina, and Fulvio Zezza. *Marmi di Puglia*. Regione Puglia: Interstone Press/Instituto Geographica de Agostini, 1982.

de los Rios Cobo, Jose Ignacio Garcia, and Juan Manuel Baez Mezquita. *La Piedra en Castilla y Leon*. Valladolid, Spain: Regional Department for the Economy, 1994.

Hamblin, W. Kenneth. *The Earth's Dynamic Systems*. Minneapolis: Burgess Publishing Co., 1978.

Hartt, Frederick. Art: *A History of Painting, Sculpture, Architecture*: Englewood Cliffs, NJ: Prentice-Hall, and New York: Harry Abrams, 1976.

Kiefer, Irene. *Global Jigsaw Puzzle: The Story of the Continental Drift*. New York: Atheneum, 1978.

Lambert, David. *A Field Guide to Geology*. Facts on File. Boston: The Diagram Group, 1996.

Lewis, Michael D. *Modern Stone Cladding*. Philadelphia: American Society for Testing and Materials, 1995.

Liberati, Anna Maria, and Fabio Bourbon. *Ancient Rome: A History of a Civilization That Ruled the World*. New York: Stewart, Tabori & Chang, 1996.

Pevsner, Nikolaus. *An Outline of European Architecture*. Baltimore: Pelican Books, 1993.

Schumann, Walter. *Minerals of the World*. New York: Sterling Publishing Company, 1992.

Sorrell, Charles A. *A Guide to Field Identification: Minerals of the World*. New York: Golden Press, 1973.

Tomio, Paolo, and Fiorino Filippi. *The Porphyry Manual.* Pergine, Valsugana (Trento): Publif tampa Arti Grafiche-S. N. C., 1994.

Uyeda, Seiya. *The New View of the Earth.* San Francisco: W. H. Freeman and Co., 1978.

Zahner, L. William. *Architectural Metals.* New York: John Wiley & Sons, 1995.

TRADE JOURNALS AND MAGAZINES

Handbook for Ceramic Tile Insulation

Indiana Limestone Institute

Architecture

Dimension Stone

Stone World Magazine

The Marble Institute of America

Index

Photography Credits

Photographer	Page number
Patrick Barta Seattle, WA	67, 69, 70–72, 84, 86, 87, 94, 95, 103, 112–115, 117, 119, 178–180, 183, 189; color insert: 9–14, 16, 24, 25
Luigi Biagini Carrara, Italy	2, 4, 6, 38, 41–43, 45–47, 49–57, 69, 74, 76, 79, 81; color insert: 4–8
Mark Chacon Seattle, WA.	59, 60, 62, 81
Michael Creighton Seattle, WA	color insert: 1
Chris Eden Seattle, WA	color insert: 20–21
Nick Fecitt Cumbria, UK	color insert: 2, 3
Rob Fraser United Kingdom	color insert: 26
Phil Loubere Seattle, WA	13–16, 19, 22, 23, 25, 48, 167, 168
Robert Pisano Seattle, WA	color insert: 17–19, 23, 27, 28, 30, 31
Ian Pleeth United Kingdom	color insert: 15, 29
Gerhard Ruf Eichstadt, Germany	10, 41, 44, 47, 58
Roger Savage United Kingdom	color insert: 32